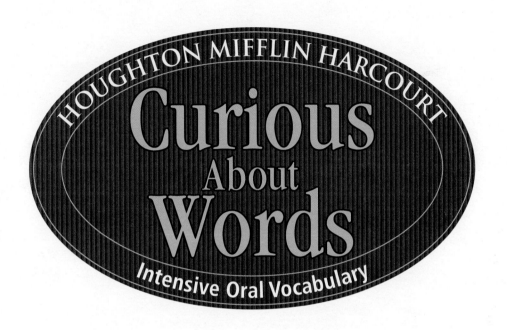

Teacher Manual

Grade 2

HOUGHTON MIFFLIN HARCOURT

School Publishers

ILLUSTRATIONS

ISBN-13:   978-0-547-32748-8
ISBN-10:   0-547-32748-X

4 5 6 7 8 9 10 0877 18 17 16 15 14 13

4500399395

Curious About Words
Grade 2

Instruction

Assessment: Pretest/Posttest

How to Use *Curious About Words*

Intensive Oral Vocabulary Instruction

Curious About Words provides intensive oral vocabulary instruction for children with limited vocabularies in Grades K through 3. These materials supplement the core vocabulary instruction in *Houghton Mifflin Harcourt Journeys*. Daily lessons use read alouds, graphic organizers, teacher-led discussion, and partner activities to develop children's listening and speaking vocabularies.

In *Curious About Words*, a wide range of meaningful, useful words are taught each week in two semantic categories. Clear, student-friendly labels help children make connections between the categories of words. All words are drawn from research-based lists of high-utility words, including academic content vocabulary from Robert Marzano's *Building Background Knowledge*. For more information, see Research Sources for Words Taught on page 158.

Read Alouds Two read alouds are the basis of instruction every week. Each read aloud introduces a new category of words. Every read aloud is accompanied by an appealing, full-page illustration or photograph, creating a collection of engaging narrative and expository texts. Oral vocabulary words are highlighted, and comprehension questions encourage discussion of the text as well as the oral vocabulary.

Daily Lessons Oral vocabulary is taught using student-friendly explanations and examples. Teacher-led discussions use graphic organizers to explore the relationships between the words in each category. Teacher-supported partner activities guide children to review and extend their understanding of all words taught in the week.

Assessments A single set of assessments is provided for each week, including the two categories of words. Each weekly assessment can support your instruction in two ways:

- **Pretest** Administer the assessment at the beginning of the week to determine which words children already know and which will require extra instructional time.
- **Posttest** Administer the assessment at the end of the week to determine how well children have learned the vocabulary that has been taught.

These assessments are administered orally to the group. Each has two components:

- **Pretest/Posttest Administration** Use this page to read aloud each item, including the answer choices. Within each item, each circle corresponds to an A, B, or C answer choice on the blackline master.
- **Pretest/Posttest Blackline Masters** Copy and distribute each page. Explain that it shows only the answer choices. Help children understand how to choose the best answer.

The Case of the Missing Book

Riley Morton is one clever kid. He has solved problems that were so *mysterious*, even teachers couldn't figure them out! He has a way of digging up answers, like a *detective*. That's why kids call him Detective Riley.

At recess yesterday, Vinnie Scarboro ran up to Riley. He looked worried. "I need your help, detective," he said.

"What's the matter?" Riley asked.

"Mr. Wilkins says I can't take any more books out of the school library," Vinnie explained. "He says I never returned the book *Plaque Attack*. But I did! I left it right on his desk."

"Very *suspicious*," Riley said. "Tell me everything you remember."

"I was out sick on Friday," Vinnie said. "And that was the day I was supposed to return the book. So on Monday, I brought it to the library."

Riley said, "Let's go to the library and look for *clues*."

Riley and Vinnie entered the library. They saw Mr. Wilkins standing at the front desk. "Hi, boys. Can I help you?" he asked.

"I think so, Mr. Wilkins," said Riley. "Vinnie is upset because he returned *Plaque Attack* to your desk Monday morning, but you say he didn't."

"Returned it to my desk?" Mr. Wilkins repeated. "Well, there's the problem. I changed the book return spot last Friday. You're supposed to leave books in this box now. The old book return spot is now for books that need to be fixed."

"Mr. Wilkins, I think I can *prove* that Vinnie returned the book," said Riley. "If you look in your back room, I think you'll find *Plaque Attack*."

The librarian disappeared into the back room. He came back out shaking his head and carrying *Plaque Attack*. "That is *puzzling*," he said. "How did that get mixed up in there? Sorry, Vincent. I was wrong. You can take books out anytime."

Outside the library, Vinnie thanked Riley. "But how did you know?" Vinnie asked.

"The book-return box was set up on Friday," Riley explained. "You were home sick that day. So you didn't know you were putting the book in the wrong place."

Suddenly, the bell rang. Riley and Vinnie had missed recess!

COMPREHENSION Which words help you understand that something strange is going on? What clues help Riley solve the mystery?

2

Days 1 and 2

"The Case of the Missing Book," Vol. 1, pp. 2–3

Owney, the Traveling Dog

Over a hundred and twenty years ago, some post-office workers in Albany, New York, found a dog. He was a stray dog who lived on the streets. Because the dog was hungry and tired, the postal workers felt sorry for him. They made a bed for him out of an empty mail bag. They fed him out of their own lunches. They let him sleep in their post office. The workers thought of the dog as a pet, so they named him Owney.

Soon, Owney started going on trips with the men when they delivered mail. His first journey was short. He went out for the day on a horse-drawn wagon. Owney liked to travel. After the first trip, he went again and again. One night, postal workers found him on a mail train! The train was headed for another part of New York. The workers made sure to transport Owney home to Albany.

It was not long before Owney hopped onto another mail train. Again, postal workers took care of him along the route and then transported him back to Albany. Owney did this over and over. He traveled to many parts of the country. People started looking forward to seeing Owney. Everyone wanted Owney to come to their city or town.

Because Owney traveled with the mail, he always ended up at a post office. His arrival caused excitement. Post-office workers gave Owney metal tags to show where he had been. They hung the tags on his collar. After a while, Owney collected so many tags that the collar got too heavy for him to wear. So the U.S. Postmaster gave Owney a fine leather harness to wear on his body. This made the tags more comfortable for him to wear. Someone who knew Owney once wrote: "Owney now wears a big bunch of tags. When he jogs along, they jingle like the bells on a junk wagon."

But the best was yet to come. The postmaster of Tacoma, Washington, decided to send Owney around the world. A postal worker accompanied Owney on his grand *tour*. They traveled on trains and steamships. One hundred and thirteen days later, Owney trotted back into the Tacoma post office.

Today, visitors to the National Postal Museum can learn more about Owney and his amazing travels. Many of the tags Owney once wore are on display. He is remembered as the Post Office's unofficial mascot: Owney, the Traveling Dog.

COMPREHENSION Which words about travel do you hear in this passage? Why do you think people were excited when Owney came to their town or city?

4

Days 3 and 4

"Owney, the Traveling Dog," Vol. 1, pp. 4–5

Assessment

Pretest/Posttest Administration p. 62
Pretest/Posttest Blackline Masters pp. 92–93

Day 1

Introduce Meanings

Assess To assess what word meanings children already know, copy and distribute the **Pretest/Posttest** on pages 92–93. Use page 62 to administer the test.

Explain Write each oral vocabulary word below on the board. Read it aloud. Offer an explanation and a brief example for each word.

Words About Solving Mysteries

clues *n.* hints that help solve a mystery *The clues led police to the criminal.*

detective *n.* person who solves a mystery *The detective found the missing car.*

mysterious *adj.* hard to explain *A mysterious sound came from her lunchbox, but when she opened it nothing was there.*

prove *v.* show to be true *She can prove she runs fast by winning the race.*

puzzling *v.* confusing *The mixed-up message was puzzling to the girl.*

suspicious *adj.* strange; making someone worry *The cat's suspicious actions made the vet think the animal was sick.*

Discuss Guide children to see the relationship between each word and the category of solving mysteries.

Read Aloud Explain that you will read aloud a story about a boy who uses clues to solve a mystery. Then read aloud "The Case of the Missing Book." Discuss the Comprehension questions.

Day 2

Categorize and Classify

Reread and Explain Reread "The Case of the Missing Book." At the end of each sentence that includes an oral vocabulary word, stop and repeat the explanation of the word. Then reread the sentence.

Use a Graphic Organizer Use the graphic organizer and the questions below to reinforce understanding of the relationship between each word and the category.

1. If a bike is missing, what job could a **detective** do? (try to find the bike)

2. Tell two things that **detectives** can do to **prove** they are good at their jobs. (Sample answers: finding something stolen; catching a criminal; solving a mystery)

3. What words might you use to describe something you cannot explain? (**puzzling; mysterious**)

Day 3

Introduce Meanings

Explain Write each oral vocabulary word below on the board. Read it aloud. Offer an explanation and a brief example for each word.

Words About Traveling

arrival *n.* reaching a place *The passengers got off the plane upon arrival at the airport.*

route *n.* a way from one place to another *A parade route must be planned in advance.*

send *v.* cause to go *We will send the letter through the mail.*

tour *n.* a trip to visit places *The visitors took a bus tour of the city.*

transport *v.* carry from one place to another *A farmer will transport corn to the market.*

travel *v.* take a journey *Her family likes to travel to the mountains.*

Discuss Guide children to see the relationship between each word and the category. Ask questions such as these: Where would you like to **travel** to? Have you ever been on a **tour**?

Read Aloud Explain that you will read aloud a story about a dog that traveled all over the world. Then read aloud "Owney, the Traveling Dog." Discuss the Comprehension questions.

Day 4

Categorize and Classify

Reread and Explain Reread "Owney, the Traveling Dog." At the end of each sentence that includes an oral vocabulary word, stop and repeat the explanation of the word. Then reread the sentence.

Use a Graphic Organizer Use the graphic organizer and the questions below to reinforce understanding of the relationship between each word and the category.

Travel Words	
Getting There	**Being There**
send transport travel	arrival tour

1. What are some ways to **travel**? (Sample answers: by car; plane; train; bus; boat)

2. How can a map help a driver plan his **route**? (Sample answer: A driver can see which roads lead to the place he is going.)

3. Name some things you might see on a **tour** of a city. (Sample answers: famous buildings; statues; parks)

Day 5

Deepen Understanding

Review Review word meanings for all oral vocabulary words. Use the definitions and examples from Day 1 and Day 3.

Guide Partner Activities Have partners work together to complete each of the activities below. Circulate and listen to partners as they work. Provide corrective feedback.

Categorize Work with a partner. List three places where your class could take a **tour**. Then list three ways to **transport** people. What form of transportation would your class use?

Describe You see a **mysterious** shadow. It is **puzzling** you. What **clues** can help you **prove** what is making the shadow? Tell a partner.

Draw Choose a real or imaginary place and draw a visitor's guide for it. In the guide, explain what there is to do upon a visitor's **arrival**. Draw the **routes** a visitor can take to **travel** there. Share with your partner.

Write What kind of message might a **detective send** to a person who looks **suspicious**? Write the message. Read it to a partner.

Assess To assess what word meanings children have learned, copy and distribute the **Pretest/ Posttest** on pages 92–93. Use page 62 to administer the test. Compare scores with Day 1 assessment.

Many McCaugheys

Do you know someone who is a twin? Twins are two babies born at the same time from the same mother. Triplets are three babies born at the same time from the same mother. When more than one baby is born at the same time to the same mother, it is called a multiple birth.

A newborn baby needs to eat every couple of hours. Also, a baby uses about ten diapers a day. Now imagine trying to take care of seven newborn babies!

Bobbi and Kenneth McCaughey did just that. On November 19, 1997, they welcomed seven babies into the world at once. They had three girls: Alexis, Natalie, and Kelsey. They also had four boys: Kenneth, Jr.; Nathan; Brandon; and Joel.

The McCaugheys had a small house. Plus, they already had a daughter named Mikayla. How could they take care of all the babies? The family got lots of help. Companies donated diapers, baby food, and even a brand-new van. The townspeople built them a bigger house. The new house has five bathrooms, two washing machines, two dryers, and two dishwashers.

In their first years as babies, the McCaugheys used more than thirty thousand diapers! These days, they eat six boxes of cereal in a week. They drink more than five gallons of milk. They eat twenty cans of vegetables and five loaves of bread. Even though they have an unusual story, in many ways the McCaugheys are like any other big family.

Now the McCaughey kids are in school. Every afternoon is like a family reunion when the septuplets come home. Despite having different hair color, they resemble one another. They also enjoy one another. They have a strong family bond. They share lots of memories from their hectic childhood!

Are there likely to be twins or triplets in your family? Look at your ancestors. Multiple births can run in families. It's a remarkable inheritance that is passed down over time.

COMPREHENSION What words about families did you hear in this passage? How are the McCaugheys like your family? How are they different?

6

Days 1 and 2

"Many McCaugheys," Vol. 1, pp. 6–7

Helping Hands

When Malia and Malcolm got home from school, they weren't ready for what they saw. Their parents were marching by the front door, holding signs and chanting.

"Less work! Less work! More fun! More fun!" they chanted.

"What's going on?" Malia and Malcolm asked.

"We're picketing the house," Mom explained. "You can't go inside until you promise to do your chores."

"Parents have rights, too," Dad said. "We're allowed to have some fun instead of working all day and night."

Malia and Malcolm traded puzzled looks. "We always do our chores," Malcolm said.

"We think you need to help out more," Mom replied. "We're not backing down from our cause."

"OK, we will," Malia said. "We promise."

So Mom and Dad laid down their signs, and everyone went inside.

In no time, Malia and Malcolm had made a mess of the family room. There were games on the floor, crumbs on the coffee table, and shoes underneath it.

An hour later, the children went into the kitchen to find Mom. "We're hungry," they announced, rubbing their stomachs.

"Did you clean up the family room?" she asked. Malia and Malcolm frowned.

"Then you're on your own," Mom said. "We're striking. We're not doing any work until you do, too."

Later, Malia and Malcolm wandered into the dining room. They found Mom and Dad reading the newspaper.

"Can you help us with our homework?" Malcolm asked.

"Sorry, we're boycotting you kids," Dad announced. "No more help with your homework—or with anything else—until you start doing your chores."

"This is an injustice!" Malcolm cried. "We're being treated unfairly!"

"Is it fair," Mom asked, "that we work so hard while you play?"

Malia and Malcolm realized their parents were right. So they set about cleaning up the house. They picked up shoes, games, toys, and books. They made their beds. When they had finished, Malia and Malcolm led their parents on a tour.

That night the family celebrated by making dinner together—and cleaning up together, too.

COMPREHENSION What words help you understand why Mom and Dad stop doing work around the house? How does this story show the importance of families working together?

8

Days 3 and 4

"Helping Hands," Vol. 1, pp. 8–9

Assessment

Pretest/Posttest Administration p. 63

Pretest/Posttest Blackline Masters pp. 94–95

Day 1

Introduce Meanings

Explain To assess what word meanings children already know, copy and distribute the **Pretest/Posttest** on pages 94–95. Use page 63 to administer the test.

Explain Write each oral vocabulary word below on the board. Read it aloud. Offer an explanation and a brief example for each word.

Words About Families

ancestors *n.* family members who lived before you *My ancestors were farmers.*

bond *n.* a feeling that holds people together *The sisters felt a close bond with each other.*

inheritance *n.* something passed on from earlier family members *His blue eyes are an inheritance from his father.*

memories *n.* things such as people, places, and events that are recalled later *We have fond memories of our childhood.*

reunion *n.* a big family get-together *All the cousins came to the family reunion.*

unusual *adj.* rare *It was unusual for the close family to spend holidays apart.*

Discuss Guide children to see the relationship between each word and the category. Ask: What do you have in common with your **ancestors**?

Read Aloud Explain that you will read aloud a story about an unusual family with eight children. Then read aloud "Many McCaugheys." Discuss the Comprehension questions.

Day 2

Categorize and Classify

Reread and Explain Reread "Many McCaugheys." At the end of each sentence that includes an oral vocabulary word, stop and repeat the explanation of the word. Then reread the sentence.

Use a Graphic Organizer Use the graphic organizer and the questions below to reinforce understanding of the relationship between each word and the category.

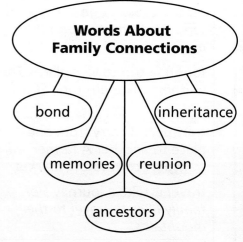

1. You might receive an **inheritance** from your _____. (**ancestors**)

2. Does your family have any **unusual** traditions? Tell about them. (Answers will vary.)

3. With which family member do you share a close **bond**? (Answers will vary.)

Day 3

Introduce Meanings

Explain Write each oral vocabulary word below on the board. Read it aloud. Offer an explanation and a brief example for each word.

Words About Being Fair

boycott *v.* to not buy something, as a punishment to the seller *We will boycott the store until the prices are fair.*

cause *n.* a goal that people work toward *Helping homeless animals is a good cause.*

injustice *n.* unfair treatment *She complained that her time-out was an injustice.*

picket *v.* to speak out against something unfair *The workers will picket to get paid more.*

rights *n.* the freedom to do something *Students have the right to ask the teacher questions.*

strike *v.* to stop working *The factory workers will strike until they are treated fairly.*

Discuss Guide children to see the relationship between each word and the category. Ask: Would you **picket** to fight **injustice**? What is one **cause** you would speak out for?

Read Aloud Explain that you will read aloud a story about parents who strike in order to get help from their children. Then read aloud "Helping Hands." Discuss the Comprehension questions.

Day 4

Categorize and Classify

Reread and Explain Reread "Helping Hands." At the end of each sentence that includes an oral vocabulary word, stop and repeat the explanation of the word. Then reread the sentence.

Use a Graphic Organizer Use the graphic organizer and the questions below to reinforce understanding of the relationship between each word and the category.

Workers Treated Unfairly	
What You Might Do	**Why You Might Do It**
picket strike boycott	rights injustice cause

1. To make the world a better place, we should speak out against _____. **(injustice)**

2. Suppose you decided to **picket** your school. What would your **cause** be? (Sample answers: less homework; more vacation)

3. If Mr. Madison loved his job at the bank, would he **strike**? Why or why not? (no; He would strike if he were unhappy.)

Day 5

Deepen Understanding

Review Repeat explanations for all oral vocabulary words. Use the definitions and examples from Day 1 and Day 3.

Guide Partner Activities Have partners work together to complete each of the activities below. Circulate and listen to partners as they work. Provide corrective feedback.

Examples Tell a partner your **memories** about a time when you felt a **bond** with a friend. Explain why you felt that way. Then tell about a **reunion** you have had with family members.

Word Parts The prefix *un-* means "not." The word **unusual** means "not usual." Use a dictionary or a glossary. Work with a partner to find and list three other examples of words with *un-*, meaning "not."

Role-Play Imagine that the students at school are going to **strike** for healthier food in the cafeteria. What might students say when they **picket**? Tell your partner.

Draw Draw a picture to show how a person today might look like his or her **ancestors**. Show an **inheritance** that was passed down from the person's ancestors.

Write Write about a **cause** you feel strongly about. Use these words: **rights, injustice, boycott**.

Assess To assess what word meanings children have learned, copy and distribute the **Pretest/Posttest** on pages 94–95. Use page 63 to administer the test. Compare scores with Day 1 assessment.

The Sparrow and the Canary

A sparrow left his friends and family in the country and flew to the nearby city. When the sparrow reached the city, he was tired and needed to rest. Up ahead, he saw a big, beautiful mansion that looked over the city. The sparrow wondered who lived in that fancy house. He noticed that the mansion had lots of windows and porches. He landed on one of the porches to take a rest.

The sparrow was surprised to see a birdcage on the porch. And inside the birdcage was a yellow canary. The canary was nibbling on a leaf of lettuce. The canary also had cups full of birdseed and water.

"You have plenty of food, I see," the sparrow said.

"Yes," the canary answered. "I have a good life. My owners give me all the food I want. And once, when I got sick, they took me to the city center to see a doctor. The doctor helped me feel better."

"How nice!" the sparrow said. "My life is not so easy. Sometimes I have trouble finding food to eat. Also, I have to watch out for cats that want to eat me."

"That's too bad," the canary said. "No cat could ever get near me here. And in cold weather, my family takes me inside where it is warm and dry."

The sparrow sighed. "I wish I could live in a place like this."

"Where do you live?" asked the canary.

"My home is in the country, where there is endless farmland and people live in small cottages," the sparrow said. "But I don't live in just one place. I move around."

"Move around?" asked the canary.

"Yes," answered the sparrow. "Sometimes I like to sit near the lake. When it rains, I go down into the basement of a building to stay dry. If you come with me, I'll show you my favorite places."

"I can't," said the canary. "My place is with my family. I fly around inside the apartment, but I don't fly around outside."

The sparrow asked, "You never fly around the city?"

"No," said the canary. "But I always have food, and I never worry about cats."

"I'd rather watch out for cats and search for food, as long as I have the freedom to fly where I want," the sparrow said. "I'm going back to the country."

COMPREHENSION Which words in the story tell about places to live? Why does the sparrow decide to go home?

10

Days 1 and 2

"The Sparrow and the Canary," Vol. 1, pp. 10–11

A Visit to the Capital

Last summer, my family traveled to Washington, D.C., for a few days. We spent most of our trip at the Mall. The Mall is a big park in Washington, D.C. The Capitol building is at one end and the Washington Monument is at the other. Most of the other landmarks in Washington are along the Mall as well.

The first day, my family and I toured the Capitol building. This is where the lawmakers work when they legislate, or make laws. We stood under the Capitol dome. The dome is the roof of a huge circular hall. Standing under the dome, you can look all the way up to the top of the very tall building. It was amazing!

Then we walked along the Mall. The Mall is lined with federal buildings. These buildings are owned by the government of the United States. They are the official offices for the people who help run our country.

There are many fun museums along the Mall, too. On the second day, we went to the Air and Space Museum. We saw the first working airplane, the 1903 Wright Flyer. We saw spaceship capsules that transported astronauts on moon missions. I touched a real moon rock at the Air and Space Museum!

We also visited the Washington Monument. It stands 550 feet tall. That's as tall as three Capitol buildings standing on top of each other! From the top, we could see over the entire city. Next, we visited the Lincoln Memorial. It has a big statue of Abraham Lincoln in it. He looks thoughtful and sad. My dad read to me some of the famous things that Lincoln said. They are carved into the wall in the Lincoln Memorial.

On the third day, we walked by the White House. This is the home of the President of the United States. It also has the President's office. It is a beautiful house. I would like to live there someday, when I am President!

Before we went home, we visited the Bureau of Engraving and Printing. This is where they print the nation's money and stamps. We saw big sheets of money coming off the printing presses. The tour guide said they make about $750 million there every day.

There are other places to see in Washington, D.C., such as the National Aquarium and the National Zoo. We didn't get to see those places on this trip. That's where we'll start next time, though!

COMPREHENSION What words about government did you hear in this passage? Would you like to visit Washington, D.C.? Why or why not?

12

Days 3 and 4

"A Visit to the Capital," Vol. 1, pp. 12–13

Assessment

Pretest/Posttest Administration p. 64

Pretest/Posttest Blackline Masters pp. 96–97

Day 1

Introduce Meanings

Assess To assess what word meanings children already know, copy and distribute the **Pretest/Posttest** on pages 96–97. Use page 64 to administer the test.

Explain Write each oral vocabulary word below on the board. Read it aloud. Offer an explanation and a brief example for each word.

Words About Places to Live

basement *n.* an underground floor of a building *My grown-up brother slept downstairs in our basement when he visited.*

city center *n.* the middle of a large town *Our apartment was right in the city center.*

cottage *n.* a small, simple house *Their tiny cottage had two bedrooms.*

country *n.* land outside the city *She likes living in the country, away from all the city noise.*

farmland *n.* land used for growing food *The city is nothing like the farmland where my friends live.*

mansion *n.* a large, expensive house *The governor's mansion has twenty-three rooms.*

Discuss Guide children to see the relationship between each word and the category.

Read Aloud Explain that you will read aloud a story about a sparrow and a canary that compare the places where they live. Then read aloud "The Sparrow and the Canary." Discuss the Comprehension questions.

Day 2

Categorize and Classify

Reread and Explain Reread "The Sparrow and the Canary." At the end of each sentence that includes an oral vocabulary word, stop and repeat the explanation of the word. Then reread the sentence.

Use a Graphic Organizer Use the graphic organizer and the questions below to reinforce understanding of the relationship between each word and the category.

Inside Places	Outside Places
basement cottage mansion	farmland country city center

1. Would you find **farmland** in a **city center**? Explain your answer. (no; A city center has lots of buildings and people.)

2. If your home has ten or more rooms, you might live in a _____. **(mansion)**

3. The Smiths never liked big houses, so they decided to live in a small _____. **(cottage)**

Day 3

Introduce Meanings

Explain Write each oral vocabulary word below on the board. Read it aloud. Offer an explanation and a brief example for each word.

Words About the Government

capitol *n.* the main government building *The governor of California works in the* capitol *building.*

federal *adj.* belonging to the United States government *The White House is a* federal *building.*

landmark *n.* something that is easy to recognize in a place *The Statue of Liberty is a* landmark *of New York City.*

legislate *v.* to make laws *The senator worked hard to* legislate *fair laws.*

memorial *n.* something to help people remember *The Jefferson* Memorial *reminds people of the great president.*

official *adj.* from the people in charge *We needed an* official *pass to visit the White House.*

Discuss Guide children to see the relationship between each word and the category. Prompt them to discuss government buildings they know about, using the vocabulary words.

Read Aloud Explain that you will read aloud a story about a trip to Washington, D.C. Then read aloud "A Visit to the Capital." Discuss the Comprehension questions.

Day 4

Categorize and Classify

Reread and Explain Reread "A Visit to the Capital." At the end of each sentence that includes an oral vocabulary word, stop and repeat the explanation of the word. Then reread the sentence.

Use a Graphic Organizer Use the graphic organizer and the questions below to reinforce understanding of the relationship between each word and the category.

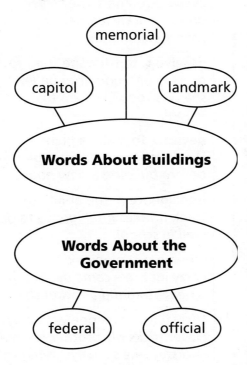

1. The government put up a statue to remember our first president. What word describes that statue? **(memorial)**

2. A statue is also a kind of _____. **(landmark)**

3. A lawmaker's job at the **capitol** is to _____. **(legislate)**

Day 5

Deepen Understanding

Review Repeat explanations for all oral vocabulary words. Use the definitions and examples from Day 1 and Day 3.

Guide Partner Activities Have partners work together to complete each of the activities below. Circulate and listen to partners as they work. Provide corrective feedback.

Examples Name some **landmarks** in your town or city. Are any of the landmarks **memorials**? Tell a partner.

Categorize Work with a partner. List three things you might see in a **city center**. Then list three things you might see on **farmland**. Tell which place is in the **country**.

Describe Pretend that your house or apartment had a **basement** that you could use for whatever you wanted. Describe to a partner how you would use the basement.

Role-Play Take turns with a partner. Pretend you are **federal** lawmakers. You work in the **capitol**. What laws would you **legislate** for students?

Draw What animal would you choose as the **official** animal of the United States? Draw and label a picture of the animal.

Compare Talk to your partner. Compare a **cottage** to a **mansion**. Think about the size of each and where you might find each.

Assess To assess what word meanings children have learned, copy and distribute the **Pretest/Posttest** on pages 96–97. Use page 64 to administer the test. Compare scores with Day 1 assessment.

Days 1 and 2

"Anansi and Turtle," Vol. 1, pp. 14–15

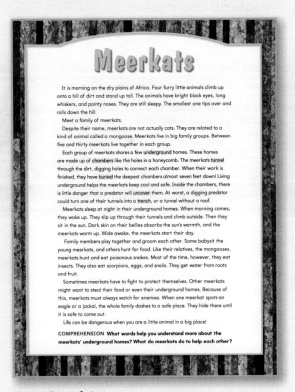

Days 3 and 4

"Meerkats," Vol. 1, pp. 16–17

Assessment

Pretest/Posttest Administration p. 65

Pretest/Posttest Blackline Masters pp. 98–99

Day 1

Introduce Meanings

Assess To assess what word meanings children already know, copy and distribute the **Pretest/Posttest** on pages 98–99. Use page 65 to administer the test.

Explain Write each oral vocabulary word below on the board. Read it aloud. Offer an explanation and a brief example for each word.

Words About Being Smart

clever *adj.* smart *The clever puppy quickly learned to follow commands.*

deceive *v.* to trick *She tried to deceive her mom into believing she was too sick to go to school.*

devise *v.* to make a plan *Workers always devise a plan before building a new house.*

intelligence *n.* the ability to think *It takes intelligence to do well in school.*

scheme *n.* a plan; a kind of crazy idea *We came up with a scheme to build a rocket ship.*

trickster *n.* someone who plays clever tricks *My brother is a real trickster—he's always trying to fool me into giving him my dessert.*

Discuss Guide children to see the relationship between each word and the category. Ask: What might show that someone is a **trickster**?

Read Aloud Explain that you will read aloud a story about a spider that doesn't want to share its dinner with a turtle. Then read aloud "Anansi and Turtle." Discuss the Comprehension questions.

Day 2

Categorize and Classify

Reread and Explain Reread "Anansi and Turtle." At the end of each sentence that includes an oral vocabulary word, stop and repeat the explanation of the word. Then reread the sentence.

Use a Graphic Organizer Use the graphic organizer and the questions below to reinforce understanding of the relationship between each word and the category.

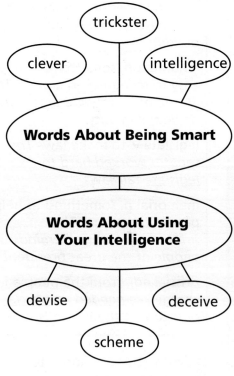

1. What words might you use to describe someone who answered every question correctly on a test? (Sample answer: **clever, intelligence**)

2. If you find out that someone is trying to **deceive** you, you might feel _____. (Sample answers: angry; upset; unhappy)

Day 3

Introduce Meanings

Explain Write each oral vocabulary word below on the board. Read it aloud. Offer an explanation and a brief example for each word.

Words About Digging

buried *v.* put in the ground and covered with earth *The children buried a shell in the sand.*

chamber *n.* a room or other space surrounded by walls *The gopher slept in a chamber under the ground.*

trench *n.* a long, narrow ditch *The farmer dug a trench to bring water to the crops.*

tunnel *v.* to dig an underground passage *The workers needed to tunnel under the river.*

uncovering *v.* taking something off the top of so the thing underneath can be seen *The dog was uncovering the bone he hid in the ground.*

underground *adj.* below the ground *A worm lives underground.*

Discuss Guide children to see the relationship between each word and the category. Ask questions such as this: What would someone do in an **underground chamber**?

Read Aloud Explain that you will read aloud a story about animals called meerkats. Then read aloud "Meerkats." Discuss the Comprehension questions.

Day 4

Categorize and Classify

Reread and Explain Reread "Meerkats." At the end of each sentence that includes an oral vocabulary word, stop and repeat the explanation of the word. Then reread the sentence.

Use a Graphic Organizer Use the graphic organizer and the questions below to reinforce understanding of the relationship between each word and the category.

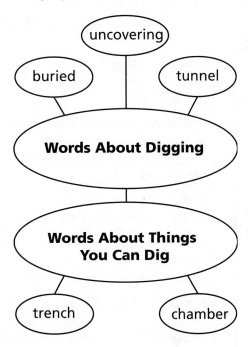

1. Name some animals that live **underground**. (Sample answer: worms, ants, moles)

2. What word might you use to describe finding something another person has **buried**? (**uncovering**)

Day 5

Deepen Understanding

Review Review word meanings for all oral vocabulary words. Use the definitions and examples from Day 1 and Day 3.

Guide Partner Activities Have partners work together to complete each of the activities below. Circulate and listen to partners as they work. Provide corrective feedback.

Compare Work with a partner. Compare a **tunnel** to a **trench**. How are a tunnel and a trench similar? How are they different? How do you think one might be used differently than the other?

Describe Talk to your partner. Describe a **clever scheme** for hiding jewels **underground**. Tell how you would keep people from **uncovering** the jewels.

Role-Play Show how you might look if your best friend acted like a **trickster** and **deceived** you. Then show how you might look if your friend apologized.

Draw Draw a picture of an animal that just **buried** something in a **chamber** in the ground.

Write Work with a partner. Write a story about a person who is very smart. Give details about his or her **intelligence**. Then write about a new invention that he or she **devised**.

Assess To assess what word meanings children have learned, copy and distribute the **Pretest/Posttest** on pages 98–99. Use page 65 to administer the test. Compare scores with Day 1 assessment.

How to Act in the Classroom

Here's a quick quiz question:
You're working at the art table in the classroom. You have markers, paints, and paper spread out around you. Suddenly the lunch bell rings. What do you do?
(a) Run to be the first person on line in the cafeteria. You're hungry!
(b) Sweep the art supplies off the table and onto the floor. The table is clean!
(c) Clean up the supplies you have used. Now, lunchtime!

You probably chose the correct answer: "Clean up the supplies you have used. Now, lunchtime!" How did you know? Because you have good manners, and that means you clean up after yourself.

Good manners are important wherever you are. You certainly need them at school, where you spend the day with many other people. It is important to be civil and respectful to people at school. Let's talk about a few ways to act in the classroom.

First, remember to give everyone a chance to speak. Even if you have an idea to share with others, self-control is important. Don't interrupt your teacher when he or she is talking with another student. Wait until the conversation has finished. Then you may speak up.

Next, if the teacher asks the whole class a question, raise your hand. That's the signal that you have an answer.

Also, in the classroom, you'll find children you don't know. When you meet someone new, make sure to introduce yourself. For example, say, "Hello, my name is Jasmine," in a friendly tone of voice.

Another thing: remember to share classroom materials with others. If someone else wants to use the supplies that you are using, invite him or her to join you. Asking someone to share with you is not only polite, it can help you make a new friend!

Finally, school is not the place to ask other children to a party or a playdate. You can do this after school hours. You can call your friends on the telephone or send a card or note with your message. Otherwise, you risk hurting the feelings of the children that you haven't asked to join you.

Remember that even the most polite children make mistakes from time to time. What do you do then? Apologize. A simple "I'm sorry" goes a long way in making up for poor manners.

COMPREHENSION Why is it important to use good manners in the classroom? Which words help you describe how you should or shouldn't act in the classroom?

18

Days 1 and 2

"How to Act in the Classroom," Vol. 1, pp. 18–19

When It Rains, It Roars

Outside, the rain was falling hard. It pounded against the roof of the house. It poured down every window. It fell, and it fell, and it kept on falling all day long.

Inside the house, Bunker was hiding beneath the couch. The rain was so loud, so fierce, and so powerful, it filled Bunker's heart with terror. He began to think frightening thoughts. What if the rain became so strong that it came alive? What would a rain monster look like? Would it be so savage that it would try to destroy the house? That's when Bunker started to panic. He whined. He howled. He crawled as far under the couch as he could go.

Bunker's owner, Marlena, walked into the room. "Bunker, what is the matter with you?" she asked the panicking puppy. "It's just rain, silly. Now come on, it's time to go for a walk."

But Bunker was imagining rain monsters outside. Their faces were mean and horrifying. When Marlena reached for him, Bunker growled.

Marlena frowned. "OK, Bunker. I'm going to the store. You can stay here by yourself."

Marlena left, and the rain kept falling. Bunker's fears grew worse. Finally, Marlena came home, and soon after, she went to bed. Bunker stayed beneath the couch and whimpered.

In the morning, Marlena found Bunker right where she'd left him. Marlena knew that Bunker was still frightened. But she had a plan.

"Bunker, I know how you can fight your fears," she said. "You just need to trust me. And you need to come out from under that couch."

Bunker crawled out slowly. Marlena scooped him up and hurried to the front door. Before Bunker could understand what was happening, they were standing outside in the cold rain.

Bunker closed his eyes and waited for the rain monsters to attack. He waited, and waited. And then he opened his eyes. Bunker barked happily. There were no rain monsters out there. He was just getting wet! He no longer felt afraid.

Bunker gave Marlena a slobbery kiss on the face.

COMPREHENSION What words help you understand how Bunker is feeling? When do Bunker's feelings change?

20

Days 3 and 4

"When It Rains, It Roars," Vol. 1, pp. 20–21

Assessment

Pretest/Posttest Administration p. 66
Pretest/Posttest Blackline Masters pp. 100–101

Day 1

Introduce Meanings

Assess To assess what word meanings children already know, copy and distribute the **Pretest/ Posttest** on pages 100–101. Use page 66 to administer the test.

Explain Write each oral vocabulary word below on the board. Read it aloud. Offer an explanation and a brief example for each word.

Words About Good Manners

apologize v. to say you are sorry *Please apologize for your rude behavior.*

civil adj. polite *You should be civil to your sister even when she bothers you.*

introduce v. to make something or someone known *Mom will introduce herself to the new neighbors.*

invite v. to ask *The boy can invite a friend for a sleepover.*

note n. a short written message *You should send a thank-you note when you receive a gift.*

self-control n. ability to control your own actions *Self-control is important at home as well as at school.*

Discuss Guide children to see the relationship between each word and the category. Ask questions such as these: Why might someone **apologize** to a friend? Why is it polite to **introduce** yourself to a new student?

Read Aloud Explain that you will read aloud a story about good manners in the classroom. Then read aloud "How to Act in the Classroom." Discuss the Comprehension questions.

Day 2

Categorize and Classify

Reread and Explain Reread "How to Act in the Classroom." At the end of each sentence that includes an oral vocabulary word, stop and repeat the explanation of the word. Then reread the sentence.

Use a Graphic Organizer Use the graphic organizer and the questions below to reinforce understanding of the relationship between each word and the category.

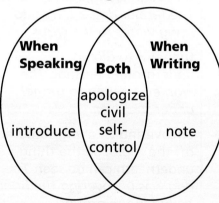

Words About Being Polite

When Speaking — Both — When Writing

introduce / apologize civil self-control / note

1. Think about this sentence: *Pam apologized for not sharing the crayons.* Which action showed Pam's good manners? Why? (apologizing; Sample answer: Pam felt badly about not sharing.)

2. Suppose you tell a new student your name. What word describes that? (**introduce**)

3. At lunchtime, what could you do to be **civil** to a new student? (Sample answer: You could **invite** the student to sit next to you at lunch.)

Day 3

Introduce Meanings

Explain Write each oral vocabulary word below on the board. Read it aloud. Offer an explanation and a brief example for each word.

Words About Scary Things

fierce *adj.* wild and dangerous *The fierce storm knocked out power for hours.*

frightening *adj.* scary *A frightening movie can cause bad dreams.*

horrifying *adj.* causing very strong fear *Some monsters can be horrifying.*

panicking *adj.* having a sudden feeling of fear *The teacher calmed the panicking boy.*

savage *adj.* cruel and uncontrolled *The savage lion attacked the smaller animal.*

terror *n.* strong fear *Because she was afraid of the dark, the girl felt terror at night.*

Discuss Guide children to see the relationship between each word and the category. Ask questions such as these: What scary things cause you to feel **terror**? What scary things might cause a person to **panic**? Name something that you think is **frightening**.

Read Aloud Explain that you will read aloud a story about a dog that is afraid of a rainstorm. Then read aloud "When It Rains, It Roars." Discuss the Comprehension questions.

Day 4

Categorize and Classify

Reread and Explain Reread "When It Rains, It Roars." At the end of each sentence that includes an oral vocabulary word, stop and repeat the explanation of the word. Then reread the sentence.

Use a Graphic Organizer Use the graphic organizer and the questions below to reinforce understanding of the relationship between each word and the category.

1. Meeting a bear in the woods would be _____. (Sample answers: **frightening; horrifying**)

2. This experience might cause you to be filled with _____. (**terror**)

3. How might you help a **panicking** person? (Sample answer: I could tell the person to take a deep breath.)

Day 5

Deepen Understanding

Review Repeat explanations for all oral vocabulary words. Use the definitions and examples from Day 1 and Day 3.

Guide Partner Activities Have partners work together to complete each of the activities below. Circulate and listen to partners as they work. Provide corrective feedback.

Categorize Work with a partner. List three animals that are **fierce**. Then list three things that can cause **terror**. Which animal on your list would most cause a person to **panic**? Why?

Role-Play Work with a partner. Take turns acting out a conversation in which you **apologize** for not being **civil** to your partner.

Examples What are some things that are **savage**? Tell your partner. Then name some ways to practice **self-control**.

Draw Draw a picture of a **frightening** monster. What details would make the monster look **horrifying**?

Write Imagine you are having a party. Write a **note** to **invite** a frightening monster to the party. Tell a partner how you would **introduce** the monster to your friends.

Assess To assess what word meanings children have learned, copy and distribute the **Pretest/Posttest** on pages 100–101. Use page 66 to administer the test. Compare scores with Day 1 assessment.

Birds of Prey

Birds of prey, or raptors, are birds that capture other birds and animals for food. Raptors use sharp claws called talons and sharp beaks to help them catch their food. Their eyesight is also very good. They are able to see the animals they hunt from very high in the air.

When baby raptors hatch from their eggs, they cannot fly. They cannot catch their own food either. The parents find food for their babies as well as for themselves. Soon, the young raptors are able to fly and hunt for themselves.

Many birds of prey are active during the day. Others are nocturnal and stay awake at night. Owls are one kind of nocturnal bird. They can see and hear very well. This is important because they hunt at night in the dark. Also, owls make almost no noise when they fly, which helps them catch other animals by surprise.

Eagles are large raptors. These birds look for prey by gliding on air currents, without needing to flap their wings. This helps them save energy so they can hunt for longer periods of time.

Hawks are also birds of prey. They are smaller than eagles. While eagles glide on air currents looking for food, hawks perch where animals can't see them. Hawks listen for greeting calls and other chatter among the animals. Then they swoop down and surprise the animals they want to catch.

Many raptors eat animals that sleep through the winter. For this reason, these raptors have to migrate. That means they fly to warmer lands where they can find food. During their travel, the raptors' feathers usually molt and new ones grow to replace them.

Some people think that birds of prey are cruel because they kill and eat small animals. This is a mistake. Like other animals that hunt for food, raptors act out of natural instinct. Also, because some of the animals they hunt can damage farmers' crops, birds of prey can actually be helpful. They play an important role in the balance of nature.

COMPREHENSION How do different birds of prey catch animals? Why do some birds of prey migrate?

Days 1 and 2

"Birds of Prey," Vol. 1, pp. 22–23

A Shelter for the Winter

Winter was on its way. The bears could feel it in the wind. Suddenly, it was too cold to sleep outside on the grass. They knew that the grass would soon be covered with snow.

Bruce the bear said to his friends, "Bears, we must construct shelters! We need to build places to stay warm when the chill, the snow, and the storms come. Let's get moving!"

And they did. They did so in many different ways.

Bruce gathered loads of leaves into a giant mound. He crawled deep into the mound until only his ears were sticking out.

Bertha the bear chopped timber from the strongest-looking trees. Then she stacked the slabs of wood into a fort. Bertha crawled inside and curled up.

Now, Buddy the bear sat down to think. The ground felt warm beneath him. A thought came to him: "What would happen if I hid under the ground in order to survive this winter?"

So Buddy began to dig. He dug a big tunnel into the earth. And then he covered the tunnel with rocks and dirt as a brace against the cold. He made sure to pack the rocks and dirt firmly together to reinforce their strength.

Then Bruce, Bertha, and Buddy waited.

A few days later, it snowed. The snow fell into Bruce's mound of leaves. The leaves became wet and heavy. "Gosh, I'm all wet and chilly!" Bruce thought. "I think Buddy had the right idea." And he began to dig into the earth.

A few days after that, strong winds came. The winds whipped against Bertha's soggy fort, splintering her slabs of timber. "Oh no, I must find a new shelter!" Bertha thought. "I will follow Bruce and Buddy underground." And that's what she did.

Weeks went by. The snow kept falling. The winds continued to whip. But the bears slept peacefully in their warm tunnels. They were happy that Buddy the bear was so clever.

COMPREHENSION Why did the bears need to build shelters? What words helped you understand which shelter was the strongest?

24

Days 3 and 4

"A Shelter for the Winter," Vol. 1, pp. 24–25

Assessment

Pretest/Posttest Administration p. 67

Pretest/Posttest Blackline Masters pp. 102–103

Day 1

Introduce Meanings

Assess To assess what word meanings children already know, copy and distribute the **Pretest/Posttest** on pages 102–103. Use page 67 to administer the test.

Explain Write each oral vocabulary word below on the board. Read it aloud. Offer an explanation and a brief example for each word.

Words About Birds

gliding v. when a bird flies without moving its wings *Hawks were gliding in the wind.*

greeting n. a message that says hello *The dove's greeting to the morning sounded beautiful.*

hatch v. to come out of an egg *Baby birds are helpless when they first hatch.*

migrate v. to travel long distances to find food *Some geese migrate thousands of miles.*

molt v. to lose feathers *Birds molt and then grow new feathers.*

nocturnal adj. awake at night and asleep during the day *Owls are nocturnal birds.*

Discuss Guide children to see the relationship between each word and the category. Ask a volunteer to come to the front of the room and show the class what a **gliding** bird looks like.

Read Aloud Explain that you will read aloud a story about birds that hunt other birds and animals for food. Then read aloud "Birds of Prey." Discuss the Comprehension questions.

Day 2

Categorize and Classify

Reread and Explain Reread "Birds of Prey." At the end of each sentence that includes an oral vocabulary word, stop and repeat the explanation of the word. Then reread the sentence.

Use a Graphic Organizer Use the graphic organizer and the questions below to reinforce understanding of the relationship between each word and the category.

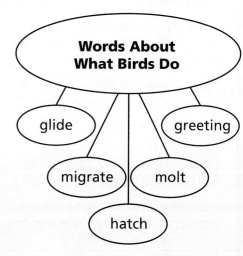

1. A bird may sing a **greeting** to another bird. When else might a bird use its voice? (Sample answer: to warn other birds)

2. Name some birds or animals that **migrate**. (Sample answer: ducks, whales)

3. Are you a **nocturnal** animal? (no) Name some nocturnal birds and animals. (Sample answer: owls, bats)

Day 3

Introduce Meanings

Explain Write each oral vocabulary word below on the board. Read it aloud. Offer an explanation and a brief example for each word.

Words About Building

brace *n.* a support *We put a brace against the wall to hold up the roof.*

construct *v.* to build *You can construct a hut from sticks and branches.*

reinforce *v.* to make stronger *Reinforce the roof with extra wood to make it stronger.*

slab *n.* a thick, flat piece *A slab of ice covered the sidewalk.*

splintering *v.* breaking into tiny pieces *I dropped a glass, splintering it on the floor.*

timber *n.* wood *Many houses are made of timber.*

Discuss Guide children to see the relationship between each word and the category. Ask questions such as these: Would you rather have a **splintering** roof or a roof that is **reinforced**? Would you rather live in a house made of **timber** or one made of sticks and branches? Explain.

Read Aloud Explain that you will read aloud a story about building shelters. Then read aloud "A Shelter for the Winter." Discuss the Comprehension questions.

Day 4

Categorize and Classify

Reread and Explain Reread "A Shelter for the Winter." At the end of each sentence that includes an oral vocabulary word, stop and repeat the explanation of the word. Then reread the sentence.

Use a Graphic Organizer Use the graphic organizer and the questions below to reinforce understanding of the relationship between each word and the category.

Words About Things Used to Build	Words About Ways to Build
brace slab timber	construct reinforce

1. What word might you use to describe what a **brace** can do to a wall? **(reinforce)**

2. What could you use as a brace against the wind if you were building a fort? **(Sample answer: rocks, a tarp)**

3. A small piece of ice could be a cube; a large piece could be a _____. **(slab)**

4. What would happen to a building if a bulldozer tore it down? **(splintering)**

Day 5

Deepen Understanding

Review Repeat explanations for all oral vocabulary words. Use the definitions and examples from Day 1 and Day 3.

Guide Partner Activities Have partners work together to complete each of the activities below. Circulate and listen to partners as they work. Provide corrective feedback.

Categorize Work with a partner. Tell about three ways you might use a **slab** of wood. Tell about three ways you might use pieces of **timber**. Would you use them differently? Why or why not?

Examples Name one animal that can **molt**. Name one object that can **splinter**. Can an object molt? Can an animal splinter? If so, give an example. It not, explain.

Draw Draw a picture of a building people might **construct**. Show how you could **reinforce** parts of the building with a **brace**.

Write Suppose you were a **nocturnal** animal. When would you sleep? When would you go to school? Write about how your life would be different.

Describe Imagine that you are a bird. Describe to your partner what it was like to **hatch,** and what **gliding** and **migrating** is like. Do you ever sing a **greeting** to other birds around you?

Assess To assess what word meanings children have learned, copy and distribute the **Pretest/Posttest** on pages 102–103. Use page 67 to administer the test. Compare scores with Day 1 assessment.

How to Help the Environment

We all need to help the global environment. This means that we need to think about keeping the whole world healthy, not just our own yard or neighborhood. Without our help, our planet, Earth, will suffer. And the people, animals, and plants living on Earth will suffer, too. What's good is that there are many easy ways that we can all help the environment.

One way we can help is to save energy. We can do this by turning off the lights when we leave a room. When we turn off the lights, power, or electricity, stops flowing to the light bulbs. And the less electricity we use, the more energy we'll save.

We can also help our environment by using less water. One easy way we can do this is to turn off the faucet when we brush our teeth. When we leave the water running, we use an excess of water, which is more than we need. We should save the water we have for important things like bathing, cooking, and watering the plants.

Another thing we can all do is cut down on the amount of pollution we create. Cars can cause pollution by sending unhealthy gases into the air. So if we drive our cars less, we can keep our air cleaner. The next time your family has an errand, you could ask your parents if you can walk or ride bikes instead of using the car.

The less pollution we put into the air, the healthier Earth's atmosphere will be. The atmosphere is high in the sky, and it surrounds the Earth. It is made of many different kinds of gas. These gases help protect our planet from the sun's strong rays. Many people believe that if our atmosphere becomes polluted, the sun's rays will break through more easily and make the Earth a lot warmer than it should be. This kind of global warming could hurt our planet.

Look around your own home. Can you think of other ways that you can help the environment?

COMPREHENSION Why is it important to help the environment? What words in this selection describe ways to help the environment?

26

Days 1 and 2

"How to Help the Environment," Vol. 1, pp. 26–27

A Neighbor in Need

"Hey Mikey, Fred Jarvis came home from the hospital today," my mother told me. "But I'm sure he's still in a lot of pain from his back injury."

"Great," I muttered, under my breath. Luckily, my mom didn't hear me.

Later, I said to my friend Ariana, "Mr. Jarvis came home from the hospital today. My mom said his back hurts. I bet he is meaner than ever now." None of the kids in the neighborhood liked Mr. Jarvis. He always kept our balls if they landed in his vegetable garden. Once, he even yelled at me for riding my bike too loud! I'm still trying to figure that one out.

"I feel bad for him. It must be hard to live all alone like Mr. Jarvis does," said Ariana. "You would have no one to help you out. It must be even harder when you're hurt. Maybe we should offer to help him out."

"Oh no," I said. "Don't you utter another word. I won't do it."

"You will do it. It's the right thing to do," Ariana insisted.

Ariana rounded up some other kids. Then she took us all to Mr. Jarvis's house. We all held our breath as she knocked on his door.

After a few moments, Mr. Jarvis opened the door. "What do you want?" he snapped.

"Hi, Mr. Jarvis. We heard that your back was hurting, so we're here to help. We thought we could take care of your garden for you," Ariana explained.

Mr. Jarvis looked surprised. "You don't need to do that."

"Now, sir, please don't argue," said Ariana. "Gardening requires a lot of bending and stooping. You can't do that if your back is hurting."

"Well, now that you mention it, my garden does need some work. I guess you kids could help," Mr. Jarvis agreed.

For the next hour, we weeded his garden and picked his vegetables. When we finished, his garden looked better than new.

"You kids did a great job," said Mr. Jarvis. We couldn't believe it! It wasn't like him to give us praise. We walked away from Mr. Jarvis's house with proud feelings—and a big bag of vegetables!

COMPREHENSION Which words help you understand how people in the story speak? What do Ariana and the other kids learn about Mr. Jarvis?

28

Days 3 and 4

"A Neighbor in Need," Vol. 1, pp. 28–29

Assessment

Pretest/Posttest Administration p. 68

Pretest/Posttest Blackline Masters pp. 104–105

Day 1

Introduce Meanings

Assess To assess what word meanings children already know, copy and distribute the **Pretest/Posttest** on pages 104–105. Use page 68 to administer the test.

Explain Write each oral vocabulary word below on the board. Read it aloud. Offer an explanation and a brief example for each word.

Words About the Environment

atmosphere *n.* a mix of gases surrounding Earth; the air and sky *The spaceship flew down through Earth's* <u>atmosphere</u>.

electricity *n.* the power that makes light bulbs and televisions turn on *If the* <u>electricity</u> *goes off, the lights will go out.*

excess *n.* more than you need *We should save energy instead of using* <u>excess</u>.

global *adj.* worldwide *Clean air and clean water are* <u>global</u> *needs.*

planet *n.* a very large object in space that circles around the Sun *Earth, Venus, and Jupiter are* <u>planets</u>.

pollution *n.* what makes air or water dirty *The bay was filled with* <u>pollution</u> *after the oil spill.*

Discuss Guide children to see the relationship between each word and the category. Ask: What does **pollution** do to our **planet**? Why is it important to not use natural energy in **excess**?

Read Aloud Explain that you will read aloud a story about ways to save energy and water. Then read aloud "How to Help the Environment." Discuss the Comprehension questions.

Day 2

Categorize and Classify

Reread and Explain Reread "How to Help the Environment." At the end of each sentence that includes an oral vocabulary word, stop and repeat the explanation of the word. Then reread the sentence.

Use a Graphic Organizer Use the graphic organizer and the questions below to reinforce understanding of the relationship between each word and the category.

Words About Earth	Words About What Can Hurt Earth
atmosphere global planet	excess pollution

1. What are some examples of **pollution**? (Sample answer: car fumes, litter)

2. How can you keep from using an **excess** of **electricity**? (Sample answers: turn off lights; don't watch as much TV)

Day 3

Introduce Meanings

Explain Write each oral vocabulary word below on the board. Read it aloud. Offer an explanation and a brief example for each word.

Words About Speaking

insisted *v.* said firmly *Taryn was tired, so I insisted I would carry her books.*

mention *v.* to briefly speak of *Please don't mention this to anyone.*

muttered *v.* mumbled *Joe muttered that he wasn't hungry because he ate a big snack.*

praise *n.* words that tell how good someone is *His praise made me feel proud.*

snapped *v.* spoke sharply *"I don't have time for this!" she snapped.*

utter *v.* to speak *Don't utter a word about the surprise.*

Discuss Guide children to see the relationship between each word and the category.

Read Aloud Explain that you will read aloud a story about children who help a neighbor. Then read aloud "A Neighbor in Need." Discuss the Comprehension questions.

Day 4

Categorize and Classify

Reread and Explain Reread "A Neighbor in Need." At the end of each sentence that includes an oral vocabulary word, stop and repeat the explanation of the word. Then reread the sentence.

Use a Graphic Organizer Use the graphic organizer and the questions below to reinforce understanding of the relationship between each word and the category.

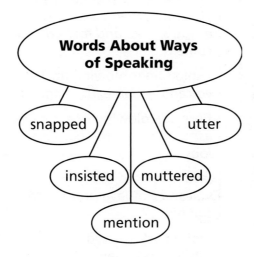

1. Do people who are sure of themselves **mutter** or **insist**? (**insist**)

2. What are some actions that deserve **praise**? (Sample answer: helping others without asking, doing well on a test)

3. If you were telling someone about your neighborhood, what kinds of things would you **mention**? (Answers will vary.)

Day 5

Deepen Understanding

Review Repeat explanations for all oral vocabulary words. Use the definitions and examples from Day 1 and Day 3.

Guide Partner Activities Have partners work together to complete each of the activities below. Circulate and listen to partners as they work. Provide corrective feedback.

Categorize Think about these words: **snapped, insist, mention, mutter, utter.** What do they sound like? Now put them in order from soft to loud. Explain your order to your partner.

Draw Show a scene where people are using an **excess** of energy and sending **pollution** into our **atmosphere.** Then show a scene where people are taking care of our **planet.**

Describe Tell how **electricity** allows us to hear about **global** events and speak with people all over the world.

Write Write about a time you received **praise** for something you did. Remember to use a lot of detail.

Assess To assess what word meanings children have learned, copy and distribute the **Pretest/Posttest** on pages 104–105. Use page 68 to administer the test. Compare scores with Day 1 assessment.

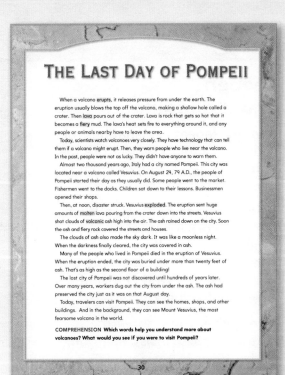

THE LAST DAY OF POMPEII

When a volcano **erupts**, it releases pressure from under the earth. The eruption usually blows the top off the volcano, making a shallow hole called a crater. Then **lava** pours out of the crater. Lava is rock that gets so hot that it becomes a **fiery** mud. The lava's heat sets fire to everything around it, and any people or animals nearby have to leave the area.

Today, scientists watch volcanoes very closely. They have technology that can tell them if a volcano might erupt. Then, they warn people who live near the volcano. In the past, people were not as lucky. They didn't have anyone to warn them.

Almost two thousand years ago, Italy had a city named Pompeii. This city was located near a volcano called Vesuvius. On August 24, 79 A.D., the people of Pompeii started their day as they usually did. Some people went to the market. Fishermen went to the docks. Children sat down to their lessons. Businessmen opened their shops.

Then, at noon, disaster struck. Vesuvius **exploded**. The eruption sent huge amounts of **molten** lava pouring from the crater down into the streets. Vesuvius shot clouds of **volcanic** ash high into the air. The ash rained down on the city. Soon the ash and fiery rock covered the streets and houses.

The clouds of ash also made the sky dark. It was like a moonless night. When the darkness finally cleared, the city was covered in ash.

Many of the people who lived in Pompeii died in the eruption of Vesuvius. When the eruption ended, the city was buried under more than twenty feet of ash. That's as high as the second floor of a building!

The lost city of Pompeii was not discovered until hundreds of years later. Over many years, workers dug out the city from under the ash. The ash had preserved the city just as it was on that August day.

Today, travelers can visit Pompeii. They can see the homes, shops, and other buildings. And in the background, they can see Mount Vesuvius, the most fearsome volcano in the world.

COMPREHENSION Which words help you understand more about volcanoes? What would you see if you were to visit Pompeii?

30

Days 1 and 2

"The Last Day of Pompeii," Vol. 1, pp. 30–31

Learning About a Natural Disaster

It was time for dinner. Nika and her mother sat down at the kitchen table. Nika's mother had made spaghetti and meatballs, Nika's favorite! Only Nika wasn't eating much. She dragged her fork through the strands of spaghetti. After a few minutes, her mother asked, "Nika, what's the matter?"

Nika took a deep breath. "Well, today in class we learned about a horrible natural disaster. There was a huge **earthquake**. It happened a long time ago in San Francisco, California."

"Ah yes, in 1906," said Nika's mother. "I remember learning about that."

"It happened while most people were still sleeping, at five o'clock in the morning," Nika explained. "The earthquake happened because the earth shifted quickly. This caused **trembles** underground. Above the ground, people heard a loud rumble. The rumble sounded like thunder."

"That sounds scary," said Nika's mother. "Do you remember what the earthquake did?"

Nika replied sadly, "It had a terrible **impact** on the city. Houses caved in and **collapsed** to the ground. Trees fell down on top of cars and bridges fell on top of roads, creating piles of useless **wreckage**. And people ran in every direction. They were scared for their lives."

Nika's mother was quiet for a while. And then she said, "It is terrible that such a bad disaster happened. Nature can be a powerful thing. It can bring us days full of sunshine and cool breezes. But it can also bring days when the earth trembles beneath us. Nature is something we can't control."

Nika nodded silently.

Her mother continued, "But that doesn't mean we can't be prepared. You and I can make a plan right now. We can plan out what we would do if a natural disaster happened here. Knowing what to do might make us feel safer if something bad ever happened."

"That's a great idea!" Nika said. "Let's start planning now!"

COMPREHENSION Which words help you understand how terrible an earthquake can be? What do you think Nika and her mother will do to plan for an emergency?

32

Days 3 and 4

"Learning About a Natural Disaster," Vol. 1, pp. 32–33

Assessment

Pretest/Posttest Administration p. 69
Pretest/Posttest Blackline Masters pp. 106–107

Day 1

Introduce Meanings

Assess To assess what word meanings children already know, copy and distribute the **Pretest/Posttest** on pages 106–107. Use page 69 to administer the test.

Explain Write each oral vocabulary word below on the board. Read it aloud. Offer an explanation and a brief example for each word.

Words About Volcanoes

erupt *v.* to burst suddenly or violently *When volcanoes erupt, smoke and melted rock come out.*

exploding *v.* blowing up *The volcano began exploding.*

fiery *adj.* glowing like fire *Fiery ashes fell from the burning logs.*

lava *n.* melted rock from a volcano *Hot lava poured down the hillside.*

molten *adj.* melted by heat *Molten rock may not be hard, but it's very hot.*

volcanic *adj.* made by a volcano *Volcanic ash fell from the top of the mountain.*

Discuss Guide children to see the relationship between each word and the category. Ask: What do you know about volcanoes? Prompt children to use some of the words.

Read Aloud Explain that you will read aloud a story about a volcano that erupted long ago. Then read aloud "The Last Day of Pompeii." Discuss the Comprehension questions.

Day 2

Categorize and Classify

Reread and Explain "The Last Day of Pompeii." At the end of each sentence that includes an oral vocabulary word, stop and repeat the explanation of the word. Then reread the sentence.

Use a Graphic Organizer Use the graphic organizer and the questions below to reinforce understanding of the relationship between each word and the category.

Words About What a Volcano Does	Words About What Comes from a Volcano
erupt exploding	fiery lava molten volcanic

1. What is something **fiery** that comes from a volcano? **(lava)**

2. Most rocks are hard and cool, but what kind of rock is melted and hot? **(molten)**

3. What words might you use to describe a volcano blowing up? **(erupt, exploding)**

Day 3

Introduce Meanings

Explain Write each oral vocabulary word below on the board. Read it aloud. Offer an explanation and a brief example for each word.

Words About Earthquakes

collapse *v.* to fall down suddenly *Buildings may collapse in an earthquake.*

disaster *n.* an event that harms many people and things *An earthquake can be a terrible disaster.*

earthquake *n.* a shaking of the ground *Some earthquakes aren't strong enough to cause much damage.*

impact *n.* the strong effect made by something *A big earthquake makes a horrible impact on the lives of many people.*

trembles *n.* acts of shaking *An earthquake sends trembles through the ground.*

wreckage *n.* broken pieces *After the earthquake, there were broken dishes among the wreckage.*

Discuss Guide children to see the relationship between each word and the category. Prompt children to tell how each word tells about **earthquakes.**

Read Aloud Explain that you will read aloud a story about an earthquake. Then read aloud "Learning About a Natural Disaster." Discuss the Comprehension questions.

Day 4

Categorize and Classify

Reread and Explain Reread "Learning About a Natural Disaster." At the end of each sentence that includes an oral vocabulary word, stop and repeat the explanation of the word. Then reread the sentence.

Use a Graphic Organizer Use the graphic organizer and the questions below to reinforce understanding of the relationship between each word and the category.

Words About Things During an Earthquake	Words About Things After an Earthquake
collapse trembles	disaster impact wreckage

1. What word might you use to describe how an earthquake feels? (**trembles**)

2. If you dented a car, what did you make? (**impact**)

3. If an earthquake makes a building **collapse**, what will be left? (**wreckage**)

Day 5

Deepen Understanding

Review Repeat explanations for all oral vocabulary words. Use the definitions and examples from Day 1 and Day 3.

Guide Partner Activities Have partners work together to complete each of the activities below. Circulate and listen to partners as they work. Provide corrective feedback.

Compare Work with a partner. Compare an **earthquake** to an **exploding** volcano.

Role-Play Pretend you are a reporter. Interview your partner about a natural **disaster.** Describe what he or she saw, heard, and felt.

Draw Draw a picture of a **fiery** volcano. It can be one you have heard about, such as Vesuvius. It can be one you and your partner make up.

Examples When might you feel **trembles**? Where might you see **wreckage**? What are some things that can **collapse**? Tell your partner.

Write Now write a description of your volcano. Use these words: **erupt, impact, lava, molten, volcanic.**

Assess To assess what word meanings children have learned, copy and distribute the **Pretest/Posttest** on pages 106–107. Use page 69 to administer the test. Compare scores with Day 1 assessment.

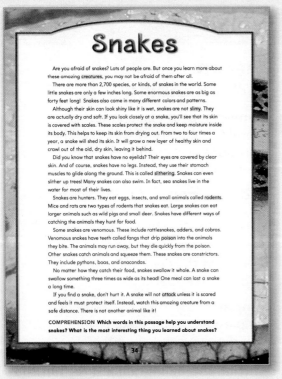

Snakes

Are you afraid of snakes? Lots of people are. But once you learn more about these amazing creatures, you may not be afraid of them after all.

There are more than 2,700 species, or kinds, of snakes in the world. Some little snakes are only a few inches long. Some enormous snakes are as big as forty feet long! Snakes also come in many different colors and patterns.

Although their skin can look shiny like it is wet, snakes are not slimy. They are actually dry and soft. If you look closely at a snake, you'll see that its skin is covered with scales. These scales protect the snake and keep moisture inside its body. This helps to keep its skin from drying out. From two to four times a year, a snake will shed its skin. It will grow a new layer of healthy skin and crawl out of the old, dry skin, leaving it behind.

Did you know that snakes have no eyelids? Their eyes are covered by clear skin. And of course, snakes have no legs. Instead, they use their stomach muscles to glide along the ground. This is called slithering. Snakes can even slither up trees! Many snakes can also swim. In fact, sea snakes live in the water for most of their lives.

Snakes are hunters. They eat eggs, insects, and small animals called rodents. Mice and rats are two types of rodents that snakes eat. Large snakes can eat larger animals such as wild pigs and small deer. Snakes have different ways of catching the animals they hunt for food.

Some snakes are venomous. These include rattlesnakes, adders, and cobras. Venomous snakes have teeth called fangs that drip poison into the animals they bite. The animals may run away, but they die quickly from the poison. Other snakes catch animals and squeeze them. These snakes are constrictors. They include pythons, boas, and anacondas.

No matter how they catch their food, snakes swallow it whole. A snake can swallow something three times as wide as its head! One meal can last a snake a long time.

If you find a snake, don't hurt it. A snake will not attack unless it is scared and feels it must protect itself. Instead, watch this amazing creature from a safe distance. There is not another animal like it!

COMPREHENSION Which words in this passage help you understand snakes? What is the most interesting thing you learned about snakes?

34

Days 1 and 2

"Snakes," Vol. 1, pp. 34–35

"Amanhã"
So Say the Little Monkeys

Squirrel Monkey lives with his friends and family in the rainforests of Brazil. Lots of rain falls in a rainforest. But there are also many sunny days.

On sunny mornings, Squirrel Monkey chatters and jumps. He swings through the treetops with his family. He runs along the tree branches with friends. Together, they munch on ripe, juicy fruit for breakfast.

All day long, Squirrel Monkey plays. He squawks and he screams. He chatters and he peeps. If he climbs a tree, the other squirrel monkeys follow him. Then they leap from one branch to another, all in a row. They snack on more fruit and munch on leaves. Life is fun in the warm afternoon sun.

But on other days, the sky gets dark and rain starts to pour like it was coming from buckets. The rainfall makes Squirrel Monkey and his friends all wet. Soon, water is dripping from their ears and faces, and from their arms and legs. Squirrel Monkey does not like to be covered in liquid, so he whimpers and cries. He and all his friends and family wrap their long tails around their bodies, and they huddle together to try to keep dry.

The rain falls all night without stopping. Squirrel Monkey feels soggy from all the water on his fur. As the rain pounds, he wonders, "Will this monsoon never end?"

Their leader says, "We must build a house tomorrow, amanhã. A house will keep us dry when it rains."

Squirrel Monkey agrees. So does everyone else. Until they fall asleep, they all chatter to each other, "Amanhã, tomorrow, we will build a house."

Then, surprise! It is daytime again. The sun is shining. Soggy Squirrel Monkey and his friends and family open their eyes and stretch. "Look, the sun is out again! Come, let's play," they chatter to each other. Then Squirrel Monkey runs up and down the trees, moist from last night's rain. He and his friends and family pick ripe, juicy fruit for breakfast. Tomorrow, amanhã, they will build a house. Why waste a sunny day working? Squirrel Monkey knows that sunny days are for playing and having fun.

COMPREHENSION Which words help you understand what the rainforest weather is like? Do you think that Squirrel Monkey and his family and friends will ever build a house? Why or why not?

36

Days 3 and 4

**"'Amanhã,' So Say the Little Monkeys,"
Vol. 1, pp. 36–37**

Assessment

Pretest/Posttest Administration p. 70
Pretest/Posttest Blackline Masters
pp. 108–109

Day 1

Introduce Meanings

Assess To assess what word meanings children already know, copy and distribute the **Pretest/ Posttest** on pages 108–109. Use page 70 to administer the test.

Explain Write each oral vocabulary word below on the board. Read it aloud. Offer an explanation and a brief example for each word.

Words About Snakes

attack *v.* to try to hurt *We saw a snake attack a mouse.*

creatures *n.* living things *Most animals and insects are creatures that live outdoors.*

poison *n.* something that gets inside living things and hurts or kills them *Some snakes kill other animals with poison.*

rodent *n.* a small animal with large front teeth *Mice and squirrels are rodents.*

slimy *adj.* slippery and sticky *Some people think snakes feel slimy.*

slither *v.* to move by sliding *Snakes slither along the ground.*

Discuss Guide children to see the relationship between each word and the category. Ask: What do you know about snakes? Prompt children to use the words in their answers.

Read Aloud Explain that you will read aloud a story about snakes. Then read aloud "Snakes." Discuss the Comprehension questions.

Day 2

Categorize and Classify

Reread and Explain Reread "Snakes." At the end of each sentence that includes an oral vocabulary word, stop and repeat the explanation of the word. Then reread the sentence.

Use a Graphic Organizer Use the graphic organizer and the questions below to reinforce understanding of the relationship between each word and the category.

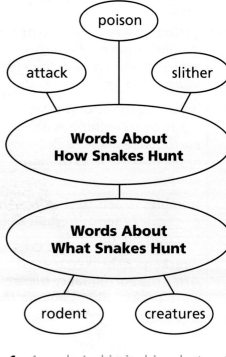

1. A snake's skin is shiny, but not _____. (**slimy**)

2. What other **creatures** do you think snakes hunt? **Add these words to the graphic organizer.** (Sample answer: insects)

3. What comes out of the fangs of some snakes? (**poison**)

4. What word tells how a snake moves? (**slither**)

Day 3

Introduce Meanings

Explain Write each oral vocabulary word below on the board. Read it aloud. Offer an explanation and a brief example for each word.

Words About Water

dripping *v.* coming down in drops *Rain was <u>dripping</u> from my hat.*

liquid *n.* anything that can flow like water does *Water is a <u>liquid</u>.*

moist *adj.* damp; a bit wet *My skin was <u>moist</u> from the sticky weather.*

monsoon *n.* a season of heavy rains *Many inches of rain fall during the <u>monsoon</u>.*

rainfall *n.* a shower of rain *Dark clouds often mean <u>rainfall</u> will follow soon.*

soggy *adj.* soaked *I stepped in a puddle and now my socks are <u>soggy</u>.*

Discuss Guide children to see the relationship between each word and the category. Ask questions such as these: Can you name something other than water that is a **liquid**? What is the difference between **moist** and **soggy**?

Read Aloud Explain that you will read aloud a story about monkeys that don't like the rain. Then read aloud "'Amanhã,' So Say the Little Monkeys." Discuss the Comprehension questions.

Day 4

Categorize and Classify

Reread and Explain Reread "'Amanhã,' So Say the Little Monkeys." At the end of each sentence that includes an oral vocabulary word, stop and repeat the explanation of the word. Then reread the sentence.

Use a Graphic Organizer Use the graphic organizer and the questions below to reinforce understanding of the relationship between each word and the category.

Words About Kinds of Rain	Words About Being Wet
monsoon rainfall	soggy moist dripping

1. Is a **monsoon** a time of dry weather or lots of **rainfall**? (lots of **rainfall**)

2. Your socks might get **soggy** if you _____. (Sample answer: step in a puddle)

3. What **liquid** can be found in a kitchen? What **liquid** comes from the sky? (juice; rain)

4. Would the ground feel **moist** before or after a rainstorm? (after)

Day 5

Deepen Understanding

Review Repeat explanations for all oral vocabulary words. Use the definitions and examples from Day 1 and Day 3.

Guide Partner Activities Have partners work together to complete each of the activities below. Circulate and listen to partners as they work. Provide corrective feedback.

Categorize Work with a partner. Put these words in order from driest to wettest: **dripping, moist, soggy, liquid**. Give reasons for the order you chose.

Examples Tell about times you touched something **slimy** and saw something **slither**. Name two kinds of **rodents**.

Role-Play Pretend you and your partner are squirrel monkeys. Talk about whether you should build a home on a sunny day. Use these words: **monsoon, rainfall, dripping, soggy**.

Draw Draw a picture of a rainforest. Show some **creatures** that live there.

Write Now write a description of the rainforest you drew. Use these words: **attack, creatures, poison**.

Assess To assess what word meanings children have learned, copy and distribute the **Pretest/Posttest** on pages 108–109. Use page 70 to administer the test. Compare scores with Day 1 assessment.

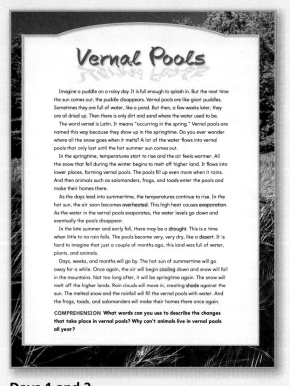

Days 1 and 2

"Vernal Pools," Vol. 1, pp. 38–39

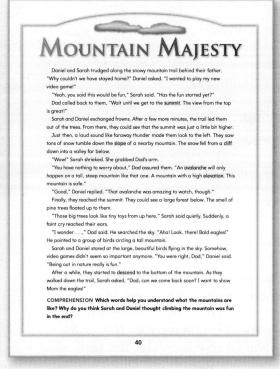

Days 3 and 4

"Mountain Majesty," Vol. 1, pp. 40–41

Assessment

Pretest/Posttest Administration p. 71

Pretest/Posttest Blackline Masters
pp. 110–111

Day 1

Introduce Meanings

Assess To assess what word meanings children already know, copy and distribute the **Pretest/ Posttest** on pages 110–111. Use page 71 to administer the test.

Explain Write each oral vocabulary word below on the board. Read it aloud. Offer an explanation and a brief example for each word.

Words About Weather Conditions

cooling *v.* making colder *The breeze began <u>cooling</u> our overheated guests.*

deserts *n.* large, dry, sandy areas *<u>Deserts</u> do not grow many plants because they are so dry.*

drought *n.* a long period of little or no rain *The <u>drought</u> was killing the farmer's crops.*

evaporation *n.* when water changes from a liquid to a gas *The <u>evaporation</u> of the water was caused by heat.*

overheated *adj.* too hot *Drink plenty of water so you don't get <u>overheated</u> when you exercise.*

shade *n.* an area where sunlight is blocked *Sitting in <u>shade</u> is cooler than sitting in sunlight.*

Discuss Guide children to see the relationship between each word and the category. Ask: Can you find **shade** in **deserts**?

Read Aloud Explain that you will read aloud a story about how changes in weather affect certain places. Then read aloud "Vernal Pools." Discuss the Comprehension questions.

Day 2

Categorize and Classify

Reread and Explain Reread "Vernal Pools." At the end of each sentence that includes an oral vocabulary word, stop and repeat the explanation of the word. Then reread the sentence.

Use a Graphic Organizer Use the graphic organizer and the questions below to reinforce understanding of the relationship between each word and the category.

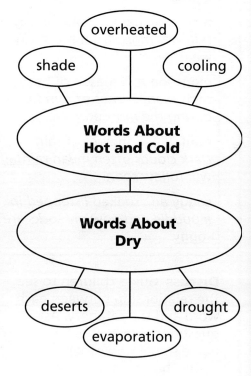

1. Where can you find **shade** on hot days? (Sample answer: under tree branches or umbrellas)

2. Suppose you are running and you get **overheated**. What should you do? (Sample answers: drink water; sit down)

Day 3

Introduce Meanings

Explain Write each oral vocabulary word below on the board. Read it aloud. Offer an explanation and a brief example for each word.

Words About Mountains

avalanches *n.* large amounts of snow falling down a mountain *Skiers learn how to stay safe from* <u>avalanches</u>.

cliffs *n.* steep, rocky sides of a mountain *We stood above the* <u>cliffs</u> *and looked at the town below.*

descend *v.* to move down *Step carefully as you* <u>descend</u> *the hill.*

elevation *n.* how high a place is *The* <u>elevation</u> *of Mount Everest is almost thirty thousand feet.*

slopes *n.* hills *The* <u>slopes</u> *were perfect for sledding.*

summit *n.* the top of a mountain *The climbers could see across two towns from the* <u>summit</u>.

Discuss Guide children to see the relationship between each word and the category. Ask: Would you **descend** toward a **summit**? Explain your answer.

Read Aloud Explain that you will read aloud a story about a family who bonds over a hiking trip. Then read aloud "Mountain Majesty." Discuss the Comprehension questions.

Day 4

Categorize and Classify

Reread and Explain Reread "Mountain Majesty." At the end of each sentence that includes an oral vocabulary word, stop and repeat the explanation of the word. Then reread the sentence.

Use a Graphic Organizer Use the graphic organizer and the questions below to reinforce understanding of the relationship between each word and the category.

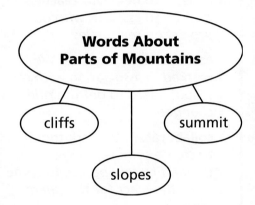

1. It is not safe to walk on a mountain in an _____. (**avalanche**)

2. What are some places that have a high **elevation**? (Sample answer: mountain-tops, tall buildings)

3. If you hiked to a mountain **cliff**, what would you have to do to get back home? (**descend**)

Day 5

Deepen Understanding

Review Repeat explanations for all oral vocabulary words. Use the definitions and examples from Day 1 and Day 3.

Guide Partner Activities Have partners work together to complete each of the activities below. Circulate and listen to partners as they work. Provide corrective feedback.

Role-Play Pretend that you are a farmer. Explain to your partner how a **drought** is hurting your crops. Use the following words: **cooling, deserts, evaporation, overheated.**

Compare Talk to your partner. Compare how it feels in the **shade** of a large tree to how it feels in the sunshine on an open beach. Tell where you like to be.

Draw Draw a picture of what you think an **avalanche** would look like. Show how the snow falls down the **slope** from a very high **elevation**. Explain your picture to a partner.

Describe Imagine that you are climbing the tallest mountain in the world. Describe your journey to a partner, using the following words: **cliffs, summit, descend.**

Assess To assess what word meanings children have learned, copy and distribute the **Pretest/Posttest** on pages 110–111. Use page 71 to administer the test. Compare scores with Day 1 assessment.

Petitions: Let Your Voice Be Heard!

What can you do if you think a rule or law is wrong? How can you try to make a change? One way you could tell your opinion is by creating a petition. A petition is a special piece of writing. It usually explains a problem. Then it tells what should be done to make the problem better. For example, let's say your school stopped letting students borrow books from the library. A petition could explain why this rule is unfair and why it should be changed.

A petition can be very powerful. This is because it lets many people give the same opinion together. Anyone who wants to can sign his or her name on the petition. Signatures show that these people agree with the opinion that is written on the petition. Let's say almost all the students in school signed the petition about borrowing from the library. The principal would probably take the petition very seriously. If only a few students signed it, the principal might take the petition less seriously. By working in association with others, you have a better chance of getting your opinion heard. Then maybe you can make a change!

Working on a petition is not an easy task. But it can be easier if you collaborate with others. You can all work together to write the petition. You can assist one another if you need help thinking of the best way to say your opinion. Then you can work together to get others to sign your petition. Your group should carefully plan how to get people to sign your petition. Everyone working on the petition can go to different places where people hang out. You can each ask people to sign a copy of the petition. Then you can get together and count how many people signed it.

There's one more thing you should know. Just because a lot of people sign a petition doesn't mean anything will change. But even if it doesn't make a change right away, a petition is still a great way of making your opinion known.

Is there a rule or law in your school or town that you think should be changed? If so, get together with some friends and make a petition! If you cooperate with one another, you could make a difference!

COMPREHENSION Which words help you understand how people work on petitions? Why do people make petitions?

42

Days 1 and 2

"Petitions: Let Your Voice Be Heard!"
Vol. 1, pp. 42–43

Billy and the Big Bully

Billy the bunny loved hopping and sniffing and walking around in the barn. He also loved dinnertime. He would chew on carrots and hay. And best of all, he would eat lettuce. It tasted so sweet and fresh. When he ate it, he felt healthy.

One day, just as Billy was about to eat his lettuce, Ron the rooster reached over and grabbed a handful of lettuce leaves.

"Those look good," said Ron. "I think I'll have them." Ron the rooster was well known by all the farm animals because he was a big bully. In fact, his fame as a bully didn't end at the farm. He was known as a bully at every nearby farm and ranch. Even most farmers were afraid of him.

Billy felt angry for a moment as he watched Ron puff out his feathers and chew on the lettuce. Then Billy the bunny had an idea.

"Has anyone ever told you how respected you are at this barn?" Billy asked, smiling kindly.

"What do you mean?" answered Ron, frowning.

"Every animal on the farm has a great deal of admiration for you, Ron. After all, you are the most prominent, widely known rooster around. We see you as our local expert at bullying. Everyone is afraid of you, and that must make you very proud."

Suddenly the lettuce didn't taste very good to Ron. He began to feel lonely and sad.

"I want you to have my last carrot as an honor," Billy continued. "An honor for being the scariest bully ever."

Then Billy began to clap. Others joined in. Soon, the whole barn was clapping. All the animals took the food scraps they had saved and placed them in front of Ron, who by this time had a horrible bellyache.

Then everyone was quiet. The only sound was Ron gulping as he swallowed the big lump of lettuce leaves he'd been chewing. Ron thought for a moment and knew that he didn't want to be famous because people were afraid of him. He just wanted people to like him.

"I'm sorry, Billy. I won't bother you anymore," said Ron. He handed back the last of the lettuce leaves.

"It's OK, Ron. I'll split this with you," said Billy, smiling.

COMPREHENSION How does Billy use words to make Ron feel bad about being a bully? What does Billy teach Ron?

44

Days 3 and 4

"Billy and the Big Bully," Vol. 1, pp. 44–45

Assessment

Pretest/Posttest Administration p. 72

Pretest/Posttest Blackline Masters pp. 112–113

Day 1

Introduce Meanings

Assess To assess what word meanings children already know, copy and distribute the **Pretest/ Posttest** on pages 112–113. Use page 72 to administer the test.

Explain Write each oral vocabulary word below on the board. Read it aloud. Offer an explanation and a brief example for each word.

Words About Teamwork

assist *v.* to help *Our teacher offered to* <u>assist</u> *us with our project on sea turtles.*

association *n.* together *We worked in* <u>association</u> *with the school board to get the rule changed.*

collaborate *v.* to work together to create something *We decided to* <u>collaborate</u> *to come up with an act for the talent show.*

cooperate *v.* to work together for a common purpose *Mr. Brodeur got everyone to* <u>cooperate</u> *and raise money.*

plan *v.* to work out ahead of time *We* <u>planned</u> *the class presentation carefully.*

task *n.* a job *My first* <u>task</u> *today will be to help clean up around the house.*

Discuss Guide children to see the relationship between each word and the category. Prompt them to tell about experiences they have had working in teams.

Read Aloud Explain that you will read aloud a story about how teamwork can help create change. Then read aloud "Petitions: Let Your Voice Be Heard!" Discuss the Comprehension questions.

Day 2

Categorize and Classify

Reread and Explain Reread "Petitions: Let Your Voice Be Heard!" At the end of each sentence that includes an oral vocabulary word, stop and repeat the explanation of the word. Then reread the sentence.

Use a Graphic Organizer Use the graphic organizer and the questions below to reinforce understanding of the relationship between each word and the category.

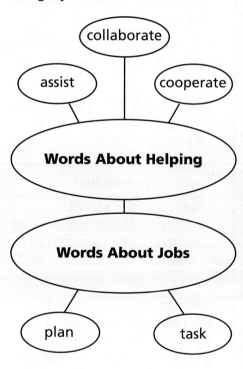

1. If you do something in **association** with others, do you all work on the same thing or do you all work on your own thing? (all work on the same thing)

2. Name some **tasks** you do at home. (Sample answer: clean my room, do homework)

Day 3

Introduce Meanings

Explain Write each oral vocabulary word below on the board. Read it aloud. Offer an explanation and a brief example for each word.

Words About Being Well Known

admiration *n.* when someone has a high opinion of someone else *I feel a lot of <u>admiration</u> for firefighters.*

expert *n.* a person who knows a lot about a topic *My teacher is a grammar <u>expert</u>.*

fame *n.* being known by many people *His <u>fame</u> meant that people knew who he was wherever he went.*

honor *n.* an award *Olivia was given a trophy as an <u>honor</u> for her hard work.*

prominent *adj.* important *Milo is a <u>prominent</u> artist in his city.*

respected *adj.* well-liked *The mayor is a very <u>respected</u> member of the community.*

Discuss Guide children to see the relationship between each word and the category. Prompt them to give examples of **respected** people with whom they are familiar.

Read Aloud Explain that you will read aloud a story about a person who is famous for the wrong reasons. Then read aloud "Billy and the Big Bully." Discuss the Comprehension questions.

Day 4

Categorize and Classify

Reread and Explain Reread "Billy and the Big Bully." At the end of each sentence that includes an oral vocabulary word, stop and repeat the explanation of the word. Then reread the sentence.

Use a Graphic Organizer Use the graphic organizer and the questions below to reinforce understanding of the relationship between each word and the category.

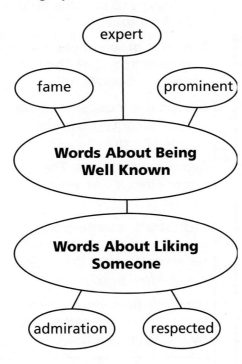

1. Name some people for whom you feel **admiration**. (Answers will vary.)

2. Imagine you were given a special gift for doing something good. What word might describe the gift? **(honor)**

Day 5

Deepen Understanding

Review Repeat explanations for all oral vocabulary words. Use the definitions and examples from Day 1 and Day 3.

Guide Partner Activities Have partners work together to complete each of the activities below. Circulate and listen to partners as they work. Provide corrective feedback.

Draw Draw a picture of a **respected** person in your town. Show your picture to a partner. Then draw someone who is an **expert** at something you're interested in.

Write Think about someone who has a lot of **fame**. Write about this person, using these words: **admiration, prominent.**

Describe Imagine you are part of a team that must **collaborate** to think of a new school mascot. Describe how the team should **cooperate.** Use these words: **assist, association, plan.**

Examples Talk to a partner. Give examples of school projects you have enjoyed. Then give examples of **tasks** you do not enjoy. Have you ever been given an **honor** for something you have worked on?

Assess To assess what word meanings children have learned, copy and distribute the **Pretest/ Posttest** on pages 112–113. Use page 72 to administer the test. Compare scores with Day 1 assessment.

The Amazing Voice

When Marian Anderson was young, she was known as the little girl with a great big voice. Little Marian could sing any song beautifully. What amazed people more was that she could sing any part of a song. She could sing parts usually sung by men as well as parts usually sung by women.

Marian Anderson was born in Pennsylvania in 1897. When she was just six years old, Marian joined the junior choir at a local church. People loved to listen to her sing. When Marian was a teenager, she decided that she wanted to learn how to sing even better. For one year Marian went to music school for vocal lessons. That was the beginning of her great career.

After her year at music school, Marian studied with a great Italian music teacher. The teacher was so amazed by her voice that he taught her for a year and did not make her pay for the lessons.

Later, Marian entered a contest to sing with the New York Philharmonic Orchestra. This was a very popular group of musicians. Lots of people wanted the chance to sing along with the different instruments that made up the orchestra. After auditioning, or trying out, Marian won. She beat three hundred other singers!

Marian spent many years traveling around the United States and Europe, where she performed in concerts. Many people gathered to hear Marian sing. She was not just a singer in a band. Marian's voice was pure and perfect for singing opera.

Even though Marian had an amazing voice that everyone loved to listen to, some concert halls at the time would not let her perform. This was because she was African American. One of these halls was Constitution Hall, in Washington, D.C. The hall was owned by a women's group called the Daughters of the American Revolution. First Lady Eleanor Roosevelt was a member of this group. Eleanor was so upset that Marian was not allowed to sing at Constitution Hall that she left the group. Eleanor got Marian a chance to sing outside at the Lincoln Memorial. This was Marian's debut in Washington, D.C. It was her first public concert there. A huge crowd of 75,000 people came to hear her sing.

Marian Anderson continued to sing for many years. She won many prizes and awards. Today she is remembered as having one of the most beautiful voices ever.

COMPREHENSION Which words in this passage are about singing and music? How did Marian's love of music help her become a great singer?

46

Days 1 and 2

"The Amazing Voice," Vol. 1, pp. 46–47

The Bremen Town Musicians

Long ago in Germany, there lived a donkey who wanted to be a musician. He told his friends, the dog, the cat, and the rooster, that he was leaving. He said, "I am going to Bremen because it's a good place for musicians to work. You should come with me because you sing as beautifully as I do. We can form a band and call ourselves the Bremen Town Musicians!"

The dog, the cat, and the rooster thought this was a great idea. So they started walking to Bremen with the donkey. But by nighttime the animals were only halfway to Bremen, and they were deep in a strange forest.

"I see a cottage," said the donkey. "Let's see if we can sleep there tonight." The animals peeked in the window of the cottage. They saw a man and a woman making dinner.

The cat said, "I know! Let's sing for the people. They might thank us by giving us food and a place to sleep."

So the animals got ready to sing. The donkey jumped onto the donkey's back. Then the cat jumped onto the dog's back, and the rooster flew onto the cat's back.

At the count of three, the animals began to sing. The donkey brayed. His braying sounded like a trumpet blaring off-key. The dog barked. His barking sounded like the pounding rumble of drums. The cat meowed. Her meowing sounded like a wailing police siren. The rooster crowed. His crowing sounded like a tree splitting in half. As the animals sang, the volume of their singing became louder. Soon the singing was so thunderous that the people in the cottage covered their ears.

"What is that horrible racket?" yelled the woman.

"I don't know, but let's get away from the noise and go someplace quiet and peaceful," answered the man. And he and the woman ran away from the cottage. When the animals finished singing, they saw that the cottage was empty.

"I think our music amazed the people, because they left us their dinner," said the donkey.

"They probably want us to sleep here, too," said the dog. And that is just what the Bremen Town Musicians did. The next morning, the animals continued on their way to Bremen, well rested and well fed.

COMPREHENSION What do the four animal friends like to do together? What words help you understand how the animals' music sounds?

48

Days 3 and 4

"The Bremen Town Musicians," Vol. 1, pp. 48–49

Assessment

Pretest/Posttest Administration p. 73
Pretest/Posttest Blackline Masters
pp. 114–115

Day 1

Introduce Meanings

Assess To assess what word meanings children already know, copy and distribute the **Pretest/ Posttest** on pages 114–115. Use page 73 to administer the test.

Explain Write each oral vocabulary word below on the board. Read it aloud. Offer an explanation and a brief example for each word.

Words About Music

auditioning *v.* trying out *I am auditioning to play the flute in the school show.*

band *n.* a group of people who play music together *The band played my favorite song.*

concert *n.* a musical program or show *The concert is in the school auditorium.*

debut *n.* a first show *The singer's debut was a huge success.*

orchestra *n.* a large group of people who play instruments together *He plays the violin in the children's orchestra.*

vocal *adj.* having to do with the voice *She learned to sing by taking vocal lessons.*

Discuss Guide children to see the relationship between each word and the category. Ask questions such as these: What is your favorite **band**? What kind of music do they play? Do you think you would like to **audition** to be in a **concert**? Why or why not?

Read Aloud Explain that you will read aloud a story about a very talented singer. Then read aloud "The Amazing Voice." Discuss the Comprehension questions.

Day 2

Categorize and Classify

Reread and Explain Reread "The Amazing Voice." At the end of each sentence that includes an oral vocabulary word, stop and repeat the explanation of the word. Then reread the sentence.

Use a Graphic Organizer Use the graphic organizer and the questions below to reinforce understanding of the relationship between each word and the category.

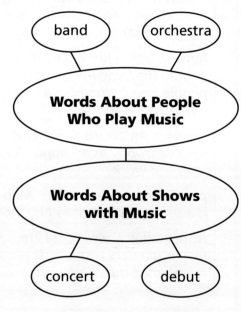

1. Do you think you would want to practice playing your instrument a lot before **auditioning** to be in an **orchestra**? (yes)

2. What type of lessons might a singer take? (**vocal**)

Day 3

Introduce Meanings

Explain Write each oral vocabulary word below on the board. Read it aloud. Offer an explanation and a brief example for each word.

Words About Noises

blare *v.* to make a loud, harsh sound *I covered my ears when I heard the whistle <u>blare</u>.*

peaceful *adj.* calm *When I'm tired, I like to listen to soft, <u>peaceful</u> music.*

racket *n.* a loud, unpleasant noise *The dog's barking made quite a <u>racket</u>.*

rumble *n.* a deep rolling sound *I can hear the <u>rumble</u> of trains going down the track.*

thunderous *adj.* loud and deep *The hall was filled with <u>thunderous</u> clapping at the end of the show.*

volume *n.* the loudness of a sound *I could not hear the music because the <u>volume</u> was too low.*

Discuss Guide children to see the relationship between each word and the category. Ask questions such as these: What words would you use to talk about sounds that you like? What words would you use to talk about sounds that you do not like?

Read Aloud Explain that you will read aloud a story about the noises that a group of animals make. Then read aloud "The Bremen Town Musicians." Discuss the Comprehension questions.

Day 4

Categorize and Classify

Reread and Explain Reread "The Bremen Town Musicians." At the end of each sentence that includes an oral vocabulary word, stop and repeat the explanation of the word. Then reread the sentence.

Use a Graphic Organizer Use the graphic organizer and the questions below to reinforce understanding of the relationship between each word and the category.

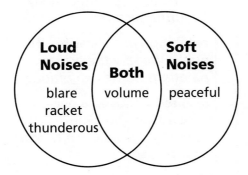

Loud Noises: blare, racket, thunderous
Both: volume
Soft Noises: peaceful

1. If you cannot hear the radio, you can turn up the _____. (**volume**)

2. What other words can you use to talk about soft noises? Add these to the graphic organizer as children suggest them. (Sample answers: quiet; low; hum)

3. What is a noise that sounds like a **rumble**? (Sample answers: thunder; a car's engine)

Day 5

Deepen Understanding

Review Repeat explanations for all oral vocabulary words. Use the definitions and examples from Day 1 and Day 3.

Guide Partner Have partners work together to complete each of the activities below. Circulate and listen to partners as they work. Provide corrective feedback.

Examples Talk to your partner. List some things that make a **racket**.

Compare Talk to your partner. Compare a **rumble** of thunder with a sudden flash of lightning. Which bothers you more?

Describe Talk to your partner. Describe how a musician might feel when **auditioning** to be in an **orchestra**. Then talk about how the musician might feel during his or her **debut**.

Write Work with your partner. Imagine you saw your favorite **band** perform. Use these words to write about the show: **concert, vocal, blare, thunderous, volume**.

Word Parts The suffix *-ful* means "full of." *Peace* means "when things are calm and there is nothing bothering you." Something that is **peaceful** is calm and makes you feel full of peace. Use a dictionary or a glossary. Work with your partner to find and list three other examples of words with *-ful*, meaning "full of."

Assess To assess what word meanings children have learned, copy and distribute the **Pretest/Posttest** on pages 114–115. Use page 73 to administer the test. Compare scores with Day 1 assessment.

The Man Who Painted Birds

What do you like to draw? A man named John J. Audubon loved to draw birds. Maybe you have even seen some of his famous pictures!

John J. Audubon was born in 1785 in what is now called Haiti. When he was a child, Audubon lived in France with his father. There he spent a lot of time exploring the outdoors. Audubon loved collecting and drawing birds' eggs, nests, and other things he found in nature. When he was eighteen years old, Audubon moved to the United States.

For a while, Audubon was put in charge of a farm that his father owned. But even while he was working on the farm, he still loved to draw birds. Spending time outside watching birds inspired Audubon. It made him want to draw even more. Later, he realized that he had more talent for art than he did for running the farm. So he went on a journey to explore and paint pictures of birds. His goal was to publish his paintings. This way, many people would be able to buy them.

When Audubon painted, he used many of the same paints, colors, and materials as other artists. But his techniques were different from those of other artists. He didn't work the same way they did. His studio where he painted was the outdoors. He made his birds look as real as he could. Most artists showed birds standing against blank backgrounds. Audubon showed birds doing natural things, such as flapping their wings or squawking at each other. He showed birds in trees or bushes or against backgrounds that were just like the outdoors. He even included small creatures like insects in order to make his paintings look real.

In 1826, Audubon had an exhibition of his paintings in London, England. Many people came to see his paintings. They loved them! Then Audubon found an expert printer in London. The printer made prints, or copies, of Audubon's paintings. Finally Audubon had published his paintings. His collection of pictures was called *The Birds of America*.

Today, Audubon's paintings are in museums. People still enjoy looking at them. Many people think of John J. Audubon as one of the greatest wildlife artists ever. In addition to painting birds, Audubon gave his name to a group that works to protect and preserve birds and their natural habitats. It is called the Audubon Society.

COMPREHENSION Which words in this passage help you understand Audubon's life as an artist? Do you think that Audubon's work helps people learn more about nature? Why or why not?

50

Days 1 and 2

"The Man Who Painted Birds," Vol. 1, pp. 50–51

The School Play

Amelia loved to be on a stage. She usually performed in front of large crowds. She could make people laugh out loud or sob quietly. She could even make them think deep thoughts. Amelia always knew exactly how to say her lines. The audience loved her, but only Amelia could hear their applause. Her audience was not real.

Amelia was very shy. She was too shy to act in front of people, so she would stand alone on the stage and act for a pretend audience. Sometimes, she helped her classmates who were getting ready to act in a play. She helped them practice their dialogues, even using different character voices. She helped them remember when to go onstage. But Amelia would not perform if she thought someone was watching.

Every day after school, Amelia would go to the auditorium early. She would step onto the stage and act out the different roles in the play. She had memorized the lines because she had practiced them so often with her friends. But one day Amelia wasn't alone. The drama teacher had come to practice early, too. He sat at the back of the auditorium, where Amelia could not see him. Amelia acted out a scene from the play. She made the drama teacher laugh out loud. She even made him think deep thoughts. He thought she was quite a talented actor.

On the night of the play, the lead actress could not go onstage. She had a sore throat and could only whisper. The drama teacher immediately thought of Amelia. He went running up to her. "Can you act in the play tonight?" he asked. "I know you'll be great! I watched you onstage a few days ago."

Amelia hesitated. At first she was embarrassed that the teacher had seen her. But he thought she was great! So finally, she said, "Yes!" It was a dramatic moment.

Amelia was very nervous as she stepped onstage. She saw the audience of schoolmates, teachers, and parents. She took a deep breath and thought about all the times she had acted for a pretend audience. "I can do this," she said to herself. And she did.

The audience loved her. When the play was over, the audience stood and clapped. Some of them even shouted "Bravo!" to show her how much they liked her acting.

Afterward, one of Amelia's friends asked for her autograph. "You'll be a star some day!" her friend said. It was a dream come true for Amelia.

COMPREHENSION What words tell you about actors and acting? Why do you think Amelia decided to act in front of a real audience?

52

Days 3 and 4

"The School Play," Vol. 1, pp. 52–53

Assessment

Pretest/Posttest Administration p. 74

Pretest/Posttest Blackline Masters pp. 116–117

Day 1

Introduce Meanings

Assess To assess what word meanings children already know, copy and distribute the **Pretest/ Posttest** on pages 116–117. Use page 74 to administer the test.

Explain Write each oral vocabulary word below on the board. Read it aloud. Offer an explanation and a brief example for each word.

Words About Artists

artist *n.* a person who makes art *The <u>artist</u> painted many beautiful pictures.*

exhibition *n.* a show for the public *We saw the artist's paintings at the <u>exhibition</u>.*

inspired *v.* moved a person to take action *The beautiful paintings <u>inspired</u> me to learn how to paint.*

studio *n.* the place where an artist works *The artist's <u>studio</u> is filled with paints and brushes.*

talent *n.* an ability to do something well *He has <u>talent</u> as a painter.*

techniques *n.* ways of doing something *I try to copy the artist's painting <u>techniques</u>.*

Discuss Guide children to see the relationship between each word and the category. Ask questions such as these: What might **inspire** **artists** to create art? Do you think it takes **talent** to be an artist? Why or why not?

Read Aloud Explain that you will read aloud a story about a famous artist. Then read aloud "The Man Who Painted Birds." Discuss the Comprehension questions.

Day 2

Categorize and Classify

Reread and Explain Reread "The Man Who Painted Birds." At the end of each sentence that includes an oral vocabulary word, stop and repeat the explanation of the word. Then reread the sentence.

Use a Graphic Organizer Use the graphic organizer and the questions below to reinforce understanding of the relationship between each word and the category.

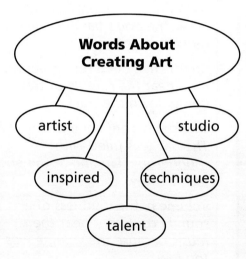

1. Imagine you heard a song and it made you want to make music. What would the song have done to you? (**inspired**)

2. The **artist** showed her photographs at an _____. (**exhibition**)

3. What might a painter's **studio** look like? (Sample answer: messy with paints and brushes on tables, drops of paint on the floor, paintings on easels)

Day 3

Introduce Meanings

Explain Write each oral vocabulary word below on the board. Read it aloud. Offer an explanation and a brief example for each word.

Words About Acting

autograph *n.* a person's handwritten name *The actor wrote his <u>autograph</u> on a piece of paper.*

bravo *interj.* well done *Someone in the audience shouted, "<u>Bravo</u>!"*

dialogue *n.* the words actors say to each other *It is a good idea for actors to practice their <u>dialogue</u> before going onstage.*

dramatic *adj.* exciting *The play had a <u>dramatic</u> ending.*

performs *v.* acts *She <u>performs</u> in the school play each year.*

scene *n.* a part of a play *The actors practiced every <u>scene</u> from the play.*

Discuss Guide children to see the relationship between each word and the category. Prompt them to use the words to talk about a play they have acted in or seen at school.

Read Aloud Explain that you will read aloud a story about a girl who wants to act. Then read aloud "The School Play." Discuss the Comprehension questions.

Day 4

Categorize and Classify

Reread and Explain Reread "The School Play." At the end of each sentence that includes an oral vocabulary word, stop and repeat the explanation of the word. Then reread the sentence.

Use a Graphic Organizer Use the graphic organizer and the questions below to reinforce understanding of the relationship between each word and the category.

Words About Actors	Words About Plays
autograph performs	dialogue dramatic scene

1. What word might you use to tell actors that they did a good job in a play? (**bravo**)

2. What word might you use to describe a **scene** that is full of amazing events? (**dramatic**)

3. The actor didn't know what to say because she had forgotten her _____. (**dialogue**)

Day 5

Deepen Understanding

Review Repeat explanations for all oral vocabulary words. Use the definitions and examples from Day 1 and Day 3.

Guide Partner Activities Have partners work together to complete each of the activities below. Circulate and listen to partners as they work. Provide corrective feedback.

Role-Play Pretend you are a famous **artist**. Explain your work to your partner. Use these words: **inspired, studio, techniques, exhibition**.

Examples What is a **talent** that you have? Tell your partner. Then name someone famous whose **autograph** you would like to get.

Describe Talk to your partner. Describe a **dramatic scene** in a movie you like.

Write Write about what it is like to watch a fun play. Use these words: **bravo, dialogue, performs**.

Assess To assess what word meanings children have learned, copy and distribute the **Pretest/Posttest** on pages 116–117. Use page 74 to administer the test. Compare scores with Day 1 assessment.

Wilma Rudolph

Few people would have thought that Wilma Rudolph would grow up to become a track star. When she was young, Wilma had to **overcome** difficult challenges in her life. She worked hard to face those challenges and beat them.

Wilma Rudolph was born in Tennessee in 1940. As a child, she had many illnesses. One of these illnesses was polio. The polio damaged Wilma's legs. She could not walk. Doctors thought that Wilma would never walk again. Eventually, she got better. But one of her legs was very weak. Wilma could only walk with the help of a metal leg brace and special shoes.

Wilma's family would not let her give up hope. Her brothers and sisters rubbed her weak leg to help it grow stronger. Wilma's mother helped her do leg-lifting exercises. Wilma worked hard to walk again. By the time she was twelve years old, she could walk without her leg brace and special shoes. That's when Wilma decided that she wanted to play sports.

In high school, Wilma became a basketball star. She was a fast runner and scored many points. One day, a college track coach saw Wilma play basketball. He asked her to run with his track team at the college. Wilma began to train with the college team. She was very fast.

When Wilma was only sixteen years old, she made the Olympic track and field team. The Olympics is a worldwide **contest**. The best athletes from countries around the world compete at different sports.

Wilma returned from her first Olympic games with a bronze medal. Her team, the USA, had come in third place in a relay race. But Wilma knew she could **succeed** and earn a gold medal. She knew that she could come in first place.

For four years, Wilma trained hard at the college. In 1960, she made the USA Olympic team again. She ran so fast that she **defeated** all the **opposing** athletes. None of the women who ran against Wilma could beat her.

Wilma came home in **triumph**. She was the first American woman to earn three gold medals at the Olympics. She was such a star that her hometown held a parade for her.

Wilma spent the rest of her life working as a teacher and coach. Her story continues to bring hope to young athletes around the world.

COMPREHENSION In what ways did Wilma face challenges in her life? What words help you understand what Wilma was like as an athlete?

54

Days 1 and 2

"Wilma Rudolph," Vol. 1, pp. 54–55

The Little Girl on the Prairie

Laura Ingalls Wilder was a **beloved** author of young adult books. She is best known for her "Little House" series, which includes *Little House on the Prairie* and *On the Banks of Plum Creek*. These stories are based on Laura's real-life experiences growing up in the Midwest.

Laura Ingalls was born in Wisconsin on February 7, 1867. There, she lived with her family in a little log cabin. The cabin was in a spot that was known as the Big Woods. When Laura was a child, her family moved many times.

When Laura was a baby, her family moved to the state of Missouri. But they didn't stay there long. One year later, they moved to Kansas. Laura's parents **devoted** themselves to making a nice home for their family. They worked hard to build a house. They also planted crops for food. But before long, the Ingalls family moved back to the Big Woods.

Laura and her sister were glad to be back in the Big Woods. Their grandparents, aunts, uncles, and cousins lived there. The children were happy playing with their cousins and going to school.

But a few years later, the Ingalls family moved again, to Walnut Grove, Minnesota. The family lived in Walnut Grove for about five years. Laura felt a great **affection** for the town. She loved Walnut Grove. Laura's book *On the Banks of Plum Creek* is based on the family's life there.

Later, when she was fifteen years old, Laura started teaching school. Then she married a man named Almanzo Wilder. They soon had a daughter named Rose. The first years of their marriage were difficult. Farming was hard, and Almanzo got very sick. He couldn't work very much anymore. So the Wilders had to move. They found a home in Missouri. They **appreciated** the new chance. Laura began writing for magazines and newspapers. And she told her daughter stories about her life.

When Rose grew older, she became a famous writer. Rose always remembered her mother's stories. She told Laura that children would enjoy reading her stories, too. So Laura wrote her first book, *Little House in the Big Woods*, about where she grew up in Wisconsin. The book is filled with **emotional** stories of Laura's early life. It was published in 1932. Laura later wrote seven more books. She **endeared** herself to readers all over the world. People loved her, and to this day, they still do.

COMPREHENSION What words help you understand that this passage is about someone people loved? How would you describe Laura Ingalls Wilder?

56

Days 3 and 4

"The Little Girl on the Prairie," Vol. 1, pp. 56–57

Assessment

Pretest/Posttest Administration p. 75

Pretest/Posttest Blackline Masters pp. 118–119

Day 1

Introduce Meanings

Assess To assess what word meanings children already know, copy and distribute the **Pretest/Posttest** on pages 118–119. Use page 75 to administer the test.

Explain Write each oral vocabulary word below on the board. Read it aloud. Offer an explanation and a brief example for each word.

Words About Competing
contest *n.* a competition, such as a race or a game *I'm going to enter the spelling <u>contest</u> at school.*
defeated *v.* beat; won over *She <u>defeated</u> all the other players and won a trophy.*
opposing *adj.* the person or team you are playing against *The <u>opposing</u> team won the game.*
overcome *v.* to deal with; to beat *I had to <u>overcome</u> my fear of being away from my parents when I started school.*
succeed *v.* to reach a goal *I know I can <u>succeed</u> if I just keep trying.*
triumph *n.* a victory or a win *It was a great <u>triumph</u> when we won the championship.*

Discuss Guide children to see the relationship between each word and the category. Ask them questions such as these: Have you ever competed in a **contest**? Did you help **defeat** an **opposing** team?

Read Aloud Explain that you will read aloud a story about a woman who competed in the Olympics. Then read aloud "Wilma Rudolph." Discuss the Comprehension questions.

Day 2

Categorize and Classify

Reread and Explain Reread "Wilma Rudolph." At the end of each sentence that includes an oral vocabulary word, stop and repeat the explanation of the word. Then reread the sentence.

Use a Graphic Organizer Use the graphic organizer and the questions below to reinforce understanding of the relationship between each word and the category.

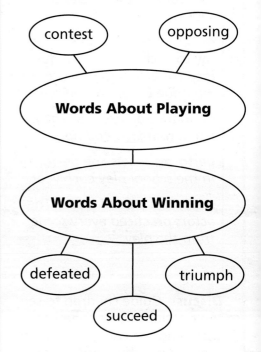

1. To **succeed**, what do you need to do to your problems? (**overcome** them)

2. Name a **contest** in which you competed against another team. (Sample answers: a soccer game; a basketball game)

3. How would you describe the team you competed against? (**opposing**)

Day 3

Introduce Meanings

Explain Write each oral vocabulary word below on the board. Read it aloud. Offer an explanation and a brief example for each word.

Words About Love

affection *n.* a great liking *I have a lot of affection for my dog.*

appreciate *v.* to be grateful *I appreciate all that my parents do for me.*

beloved *adj.* loved very much *My beloved old teddy bear is always on my pillow.*

devote *v.* to give *My older brother always tries to devote an hour to helping me with my homework.*

emotional *adj.* making people have strong feelings *It was an emotional day when my baby sister was born.*

endeared *v.* made beloved *My baby sister's smile endeared her to me.*

Discuss Guide children to see the relationship between each word and the category. Prompt them to use the words to describe members of their families. Ask: Who has **affection** for you? What about these people **endears** you to them?

Read Aloud Explain that you will read aloud a story about a writer who is loved by many children. Then read aloud "The Little Girl on the Prairie." Discuss the Comprehension questions.

Day 4

Categorize and Classify

Reread and Explain Reread "The Little Girl on the Prairie." At the end of each sentence that includes an oral vocabulary word, stop and repeat the explanation of the word. Then reread the sentence.

Use a Graphic Organizer Use the graphic organizer and the questions below to reinforce understanding of the relationship between each word and the category.

Words About Love	
What People Feel	**What People Do**
affection endeared beloved	devote appreciate

1. Name one way you **devote** time or effort to someone you care about. (Sample answers: carrying groceries; doing chores)

2. If you are loved very much, you are _____. (**beloved**)

3. What was an **emotional** thing that happened in your life? (Answers will vary.)

Day 5

Deepen Understanding

Review Repeat explanations for all oral vocabulary words. Use the definitions and examples from Day 1 and Day 3.

Guide Partner Activities Have partners work together to complete each of the activities below. Circulate and listen to partners as they work. Provide corrective feedback.

Describe Talk to your partner. Describe a **contest** you have seen or been in. Use these words: **defeated, opposing, succeed, triumph.**

Examples Do you sometimes find it hard to **overcome** your feelings and act calm? What are some things that are **emotional** for you? Work with your partner. Make a list.

Draw Draw a picture of someone who feels **affection** for you.

Write Write a description of a person you love. Use these words: **beloved, appreciate, devote, endeared.**

Assess To assess what word meanings children have learned, copy and distribute the **Pretest/Posttest** on pages 118–119. Use page 75 to administer the test. Compare scores with Day 1 assessment.

THE GOLDILOCKS CASE

It was a slow day at the police station. Inspector Hound was chasing his tail when the phone rang. It was a call from the three Bears' house.

"Come quick!" a voice cried. "It's a burglary." It was Mama Bear calling. "An intruder broke into our home and took things that didn't belong to her! She ate a bowl of porridge and broke a chair, and she's still here sleeping in our baby's bed!"

"Calm down, Mama Bear," said Inspector Hound. "I'll be there in no time."

"Please hurry!" Mama Bear cried. "Everything was just right before she broke in."

But "just right" for one person is not always the best fit for everyone. Why, just last night Inspector Hound had gone to dinner at the three Bears' home. His porridge was much too cold, and his chair was much too hard. But the Bears needed help, so he rushed out the door, hoping to catch the suspect before she could get away.

When Inspector Hound arrived, he found the Bears huddled together outside the front door.

"She's upstairs," said Papa Bear, in a voice shaking with fear.

"Sound asleep in my bed," added Baby Bear. "She frightens me!"

Inspector Hound told them to stay put while he checked it out. Then he carefully walked inside, sniffing for clues. In the kitchen were two bowls full of porridge and one empty bowl. In the living room, next to that awful hard chair, was Baby Bear's broken chair. Then he walked upstairs and saw the intruder.

There was a little blonde girl sleeping on Baby Bear's bed, snoring peacefully. Inspector Hound carefully shook her awake. He planned to interrogate her back at the police station. He would ask her questions until he learned why she had broken into the Bears' home.

She opened her eyes and smiled sweetly. "Hello, fuzzy puppy," she cooed.

Inspector Hound replied, "What are you doing here, miss? You know you're not supposed to break into someone else's home. It's illegal."

"Ohhh, a talking doggy!" cried Goldilocks happily.

As they walked downstairs, Goldilocks saw the three Bears. She screamed and fainted. Inspector Hound wondered whether she was really a criminal after all.

COMPREHENSION What words in the story might be used by a police officer? What does Inspector Hound learn about Goldilocks?

58

Days 1 and 2

"The Goldilocks Case," Vol. 1, pp. 58–59

Goldilocks on Trial

Goldilocks looked nervous as the police dog, Inspector Hound, brought her into the courthouse. Last week he had caught her sleeping inside the three Bears' home. Now they stood in front of the judge, who decided the punishments. This judge was a grumpy skunk.

"Your Honor," said Inspector Hound, "this is Goldilocks. She was sleeping in Papa and Mama Bear's home."

Grumpy Judge Skunk looked over his glasses. He glared at Goldilocks. "Well, what do you have to say for yourself, my dear?"

"I am innocent, your Honor. I have done nothing wrong," Goldilocks replied.

"I'll be the judge of that," snapped Judge Skunk. "Inspector Hound, what is your evidence against this girl? What proof do you have?"

"Well, your Honor, Mama Bear found an intruder sleeping in their house. When I arrived, I found an empty porridge bowl, a broken chair, and this girl sleeping in Baby Bear's bed."

"Do you have any witnesses?" asked Judge Skunk.

"Yes, I saw the whole thing," said Mama Bear. "This rude little girl broke into our house and ruined our things. I demand justice."

"Well, Goldilocks, do you have an alibi?" asked Judge Skunk. "Can you prove that you were somewhere else at the time?"

"No, I can't, your Honor. I was there, but I do have an excuse."

"Please, tell us your story," said the judge.

Goldilocks spoke quickly. "I got lost in the forest behind my house. It seemed as if I walked for hours. Then I saw a pretty little house. I was so tired and hungry that I knocked on the door to ask for help. There was no one home, so I went inside and ate the yummy porridge. When I sat down, I was too big, so I broke the nice chair. Then I was so sleepy from the porridge that I messed up the warm bed. I didn't mean to cause trouble. I'm sorry, Papa and Mama Bear."

Mama Bear started to cry. "It's OK, dear," she said.

Judge Skunk paused for a moment. He thought about what to do. Finally, he spoke. "Goldilocks, I have decided that you are guilty. But I have also decided that you didn't mean any harm. You can go free if you promise to help Mr. and Mrs. Bear fix their chair and make the beds."

Goldilocks happily helped the bears, and afterward, Inspector Hound helped her find her way home.

COMPREHENSION Why does Judge Skunk decide Goldilocks is guilty? Which words help you understand the law?

60

Days 3 and 4

"Goldilocks on Trial," Vol. 1, pp. 60–61

Assessment

Pretest/Posttest Administration p. 76

Pretest/Posttest Blackline Masters pp. 120–121

Day 1

Introduce Meanings

Assess To assess what word meanings children already know, copy and distribute the **Pretest/Posttest** on pages 120–121. Use page 76 to administer the test.

Explain Write each oral vocabulary word below on the board. Read it aloud. Offer an explanation and a brief example for each word.

Words About Crimes and Criminals

burglaries *n.* when someone breaks into a house or building and steals things *There have been several burglaries in our neighborhood.*

illegal *adj.* against the law *Stealing is illegal.*

inspector *n.* a police officer or detective *The inspector figured out how the thief broke in.*

interrogate *v.* to ask questions *He will interrogate all the neighbors about the crime.*

intruder *n.* somebody who goes into a place where he or she isn't supposed to be *The intruder came in through an open window.*

suspect *n.* someone people believe did something wrong *Brenda was a suspect, but she wasn't the one who broke in.*

Discuss Guide children to see the relationship between each word and the category.

Read Aloud Explain that you will read aloud a story about a police investigation. Then read aloud "The Goldilocks Case." Discuss the Comprehension questions.

Day 2

Categorize and Classify

Reread and Explain Reread "The Goldilocks Case." At the end of each sentence that includes an oral vocabulary word, stop and repeat the explanation of the word. Then reread the sentence.

Use a Graphic Organizer Use the graphic organizer and the questions below to reinforce understanding of the relationship between each word and the category

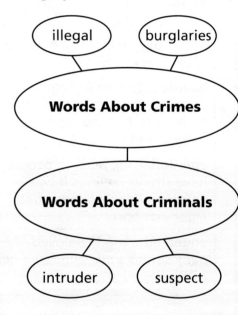

1. A person whose job is solving crimes is an _____. (**inspector**)

2. What is one thing a police officer does to find out facts about a crime? (Sample answer: **interrogate** people)

3. Is a **suspect** always a criminal? Explain. (no; The person might not have committed the crime.)

Day 3

Introduce Meanings

Explain Write each oral vocabulary word below on the board. Read it aloud. Offer an explanation and a brief example for each word.

Words About Guilty and Not Guilty

alibi *n.* when you say you did not commit a crime because you were somewhere else at the time *My alibi is that I was at my friend's house when the cookies disappeared.*

courthouse *n.* a building where judges help decide who broke the law *At the courthouse, he told the judge he was not guilty.*

evidence *n.* proof *The evidence showed that I did not do anything wrong.*

innocent *adj.* not guilty *The man was innocent of the crime, so the judge set him free.*

justice *n.* fairness *If people are punished for things they didn't do, they are not being treated with justice.*

witnesses *n.* people who saw a crime happen *The witnesses saw her take the jewels.*

Discuss Guide children to see the relationship between each word and the category. Ask questions such as this: What important **evidence** can **witnesses** give?

Read Aloud Explain that you will read aloud a story about Goldilocks and her trial. Then read aloud "Goldilocks on Trial." Discuss the Comprehension questions.

Day 4

Categorize and Classify

Reread and Explain Reread "Goldilocks on Trial." At the end of each sentence that includes an oral vocabulary word, stop and repeat the explanation of the word. Then reread the sentence.

Use a Graphic Organizer Use the graphic organizer and the questions below to reinforce understanding of the relationship between each word and the category.

Proving Someone Is Not Guilty

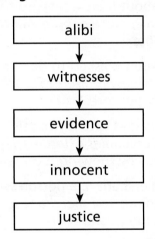

1. What is the place where trials happen? **(courthouse)**

2. Does **justice** always mean deciding that someone is not guilty? Can justice also mean deciding that someone is guilty? Explain. (yes; Justice means being fair, and it is fair to punish someone who is guilty.)

Day 5

Deepen Understanding

Review Repeat explanations for all oral vocabulary words. Use the definitions and examples from Day 1 and Day 3.

Guide Partner Activities Have partners work together to complete each of the activities below. Circulate and listen to partners as they work. Provide corrective feedback.

Role-Play Pretend you are an **inspector.** Explain your job to a partner. Use these words: **evidence, interrogate, witnesses.**

Examples Work with your partner. Imagine that there was a **burglary** at a jewelry store and the police arrested a **suspect.** What are some **alibis** that the suspect could have? How might the suspect prove that he or she is **innocent**?

Draw Draw a picture of a **courthouse.** Show a person on trial for breaking into a house.

Write Now work with your partner to write about the trial. Use these words: **intruder, illegal, justice.**

Assess To assess what word meanings children have learned, copy and distribute the **Pretest/ Posttest** on pages 120–121. Use page 76 to administer the test. Compare scores with Day 1 assessment.

Jamal's Lemonade Business

One day during summer vacation, Jamal looked out the window and saw his neighbor Marissa standing behind a table in her front yard. On the table was a big pitcher of lemonade and a sign that said, "Lemonade, 10 cents."

Jamal watched as one customer after another bought Marissa's lemonade. He started to count all the people who bought lemonade. Then, he figured out how much money Marissa was making. "I could have a lemonade stand, too," Jamal thought. "I could promote my lemonade as the cheapest in the neighborhood. And I could put up more signs than Marissa did to market my lemonade to more people!"

The next morning, Jamal went to a fruit merchant down the street and bought enough lemons to fill up the basket on his bicycle. Then Jamal hired his friend Miguel, who was a great artist, to make some cool-looking signs. These signs would help advertise his lemonade stand.

Back home in the kitchen, Jamal cut the lemons in half and squeezed the juice into a pitcher. Then he added water, and mixed the water and juice with a spoon. He added ice cubes to keep it cold. "That should do it," Jamal said to himself, but he didn't taste what he had made.

Jamal picked up the pitcher of lemonade and hurried outside. He hoped to get some customers before Marissa got started. He quickly set up his table. His friend Miguel brought the signs, and Jamal paid him a dollar.

Jamal's first customer was his next-door neighbor. Jamal watched as she took a long gulp of lemonade. She made a funny face and started to cough. "Maybe she doesn't like lemonade," thought Jamal. But still he didn't taste what he had made.

A short time later, Marissa came out and set up her lemonade stand. She said to Jamal, "I see you're in the lemonade business, too."

Jamal watched as two neighbors bought lemonade from Marissa. All day long, more and more customers went to her stand. No one bought lemonade from Jamal. When evening came, Jamal sat behind his table looking disappointed. What was Marissa's secret?

"Hey Jamal," Marissa said quietly. "Did you taste your lemonade?"

Jamal thought for a moment. Then he poured himself a cup for the first time that day. "Yuck!" he shouted. He had been selling a bad product.

"You probably forgot to add sugar," said Marissa. She felt bad for Jamal, but she smiled a little. She suggested that they could sell lemonade together the next day.

COMPREHENSION What words help you understand what Jamal did to start his lemonade business? How does Marissa help Jamal feel better about his mistake?

2

Days 1 and 2

"Jamal's Lemonade Business," Vol. 2, pp. 2–3

Winter Warmers

When winter weather strikes, what does it feel like? How about cold and chilly? Does that sound right? You feel those icy wintry winds blowing on your skin. You might even worry that your ears will freeze into ice cubes!

Not everyone lives in a place that has cold winter weather. But even if you don't, you might visit a place that does. If you are somewhere cold in the winter, there is one basic rule you must follow: bundle up! Keeping your body warm is the only way to stay safe in cold weather.

When someone loses more heat than the body can create, they can get hypothermia. This is when the body temperature becomes much colder than it should be. When this happens, the body parts that are farthest away from the heart—like fingers and toes—have the most risk of becoming freezing cold.

When you're dressing warmly for winter, the first thing you'll need to put on is a hat. Most of our body heat escapes from our heads. If you wear a nice warm hat that covers your ears, you will be able to keep your body much warmer!

Some other important items to wear are thick gloves and warm socks. It is important to keep your gloves and socks as dry as possible. Have you ever walked outside after a blizzard and gotten snow in your boots? Or have you ever made snowballs until your gloves got wet and heavy? Then you know that wet socks and gloves are no fun. They can make you feel very cold. It could even cause you to get sick with a cold.

The most important clothes to wear in wintry weather are warm pants and a jacket. You can decide how warmly you'll need to dress by looking out your window. If it's early in the morning and there is already a frosty haze in the sky, it would be smart to wear thermal pants and a heavy jacket. Or if you look outside and the sun is beginning to melt the snow, you could probably wear warm, but lighter, clothes. It is smart to dress in layers. This way, you can take something off if you feel too warm. But if you don't wear enough, then you won't have anything extra to put on if you feel too cold.

Just remember to stay safe and warm whenever winter finds you!

COMPREHENSION Which words in this selection tell you about winter weather? What can you do to stay warm when it's cold outside?

Days 3 and 4

"Winter Warmers," Vol. 2, pp. 4–5

Assessment

Pretest/Posttest Administration p. 77

Pretest/Posttest Blackline Masters pp. 122–123

Day 1

Introduce Meanings

Assess To assess what word meanings children already know, copy and distribute the **Pretest/Posttest** on pages 122–123. Use page 77 to administer the test.

Explain Write each oral vocabulary word below on the board. Read it aloud. Offer an explanation and a brief example for each word.

Words About Buying and Selling
advertise v. to tell people about *If we advertise the toy sale, more people will come to shop.*
hired v. asked to do a job *Tara's mom was hired to work in a large store.*
market v. to try to sell *Companies often market a new toy by showing it on television.*
merchant n. a person who sells things *The merchant sold us candles and soaps.*
product n. something that is sold *Many customers came to the store to buy the new product.*
promote v. to tell about how good something is *The menu used bold letters to promote the best dessert.*

Discuss Guide children to see the relationship between each word and the category. Prompt them to tell about their favorite stores, using the words.

Read Aloud Explain that you will read aloud a story about two merchants selling lemonade. Then read aloud "Jamal's Lemonade Business." Discuss the Comprehension questions.

Day 2

Categorize and Classify

Reread and Explain Reread "Jamal's Lemonade Business." At the end of each sentence that includes an oral vocabulary word, stop and repeat the explanation of the word. Then reread the sentence.

Use a Graphic Organizer Use the graphic organizer and the questions below to reinforce understanding of the relationship between each word and the category.

Words About Stores	
Words About Actions	**Words About People and Things**
advertise	product
promote	merchant
market	
hired	

1. Who are some other people you might see in a store? What are some other things people do in a store? **Add these to the graphic organizer as children suggest them.** (Sample answers: People: salespeople, managers; Actions: buy, shop, sell)

2. What can a store do to **advertise** what it is selling? (Sample answers: make posters; make commercials)

3. A merchant might sell only one kind of _____. (product)

Day 3

Introduce Meanings

Explain Write each oral vocabulary word below on the board. Read it aloud. Offer an explanation and a brief example for each word.

Words About Winter

blizzard *n.* a powerful snowstorm *We shoveled snow for hours after the <u>blizzard</u>.*

chilly *adj.* cool *I felt <u>chilly</u> without my coat on.*

freeze *v.* to change from water to ice *The winter air was cold enough to <u>freeze</u> the pond.*

haze *n.* a light fog *The <u>haze</u> made it hard for us to see far away.*

melt *v.* to change from ice to water *The warm sunshine began to <u>melt</u> the snow.*

wintry *adj.* cold like winter *It is important to bundle up during <u>wintry</u> weather.*

Discuss Guide children to see the relationship between each word and the category. Ask questions such as these: What is winter like where we live? Is it chilly? Does anything freeze? Do we ever have blizzards? Prompt children to talk about their own experiences, using the words.

Read Aloud Explain that you will read aloud a story about how to stay warm during the winter. Then read aloud "Winter Warmers." Discuss the Comprehension questions.

Day 4

Categorize and Classify

Reread and Explain Reread "Winter Warmers." At the end of each sentence that includes an oral vocabulary word, stop and repeat the explanation of the word. Then reread the sentence.

Use a Graphic Organizer Use the graphic organizer and the questions below to reinforce understanding of the relationship between each word and the category.

1. What word describes when water turns into ice? **(freeze)**

2. You might have trouble seeing far in front of you if there is _____. **(haze)**

3. Is it a good idea to wear a coat when it is **chilly**? Explain your answer. (Sample answer: yes; You'll be cold without it.)

4. Describe what you might feel and see in **wintry** weather. (Sample answer: cold temperatures, snow, darker days)

Day 5

Deepen Understanding

Review Repeat explanations for all oral vocabulary words. Use the definitions and examples from Day 1 and Day 3.

Guide Partner Activities Have partners work together to complete each of the activities below. Circulate and listen to partners as they work. Provide corrective feedback.

Categorize List three things you would need in a **blizzard**. Then list three things you would do after all the snow **melted** and it wasn't **chilly** outside.

Draw Imagine your favorite game. Now draw a picture that would help **advertise** this game to other people. Tell a partner how your drawing **promotes** the game.

Describe Talk to a partner. Describe what a beach might look like when it has a **haze** above the water. What would you see? Then describe how something might look and feel when it **freezes.**

Write Think of something you could sell to people living in **wintry** weather. Write a few sentences to explain how you would **market** your **product.**

Role-Play Work with a partner. Pretend that you are a **merchant** who has just **hired** a new worker. Help the new worker sell something to a customer.

Assess To assess what word meanings children have learned, copy and distribute the **Pretest/Posttest** on pages 122–123. Use page 77 to administer the test. Compare scores with Day 1 assessment.

The Luckiest Man on the Face of the Earth

Lou Gehrig was born in New York City in 1903. His parents had moved to America from Germany. They were poor. When he was a little boy, Gehrig loved to play baseball. He didn't know that he would grow up to become one of the greatest baseball players in history.

Gehrig went to college in New York City. He immediately joined the baseball team. One afternoon, a man from the New York Yankees came to watch a game that Gehrig was pitching. Gehrig struck out seventeen batters! The man from the Yankees was very impressed. Soon after, the New York Yankees offered Gehrig a job playing on their team.

Each week, excited Yankee fans filled the bleacher seats at Yankee Stadium. They loved to watch the players hit balls and play catch during a warm-up on the field. During the games, Gehrig ran fast around the bases. Fans cheered when he hit the ball out of the park. They also loved to hear the umpire yell "Safe!" when Gehrig reached home plate on a close play.

During his career, Gehrig competed in 2,130 straight games. He was the only baseball player ever to play so many games in a row without missing one. Only one other baseball player, Cal Ripken, Jr., has broken Gehrig's record.

In 1939, when Gehrig was thirty-nine years old, he began to feel sick. He could not play baseball as well as he once could. Doctors tried to figure out what was wrong, but they had a hard time. Finally, the doctors figured out that Gehrig had a disease they had never seen before. There was no cure for this disease. The doctors told Gehrig that this disease would make it hard for him to move. At first, he would have trouble playing baseball. Later, he would have trouble tying his shoes and even eating his food.

After learning about his illness, Lou Gehrig announced that he had to quit playing baseball. On July 4, 1939, the Yankees honored Lou Gehrig. All the Yankees, including manager Joe McCarthy, were very sad. They told Gehrig how much he meant to them. Gehrig then made a speech to his team and all the fans at Yankee Stadium. Even though he had been through so much, he said, "I consider myself the luckiest man on the face of this earth."

COMPREHENSION How do you think Lou Gehrig's story might inspire people? What words would you use to describe Lou Gehrig's baseball career?

6

Days 1 and 2

"The Luckiest Man on the Face of the Earth," Vol. 2, pp. 6–7

The Legend of Hua Mulan

Hua Mulan lived with her mother and father in a tiny village in ancient China. Life was very hard for the family because Hua Mulan was her parents' only child. Girls usually stayed at home. They learned how to take care of the house while boys helped their fathers in the fields. Since Hua Mulan had no brothers, she did both. Unlike most girls, she grew very strong.

When Hua Mulan was a young woman, a war broke out in China. The enemy's armed forces won many battles. The king was afraid that another ruler would conquer him. One day, the king's officer made an announcement. The king ordered every family to send one man to fight in the war. Hua Mulan's father was the only man in her family, and he was too old to fight. He would likely be killed. Hua Mulan knew that she would make a good warrior. So she made up her mind to take her father's place and go to war, even though women were not allowed to join the army.

That night, Hua Mulan cut her hair short. The next day, she went to the market. She used all her money to buy a horse, a saddle, and a sword. She bought some metal and then went home to make a shield, which would protect her from her enemies' swords. Then she joined the king's army.

Hua Mulan fought bravely in every battle. She learned that she was even stronger than many of the other soldiers because of her years of hard work in the fields. When the army advanced toward them, she would guard soldiers who were not as strong. The generals in the army noticed her bravery. But they never noticed that she was a woman.

The king heard of Hua Mulan's courage. When the war ended, the king offered her a high position in his court, but Hua Mulan refused it. She said that her family needed her help. If the king no longer needed her service, she wanted to return at once to her parents. The king said she could go.

By the time Hua Mulan returned to her hometown, news of her heroic actions had spread. The village gathered to watch Hua Mulan ride into town on horseback. Later, friends that Hua Mulan had made in the army came to visit her. They were surprised. It was the first time they had seen Hua Mulan wearing a dress!

COMPREHENSION What does Hua Mulan do to help others? Which words tell you about armies and battles?

8

Days 3 and 4

"The Legend of Hua Mulan," Vol. 2, pp. 8–9

Assessment

Pretest/Posttest Administration p. 78
Pretest/Posttest Blackline Masters pp. 124–125

Day 1

Introduce Meanings

Assess To assess what word meanings children already know, copy and distribute the **Pretest/ Posttest** on pages 124–125. Use page 78 to administer the test.

Explain Write each oral vocabulary word below on the board. Read it aloud. Offer an explanation and a brief example for each word.

Words About Baseball
baseball *n.* a team sport played with bats and balls *Baseball is a classic summertime sport.*
bleachers *n.* bench seats next to the field *The excited fans cheered from the bleachers.*
compete *v.* to play against *We will compete to see which baseball team is the best.*
manager *n.* the head coach of a baseball team *The manager decided that the pitcher should come out of the game.*
umpire *n.* the person who makes sure that a game is played fairly *The umpire called me out at home plate.*
warm-up *n.* a time to get ready *We stretched out during the warm-up.*

Discuss Guide children to see the relationship between each word and the category. Prompt them to use the words to discuss sports they watch or play.

Read Aloud Explain that you will read aloud a story about a famous baseball player named Lou Gehrig. Then read aloud "The Luckiest Man on the Face of the Earth." Discuss the Comprehension questions.

Day 2

Categorize and Classify

Reread and Explain Reread "The Luckiest Man on the Face of the Earth." At the end of each sentence that includes an oral vocabulary word, stop and repeat the explanation of the word. Then reread the sentence.

Use a Graphic Organizer Use the graphic organizer and the questions below to reinforce understanding of the relationship between each word and the category.

Baseball Words	
People at the Game	**Playing the Game**
manager	compete
umpire	warm-up

1. Would you need an **umpire** for a **warm-up**? Why or why not? (no; An umpire only needs to be there during the game.)

2. What do fans in the **bleachers** do? (Sample answers: cheer; yell)

3. Name some other people you might see at a **baseball** game. Then name other words about playing baseball. Add these to the graphic organizer as children suggest them. (Sample answers: People: fans, players; Playing: slide, catch, run)

Day 3

Introduce Meanings

Explain Write each oral vocabulary word below on the board. Read it aloud. Offer an explanation and a brief example for each word.

Words About Soldiers

advanced *v.* moved forward *The soldiers advanced into an unknown area of the town.*

armed forces *n.* armies of soldiers *Abraham joined the armed forces to protect his country.*

battle *n.* a long fight *They fought for days before winning the battle.*

conquer *v.* to take control of *The army fought to conquer the new land.*

shield *n.* a metal plate used to protect the body *The soldier held his shield close to his body so he wouldn't get hurt.*

warrior *n.* a fighter *The warrior had fought in many battles before this one.*

Discuss Guide children to see the relationship between each word and the category. Ask questions such as this: What do you know about **armed forces** such as the army or the navy?

Read Aloud Explain that you will read aloud a story about a woman who was one of China's most famous warriors. Then read aloud "The Legend of Hua Mulan." Discuss the Comprehension questions.

Day 4

Categorize and Classify

Reread and Explain Reread "The Legend of Hua Mulan." At the end of each sentence that includes an oral vocabulary word, stop and repeat the explanation of the word. Then reread the sentence.

Use a Graphic Organizer Use the graphic organizer and the questions below to reinforce understanding of the relationship between each word and the category.

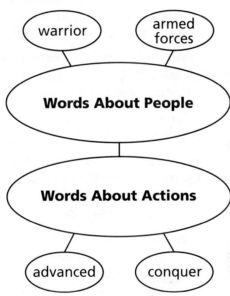

1. What word describes what a **warrior** would use to protect his or her body in a **battle**? **(shield)**

2. If an army **advanced**, did it move closer to or farther away from where it wanted to go? **(closer)**

Day 5

Deepen Understanding

Review Repeat explanations for all oral vocabulary words. Use the definitions and examples from Day 1 and Day 3.

Guide Partner Activities Have partners work together to complete each of the activities below. Circulate and listen to partners as they work. Provide corrective feedback.

Word Parts The suffix *-er* means "a person who." The word **manager** means "a person who manages." Use a dictionary or glossary. Work with a partner to find and list three other examples of words with *-er,* meaning "a person who."

Role-Play Show your partner how you would root for your favorite players as they **compete** in a **baseball** game. Show how an **umpire** would call someone out in the game.

Draw Draw a picture of a **warrior** holding a **shield.** Show the warrior doing a **warm-up** before going to fight in a **battle.**

Examples List examples of places that have **bleachers.**

Write Work with your partner. Think about what you learned about Hua Mulan's time in the **armed forces.** Write about what she might have felt knowing that an enemy army was **advancing** on her homeland and wanted to **conquer** it.

Assess To assess what word meanings children have learned, copy and distribute the **Pretest/ Posttest** on pages 124–125. Use page 78 to administer the test. Compare scores with Day 1 assessment.

A FIRST AID LESSON

Have you ever gotten a bad cut? I was over at my friend Josh's house one day. We were in-line skating in his driveway. Josh's older brother Alan was hanging out with us while their mom was at the store. We played a game called obstacle course. Josh and I drew a course with chalk and took turns racing around it. I had just finished my turn and was looking back at Josh when he fell.

"I'm OK!" he said, jumping back up. But I could see that his knee was bleeding. He had gotten a **wound** from the fall. Alan rushed over to look at Josh's cut.

"I think we should go get your mom," I said. Then I remembered that his mom was not there. I looked at Alan.

Alan could tell I was nervous, so he calmly said, "I know what to do. Don't worry. We'll take care of it together."

Then Alan showed us what to do when someone gets injured.

To treat an injury, first you must decide if the **condition** of the person you are trying to help is serious. It is always best to tell an adult when someone gets hurt. If someone is bleeding a lot, you should call 9-1-1. The operator will send an **ambulance** right away to take the injured person to the hospital. Or if the bleeding is not too serious, you can give **treatment** yourself.

To treat a minor cut, you should first press down on it lightly with a clean cloth. This will help stop the bleeding. Next, you should wash the wound with a gentle soap. This will help keep germs out of the wound so it can heal faster. Then you should put an antibiotic ointment on the wound. Medicine in the ointment kills any germs in the wound. Finally, you should cover the wound with a bandage. The bandage protects the skin while it heals. Soon the skin will heal and be as good as new.

When Josh's mom came home from the store, we told her what we did to fix the wound. She lifted the bandage and took a peek.

"It looks as if you boys did a great job!" she said.

You should always take **precautions** to avoid getting hurt. Wear protective gear when you are doing something that might cause an injury. That means always wearing a helmet and pads when you bike or skate.

COMPREHENSION What can a friend do to help another friend who is hurt? Which words help you understand how to stay safe?

10

Days 1 and 2

"A First Aid Lesson," Vol. 2, pp. 10–11

The Brave Boy of Haarlem

Many years ago, a boy named Peter lived in a town called Haarlem. The town of Haarlem was in a country called Holland, which lay beside the stormy North Sea.

Holland was a low, flat country. Some parts of the country were even lower than the sea. So the people of Holland built huge walls out of the earth. These walls were called dikes. They kept the land dry so that people could build homes and grow crops.

One day Peter asked his father if he could take dinner to an old woman in town who was sick. "Yes," his father said, "as long you promise to be back before dark." So Peter set out right away. He followed a path that ran along the base of a dike. He visited the sick old woman and gave her food and comfort.

By the time Peter started home, it was already getting dark and the wind was blowing. He knew he had to hurry, so he walked quickly along the path beneath the dike. Peter could hardly see the path. He began to feel afraid. He imagined terrible monsters were chasing him. Then he heard something really scary.

He heard the sound of water trickling through the dike. He followed the sound to a hole in the dike. Only a thin stream of water flowed through the hole, but he knew that the stormy sea was high above him on the other side of that huge earth wall. The stormy sea would make the hole bigger. More water would come through and the hole would get bigger still. The hole would keep getting bigger until the dike came crashing down, flooding the whole town. Peter ran over and stuck his finger in the hole, and the water stopped.

Peter cried for help, but no one was near. Soon his finger began to ache. He called again, but no one came. His finger quickly became sore and started to swell. Still, no one came. Peter **suffered** for hours, holding his finger in the dike. Finally, his father found him. Peter was so tired and hungry that he thought he might faint.

Peter's father saw the hole. He told people from the town, and they came to help fix the dike. It took Peter three days to **recover** from his adventure. When he was better, the people of Haarlem threw a party in his honor. He had saved the town!

COMPREHENSION How does Peter make a difference in his community? Which words help you understand the pain Peter felt that night?

12

Days 3 and 4

"The Brave Boy of Haarlem," Vol. 2, pp. 12–13

Assessment

Pretest/Posttest Administration p. 79
Pretest/Posttest Blackline Masters pp. 126–127

Day 1

Introduce Meanings

Assess To assess what word meanings children already know, copy and distribute the **Pretest/Posttest** on pages 126–127. Use page 79 to administer the test.

Explain Write each oral vocabulary word below on the board. Read it aloud. Offer an explanation and a brief example for each word.

Words About Getting Hurt

ambulance *n.* a vehicle that takes hurt or sick people to the hospital *The <u>ambulance</u> took the sick woman to the hospital.*

condition *n.* the way someone is *Dan was in good <u>condition</u> after getting over his cold.*

injured *adj.* hurt *I took care of the <u>injured</u> animal.*

precaution *n.* something you do to avoid getting sick or hurt *Wearing a seat belt is an important <u>precaution</u>.*

treatment *n.* something done to help a person who is sick or hurt *The <u>treatment</u> the doctor gave me helped me get better.*

wound *n.* a cut, bruise, or other injury to the skin *I cleaned the <u>wound</u> on my hand.*

Discuss Guide children to see the relationship between each word and the category. Ask questions such as these: When have you been **injured**? Did you have a **wound**?

Read Aloud Explain that you will read aloud a story about what to do when someone gets hurt. Then read aloud "A First Aid Lesson." Discuss the Comprehension questions.

Day 2

Categorize and Classify

Reread and Explain Reread "A First Aid Lesson." At the end of each sentence that includes an oral vocabulary word, stop and repeat the explanation of the word. Then reread the sentence.

Use a Graphic Organizer Use the graphic organizer and the questions below to reinforce understanding of the relationship between each word and the category.

Words About Getting Hurt	Words About Getting Help
wound	ambulance
injured	treatment

1. If someone were very **injured**, he or she would be in poor _____. (**condition**)

2. What are some other words about getting hurt? What are some other words about getting help when someone is hurt? Add these to the graphic organizer as children suggest them. (Sample answers: Getting Hurt: bruise, scrape; Getting Help: doctor, nurse)

3. What is a **precaution** you should take when riding a bike? (Sample answer: wear a helmet)

Day 3

Introduce Meanings

Explain Write each oral vocabulary word below on the board. Read it aloud. Offer an explanation and a brief example for each word.

Words About Feeling Hurt or Sick

ache *v.* to hurt for a while *My elbow started to ache after I bumped it on the table.*

comfort *n.* help that makes someone feel better *The mother was a comfort to her sick child.*

faint *v.* to pass out *Mrs. Abercrombie will faint when she hears the news!*

recover *v.* to get better *The doctor said that Tamika will recover soon.*

suffered *v.* felt pain or other bad feelings *I suffered a lot when I got a bad headache.*

swell *v.* to puff up *Tony's twisted ankle quickly began to swell.*

Discuss Guide children to see the relationship between each word and the category. Ask questions such as these: What could cause a part of your body to ache? What could help you recover?

Read Aloud Explain that you will read aloud a story about a boy who saves his town from being flooded. Then read aloud "The Brave Boy of Haarlem." Discuss the Comprehension questions.

Day 4

Categorize and Classify

Reread and Explain Reread "The Brave Boy of Haarlem." At the end of each sentence that includes an oral vocabulary word, stop and repeat the explanation of the word. Then reread the sentence.

Use a Graphic Organizer Use the graphic organizer and the questions below to reinforce understanding of the relationship between each word and the category.

Words About Feeling Bad	Words About Feeling Better
ache swell suffered faint	comfort recover

1. What things could give you **comfort** if you were sick? (Sample answer: Mom, soup)

2. What other words can you use to talk about feeling bad? about feeling better? Add these to the graphic organizer as children suggest them. (Sample answers: Feeling Bad: sick, pain, hurt; Feeling Better: relief, healthy, well)

Day 5

Deepen Understanding

Review Review word meanings for all oral vocabulary words. Use the definitions and examples from Day 1 and Day 3.

Guide Partner Activities Have partners work together to complete each of the activities below. Circulate and listen to partners as they work. Provide corrective feedback.

Examples Talk to a partner. Talk about a time you or someone you know was **injured.** How long did it take to **recover**? Was there a **precaution** that could have been taken to stop the injury from happening?

Role-Play Pretend you are **suffering** because you have an **ache** or a **wound.** Then ask your partner to pretend to give **treatment** and **comfort** to you.

Describe Talk to your partner. Describe what you would do if someone were in bad **condition.** Tell what would happen when the **ambulance** got there.

Compare Compare how someone would feel if he or she were about to **faint** to how the person would feel if a finger just started to **swell.**

Assess To assess what word meanings children have learned, copy and distribute the **Pretest/ Posttest** on pages 126–127. Use page 79 to administer the test. Compare scores with Day 1 assessment.

Nat Love, Cowboy and Railroad Man

Nat Love was born in 1854 in Tennessee. Nat's father passed away when Nat was young, so Nat helped his mother take care of the family. He cared for the family's garden. He picked berries and nuts to sell. Nat worked hard to earn money. Then he used that money to buy food and clothes for his family.

But after a while, Nat became restless and wanted to see the world. So, when he was fifteen years old, he went west. Nat became a cowboy. Sometimes his work was dangerous. One dark, stormy night, he had to round up cattle. Nat could hear the cattle, but he could only see them when lightning lit up the sky. It was hard to round up cattle in the dark. But Nat was stubborn and would not give up. Instead, he chased the cattle until he had caught them all.

Another time, Nat entered a roping contest. Each person in the contest had to rope, or catch, a wild horse. Then they had to put a bridle and saddle on the horse and ride it. Nat was feisty and full of energy. From the time he caught the wild horse to the time he rode it, it only took him nine minutes. No one was faster than Nat, so he won the contest.

Nat was a cowboy for more than twenty years. Then he worked as a porter for the railroad. His job was to take care of train passengers. He noticed how people were feeling. Nat did a good job of cheering people up because he was sensitive to their feelings. Sometimes Nat took care of sick passengers. He washed their faces and fed them. He made a sincere effort to make them feel better.

Nat was never jealous of others. Instead, he was happy with what he had. He was happy, too, that he was able to travel.

When Nat was fifty-four years old, he wrote a book about his life. He wrote, "I have seen a large part of America, and am still seeing it, but the life of a hundred years would be all too short to see our country. America, I love thee, sweet land of liberty, home of the brave and the free."

COMPREHENSION What did Nat Love do that made a difference in other people's lives? Which words help you understand what Nat Love was like?

14

Days 1 and 2

"Nat Love, Cowboy and Railroad Man," Vol. 2, pp. 14–15

THE HAIRCUT

Mr. Moreno was a businessman who was staying at a hotel in a small town. He needed a haircut, so he asked a hotel worker where he could find a barbershop.

The hotel worker said, "There are only two barbershops in town. One barbershop is on Elm Street. The other barbershop is on Park Street."

Mr. Moreno worked until the late afternoon. Finally, he had time to get a haircut. Mr. Moreno walked to the barbershop on Elm Street first. He looked in the window and saw the barber eating lunch. He noticed the barber's haircut. He thought, "I know I'm being negative, but this barber has the messiest haircut I've ever seen! His hair is too long on one side. It is too short on the other side. I think someone clumsy cut this barber's hair." Then he noticed the barbershop floor. It was a mess too, just like his hair! The barber hadn't swept the floor in a long time.

Next, Mr. Moreno walked to the barbershop on Park Street. That barbershop was neat. The barber there was reading a paper, and his haircut was neat. It looked great! The businessman thought, "This barber has one of the best quality haircuts I've ever seen! I want a great haircut, and after visiting both of these barbershops, I know where I'll get my hair cut."

Where do you think Mr. Moreno went for his haircut?

Mr. Moreno got a haircut from the messy barber on Elm Street—the one with the bad haircut. There were only two barbers in town. So Mr. Moreno was sure that the two barbers cut each other's hair. Because the neat barber on Park Street had a great haircut, the businessman was sure that the messy barber on Elm Street gave great haircuts. He was reluctant to go to the neat barber on Park Street. He was sure that barber gave bad haircuts.

The messy barber on Elm Street gave Mr. Moreno a great haircut. Afterward, the businessman gave the barber a genuine smile and said, "You are great! This is the best haircut I've ever had. I mean it!"

But the messy barber was modest. He said, "I'm just doing my job. But I always try to do my best."

Then Mr. Moreno said, "Tell me, why is the floor of your shop so messy?"

The barber said, "I'm too busy giving haircuts to sweep the floor. Sometimes I'm even too busy to eat lunch until late in the day."

COMPREHENSION What words help you understand what the two barbers are like? How does the businessman's choice to go to the barber on Elm Street show that you can't always believe what you see?

16

Days 3 and 4

"The Haircut," Vol. 2, pp. 16–17

Assessment

Pretest/Posttest Administration p. 80

Pretest/Posttest Blackline Masters pp. 128–129

Day 1

Introduce Meanings

Assess To assess what word meanings children already know, copy and distribute the **Pretest/ Posttest** on pages 128–129. Use page 80 to administer the test.

Explain Write each oral vocabulary word below on the board. Read it aloud. Offer an explanation and a brief example for each word.

Words That Tell What People Are Like
feisty adj. tough and full of energy *The feisty boy couldn't wait to go play hockey.*
jealous adj. wanting something someone else has *Don't be jealous of her good grades.*
restless adj. unable to stay in one place or stay doing the same thing *The restless woman moved from town to town.*
sensitive adj. aware of other people's needs or feelings *The nurse was sensitive to her patient's needs.*
sincere adj. honest *May's sincere apology made me feel much better.*
stubborn adj. not willing to quit or change your mind *My sister is so stubborn!*

Discuss Guide children to see the relationship between each word and the category. Prompt them to think of people they know and describe them using the words.

Read Aloud Explain that you will read aloud a story about a man named Nat Love. Then read aloud "Nat Love, Cowboy and Railroad Man." Discuss the Comprehension questions.

Day 2

Categorize and Classify

Reread and Explain Reread "Nat Love, Cowboy and Railroad Man." At the end of each sentence that includes an oral vocabulary word, stop and repeat the explanation of the word. Then reread the sentence.

Use a Graphic Organizer Use the graphic organizer and the questions below to reinforce understanding of the relationship between each word and the category.

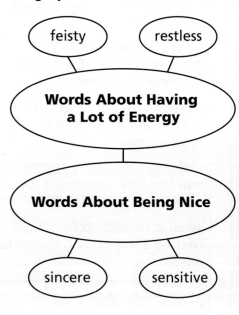

1. Would a person who is **sincere** tell a lot of lies? (no)

2. If your friend had a bike and you didn't, you might be _____. (jealous)

3. What word could you use to describe someone who won't change his or her mind? (stubborn)

Day 3

Introduce Meanings

Explain Write each oral vocabulary word below on the board. Read it aloud. Offer an explanation and a brief example for each word.

More Words That Tell What People Are Like

clumsy *adj.* not skilled; awkward *I am very clumsy in gym class.*

genuine *adj.* sincere; real *The teacher had a genuine wish for her students to do well.*

modest *adj.* not bragging *Mo is modest about how well he can draw.*

negative *adj.* thinking about things in a bad way rather than in a good way *Rico was so negative, he didn't even have fun on his vacation!*

quality *n.* how good or bad something is *The bike quickly broke because it was of poor quality.*

reluctant *adj.* not wanting to *I was reluctant to tell him I didn't like his cooking.*

Discuss Guide children to see the relationship between each word and the category. Ask questions such as this: What is something good you can do that you are **modest** about?

Read Aloud Explain that you will read aloud a story about a man who needs to decide where to get a haircut. Then read aloud "The Haircut." Discuss the Comprehension questions.

Day 4

Categorize and Classify

Reread and Explain Reread "The Haircut." At the end of each sentence that includes an oral vocabulary word, stop and repeat the explanation of the word. Then reread the sentence.

Use a Graphic Organizer Use the graphic organizer and the questions below to reinforce understanding of the relationship between each word and the category.

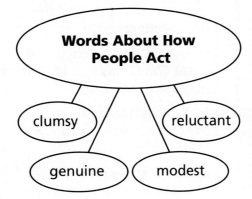

Words About How People Act — clumsy, reluctant, genuine, modest

1. Suppose you asked two people if they had fun at a party. Would a **negative** person say yes or no? (no)

2. The best meals are usually made of ingredients that are of the best _____. (quality)

3. Would you give a **clumsy** person something breakable to carry? Why or why not? (no; He or she might drop it.)

Day 5

Deepen Understanding

Review Review word meanings for all oral vocabulary words. Use the definitions and examples from Day 1 and Day 3.

Guide Partner Activities Have partners work together to complete each of the activities below. Circulate and listen to partners as they work. Provide corrective feedback.

Examples Have you ever been **jealous** of someone? Tell a partner about it. Then tell your partner about a time you were reluctant to do something.

Word Parts The suffix *-less* means "without." The word *restless* means "without rest." Work with a partner to think of some things that you might be "without." Add *-less* to three of those words. Then use a dictionary or a glossary to check the new words.

Categorize Talk with your partner. List three things a **negative** person might say to someone who is feeling sad. Then list three things a **sensitive** person might say to someone who is feeling sad.

Write Write a description of a made-up school. Talk about what the people at the school are like. Use these words: **clumsy, sincere, genuine, stubborn, feisty, modest, quality.**

Assess To assess what word meanings children have learned, copy and distribute the **Pretest/Posttest** on pages 128–129. Use page 80 to administer the test. Compare scores with Day 1 assessment.

Gabriel Lopez, Superhero

On the outside, Gabriel Lopez was just a quiet second grader. Other kids didn't think he was very special. But little did they know of the great feats that Gabriel was capable of.

One day, Gabriel sat at his desk, carefully writing his name in cursive. Suddenly, his pencil eraser began to glow. Gabriel sprang into action. He raised his hand and asked, "Mr. Wright, may I go to the restroom?"

Mr. Wright agreed, so Gabriel walked into the hall and then ran to his cubby. He reached inside of it and pressed a hidden button. A wall of his cubby opened, and Gabriel stepped onto a slide. The slide spun him around and around and then dropped him onto his bicycle. Gabriel put on his helmet, which had an earpiece that allowed him to communicate with Superhero Command Central.

"Who do I need to rescue today?" Gabriel asked Command Central.

"Your librarian, Mr. Emery," Command Central answered. "The evil villain Dr. Quizzer has captured him. You must trick Dr. Quizzer and bring Mr. Emery back to the school. Good luck!"

With that, Gabriel biked to the boathouse by the pond. He opened the boathouse door and saw a ladder behind some rowboat oars. Gabriel climbed down the ladder. Then he snuck down a hallway into Dr. Quizzer's hideout.

Mr. Emery was in distress. Dr. Quizzer had tied him up. Gabriel moved forward just as Dr. Quizzer stepped out of the shadows. "I knew you'd come to rescue your librarian!" said Dr. Quizzer with an evil laugh. "After I capture you, no one will be able to study for tests again!"

Dr. Quizzer threw a net at Gabriel. Gabriel dodged the net, flipped through the air, and said, "Hey, Dr. Quizzer, pop quiz! What's you minus us?"

As Dr. Quizzer stood thinking, Gabriel hastened to pass Mr. Emery. Then they ran down the hallway and used all their muscular strength to quickly climb the ladder up to the surface. Dr. Quizzer was left in the dust, and Gabriel had saved the day!

COMPREHENSION How does Gabriel trick Dr. Quizzer? Which words help you understand what Gabriel does when he is a superhero?

18

Days 1 and 2

"Gabriel Lopez, Superhero," Vol. 2, pp. 18–19

The Greatest Race Ever

During the winter of 1925, the people of Nome, Alaska, had an emergency. A deadly disease was quickly spreading throughout the town. The people needed medicine. But planes and ships could not get to Nome because of cold weather and ice. The only way to get the medicine to Nome was by dog sled. But the sleds would have to hurry.

At the time, dog sleds were used to carry mail to Nome. Teams of dogs pulled the sleds. The men who drove the sleds were called mushers. These mushers agreed to help deliver the medicine to Nome. But the trip was more than 650 miles! So the mushers organized a relay. Each musher would carry the medicine for part of the trip until it reached Nome.

On January 27, musher Bill Shannon began the trip. He and his team of dogs charged into the dark night. They rushed forward to meet the next team. They ran fifty-two miles. Then Shannon gave the medicine to Edgar Kallands, and Kallands was off.

The race continued. Each musher hastened to pass the medicine off to the next musher. They moved with great speed. The momentum continued across the frozen landscape. Most of the teams ran about thirty miles. But one team, Leonhard Seppala's team, ran more than ninety miles!

Leonhard Seppala and his team of dogs ran across the sea ice. Sea ice is dangerous because it can break apart. Pieces of ice can retreat, or pull away, from land. Seppala's lead dog, Togo, guided the team. The dogs ran fast, streaking across the dangerous ice. Just hours after they crossed the ice, the ice broke apart.

Then a terrible blizzard blew in. Officials decided that it was too dangerous for the dog teams to continue the trip. They sent messages telling the mushers to wait until the storm was over. But Gunnar Kaasen did not get the message. He kept on going to Nome. His lead dog, Balto, ran through the blinding snow. Balto kept his nose down, pursuing the smell of other dog teams that had traveled the trail before.

Finally, five and a half hours after Shannon started the relay, Kaasen's dog team carried the medicine into Nome. The doctor and nurses treated the sick right away. The people of Nome were saved! Brave men and brave dogs had stopped a disaster.

COMPREHENSION What words in this passage are about movement? How did the mushers and their dog teams make a difference?

20

Days 3 and 4

"The Greatest Race Ever," Vol. 2, pp. 20–21

Assessment

Pretest/Posttest Administration p. 81
Pretest/Posttest Blackline Masters pp. 130–131

Day 1

Introduce Meanings

Assess To assess what word meanings children already know, copy and distribute the **Pretest/Posttest** on pages 130–131. Use page 81 to administer the test.

Explain Write each oral vocabulary word below on the board. Read it aloud. Offer an explanation and a brief example for each word.

Words About Superheroes

captured *v.* caught *Superwoman captured the dangerous criminal.*

distress *n.* when people are upset *The family was in distress because of the fire.*

feat *n.* a brave act *Capturing the criminal was an amazing feat of bravery.*

muscular strength *n.* power that comes from muscles *The superhero had amazing muscular strength.*

rescue *v.* to save *The firefighter had to rescue the puppy.*

villain *n.* a bad guy *Can you name a villain that Superman has not defeated?*

Discuss Guide children to see the relationship between each word and the category. Prompt them to use the words to describe heroic actions. Ask: Have you ever seen or heard about someone in **distress**? What was done to **rescue** him or her?

Read Aloud Explain that you will read aloud a story about an unlikely superhero. Then read aloud "Gabriel Lopez, Superhero." Discuss the Comprehension questions.

Day 2

Categorize and Classify

Reread and Explain Reread "Gabriel Lopez, Superhero." At the end of each sentence that includes an oral vocabulary word, stop and repeat the explanation of the word. Then reread the sentence.

Use a Graphic Organizer Use the graphic organizer and the questions below to reinforce understanding of the relationship between each word and the category.

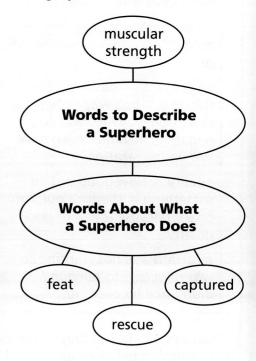

1. What other words could describe a superhero? Add these to the graphic organizer as children suggest them. (Sample answer: strong, brave, helpful)

2. The superhero tried to capture the mean _____. (**villain**)

3. What are some things that cause you **distress**? (Sample answer: mean people, not understanding what the teacher is saying)

Day 3

Introduce Meanings

Explain Write each oral vocabulary word below on the board. Read it aloud. Offer an explanation and a brief example for each word.

Words About Moving Quickly

charged *v.* rushed *The players charged onto the court as their names were called.*

hastened *v.* hurried *Jenelle hastened to get to class on time.*

momentum *n.* the speed or power something has while moving *Kara's bike gained momentum as it went down the hill.*

pursuing *v.* following *The police officer is pursuing the suspect.*

retreat *v.* to go back or move away *It is a good idea to retreat from a growling dog.*

streak *v.* to move really fast *I saw a runner streak across the park.*

Discuss Guide children to see the relationship between each word and the category. Ask them to use the words to talk about times when they moved quickly.

Read Aloud Explain that you will read aloud a story about dog teams that save a town. Then read aloud "The Greatest Race Ever." Discuss the Comprehension questions.

Day 4

Categorize and Classify

Reread and Explain Reread "The Greatest Race Ever." At the end of each sentence that includes an oral vocabulary word, stop and repeat the explanation of the word. Then reread the sentence.

Use a Graphic Organizer Use the graphic organizer and the questions below to reinforce understanding of the relationship between each word and the category.

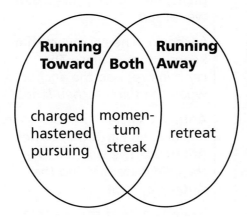

Running Toward / Both / Running Away

charged hastened pursuing | momentum streak | retreat

1. Would a dog **hasten** after a rabbit? **(yes)**

2. What word could you use to describe what a dog is doing when it is chasing a rabbit? **(pursuing)**

3. Something that is moving very fast has a lot of _____. **(momentum)**

Day 5

Deepen Understanding

Review Repeat explanations for all oral vocabulary words. Use the definitions and examples from Day 1 and Day 3.

Guide Partner Activities Have partners work together to complete each of the activities below. Circulate and listen to partners as they work. Provide corrective feedback.

Draw Draw a picture of a superhero. Your superhero might be **pursuing** a **villain** or doing a great feat, such as saving someone in **distress**.

Write Now write a story about a time your superhero needed to **capture** a criminal. Use these words: **hastened, retreat, streak.**

Role-Play With your partner, act out how you would use **muscular strength** to **rescue** someone who was trapped.

Examples Have you ever **charged** toward something with a lot of **momentum**? Tell your partner where you were running and why you were running so fast.

Assess To assess what word meanings children have learned, copy and distribute the **Pretest/Posttest** on pages 130–131. Use page 81 to administer the test. Compare scores with Day 1 assessment.

Shackleton's Amazing Journey

Imagine a story about people who lived in a bitterly cold and icy place for almost two years. Imagine that they did not have a lot of food. Imagine that they had nowhere warm to sleep. Guess what? This is a true story.

In 1914, Sir Ernest Shackleton and a crew of twenty-seven men set sail from England to Antarctica. No one had ever traveled across Antarctica before, because it was very cold and dangerous. The crew sailed on a wooden ship called the *Endurance*.

When the voyage began, the men were excited. But later, as they sailed deeper within the Antarctic Circle, the water became more and more icy. When they tried to move forward, they would sail into giant blocks of ice. Finally, a huge block of ice froze around the ship. They did not need to drop their anchor in order to stop—they were trapped by the ice.

Everyone aboard the ship hoped they would get free soon. They hoped the ocean current might rock the ship back and forth to break them loose. The crew was scared because they were very cold. They had almost finished eating all the food they had brought. But soon, the thick ice began to crush the ship. The crew knew that the *Endurance* would sink. So they took many things out of the ship and made a camp on the ice. They took tools, weapons, tents, and blankets. They also took lifeboats.

The men lived on the ice for five months. The ice block they had lived on slowly drifted through the water. At last, they had found water they could sail through! The crew used the lifeboats they had taken from the *Endurance* to sail away from the ice block. Luckily, they reached a tiny bit of land and set up camp there. This place was called Elephant Island. The bad news, however, was that no other people lived there. The men still needed to find help.

Shackleton and five other men went to find help. They sailed in a lifeboat away from the island. After a dangerous trip, the men entered a small bay. On the land near the bay, they were finally able to find people to help them. Shackleton borrowed a ship so he could go back to Elephant Island. He found his whole crew there. Everyone was alive.

COMPREHENSION What caused the *Endurance* to sink? Which words about the sea help you understand what happens to the crew of the *Endurance*?

22

Days 1 and 2

"Shackleton's Amazing Journey," Vol. 2, pp. 22–23

In Search of the Unknown

Antarctica. Have you ever heard of it? Could you find it on a map? If you looked for it, you would see that it is at the bottom of the world.

Antarctica is one of the seven continents. It is a special continent for many reasons. One reason is that it is almost completely covered by ice. Another reason is that nobody lives there. Antarctica is one of the only frontiers left on Earth. People cannot live there for long periods of time because the weather is too dangerous. Antarctica is the coldest and windiest place on Earth.

Wouldn't you be curious about a whole continent where nobody lives? What do you think you'd see there? Many people want to find out. They lead expeditions to Antarctica because they hope to learn more about the land. Some teams of scientists want to look for meteorites, or rocks that have fallen from outer space. Other teams of scientists want to study the animals that live there, like penguins. Some people, like explorers, go just for fun!

Explorers are people who find areas of wilderness and try to learn more about why nobody lives there. Sometimes explorers are sent as scouts to take notes about everything they see, and then they report back to the group of people who sent them. Most explorers who see a place for the first time will claim it, or say it is part of their country's territory. Since so many people have claimed different places in Antarctica, the continent belongs to seven different countries!

Getting to Antarctica is not easy. You cannot just schedule a flight and pack a suitcase. If you really want to go there, you will have to learn more about how to protect yourself from the dangerous weather. Then you will have to find someone to guide you. That person would be an expert, and he or she could help you stay safe.

Most people who travel to Antarctica go there to do research. Not many people go there as tourists. Do you want to go and see what it looks like?

COMPREHENSION Why can't people live on Antarctica? Which words about exploring a new land do you hear?

24

Days 3 and 4

"In Search of the Unknown," Vol. 2, pp. 24–25

Assessment

Pretest/Posttest Administration p. 82
Pretest/Posttest Blackline Masters
pp. 132–133

Day 1

Introduce Meanings

Assess To assess what word meanings children already know, copy and distribute the **Pretest/Posttest** on pages 132–133. Use page 82 to administer the test.

Explain Write each oral vocabulary word below on the board. Read it aloud. Offer an explanation and a brief example for each word.

Words About Sailing

aboard *adv.* on a ship, train, plane, etc. *Come aboard before we set sail.*

anchor *n.* a heavy object that keeps a ship in place *The captain dropped the anchor when the ship reached land.*

Antarctic Circle *n.* an imaginary line around Earth that circles Antarctica *The ship sailed in the cold water around the Antarctic Circle.*

bay *n.* a part of the sea that is partly surrounded by a curved area of land *The bay was filled with boats.*

current *n.* a steady flow of water *The sea turtles were carried along by the current.*

voyage *n.* a trip, often a long one by water *We went on a voyage across the ocean.*

Discuss Guide children to see the relationship between each word and the category. Ask questions such as these: Where would you like to go on a **voyage** to? Have you ever swum in a **bay**?

Read Aloud Explain that you will read aloud a story about a journey to Antarctica. Then read aloud "Shackleton's Amazing Journey." Discuss the Comprehension questions.

Day 2

Categorize and Classify

Reread and Explain Reread "Shackleton's Amazing Journey." At the end of each sentence that includes an oral vocabulary word, stop and repeat the explanation of the word. Then reread the sentence.

Use a Graphic Organizer Use the graphic organizer and the questions below to reinforce understanding of the relationship between each word and the category.

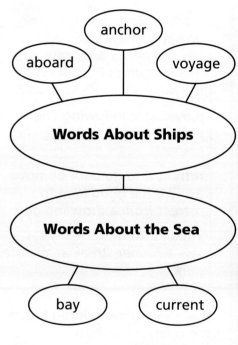

1. Name some things you might see on a **voyage** across the ocean. (Sample answers: other ships; whales; water; islands)

2. One of the coldest places on Earth is the _____. (**Antarctic Circle**)

Day 3

Introduce Meanings

Explain Write each oral vocabulary word below on the board. Read it aloud. Offer an explanation and a brief example for each word.

Words About Explorers
expedition *n.* a journey made by a group of people for a certain reason, such as to explore something *They went on an* <u>expedition</u> *to Antarctica.*
frontier *n.* a place beyond where people live *The* <u>frontier</u> *was large and unexplored.*
guided *v.* showed the way *The dog* <u>guided</u> *us through the forest.*
scout *n.* a person who goes ahead of a group to find out what is there *The* <u>scout</u> *made sure the road ahead was safe.*
territory *n.* an area of land *They were in a* <u>territory</u> *they had never been to before.*
wilderness *n.* a wild area of land that has not been lived on and changed by people *It would be easy to get lost in the* <u>wilderness</u>.

Discuss Guide children to see the relationship between each word and the category. Ask questions such as this: What might people see on an **expedition** into the **wilderness**?

Read Aloud Explain that you will read aloud a story about exploring Antarctica. Then read aloud "In Search of the Unknown." Discuss the Comprehension questions.

Day 4

Categorize and Classify

Reread and Explain Reread "In Search of the Unknown." At the end of each sentence that includes an oral vocabulary word, stop and repeat the explanation of the word. Then reread the sentence.

Use a Graphic Organizer Use the graphic organizer and the questions below to reinforce understanding of the relationship between each word and the category.

Words About Exploring	Words About Land to Explore
expedition guided scout	frontier territory wilderness

1. Juana helped her sister find her way on her first day of school. What word tells what Juana did? **(guided)**

2. They went to explore the deep sea in a submarine. Their trip was an underwater _____. **(expedition)**

3. What is a **territory** you might like to explore? (Answers will vary.)

Day 5

Deepen Understanding

Review Review word meanings for all oral vocabulary words. Use the definitions and examples from Day 1 and Day 3.

Guide Partner Activities Have partners work together to complete each of the activities below. Circulate and listen to partners as they work. Provide corrective feedback.

Role-Play Pretend you are a scout on an **expedition** into a forest. Show how you might go ahead to find out where everyone should go next. Then show how you would **guide** the rest of your group on the path you found.

Describe Talk with your partner. Imagine you were going on a **voyage** to the **Antarctic Circle**. Describe what you might see.

Write Now write a description of your travels. Use these words: **aboard, frontier, wilderness, territory.**

Draw Draw a picture of a **bay**. Show a ship with its **anchor** down and show the **current** moving in the bay.

Assess To assess what word meanings children have learned, copy and distribute the **Pretest/Posttest** on pages 132–133. Use page 82 to administer the test. Compare scores with Day 1 assessment.

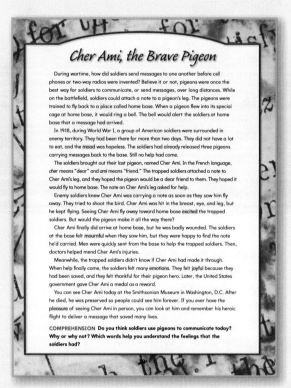

THE SPOILED PRINCESS

There was once a princess who had everything she could ever want. She had pretty ponies and swimming pools, beautiful dresses and mountains of candy. But those things didn't make her happy. She always wanted more. In fact, she was a mean little girl who treated everyone badly.

One day, the princess saw a little girl playing happily with a dirty doll. The princess called her fairy godmother right away.

"Fairy godmother, come here now!" she ordered. Her fairy godmother appeared at once in a puff of smoke.

"What took you so long, Judy?" sneered the princess. "Can't you hear anymore?"

Her fairy godmother could hardly hide her disgust at the little girl's bad manners.

"Your insults harm you more than they hurt my feelings. Now, how can I help you dear?"

"That little girl playing in the street seems happy!" shouted the princess. "The doll must make her happy. I want it now!"

"But she is a poor little girl. That's her only doll, and you have hundreds of dolls," her fairy godmother pleaded.

"You work for me, Judy," the princess said with scorn. "Get me the doll now!"

Taking the doll away from the little girl embarrassed the fairy godmother and made her feel sad. But she did as she was told.

At first, the princess felt happy playing with the dirty old doll, but soon she was angry and sad again. "That girl must have a secret that makes her happy," thought the princess. She ordered her fairy godmother to bring the girl to her room.

"Why are you so happy?" the princess demanded.

"I am happy because I have friends and family who love me," said the little girl, smiling shyly. "What is your name? Maybe we could be friends."

Finally, the princess realized that possessions would not make her happy. From that day on, the princess was nice to everyone. She had learned that kindness was the real key to happiness.

COMPREHENSION What words help you understand the bad behavior of the princess? How is the princess different at the end the story?

26

Days 1 and 2

"The Spoiled Princess," Vol. 2, pp. 26–27

Cher Ami, the Brave Pigeon

During wartime, how did soldiers send messages to one another before cell phones or two-way radios were invented? Believe it or not, pigeons were once the best way for soldiers to communicate, or send messages, over long distances. While on the battlefield, soldiers could attach a note to a pigeon's leg. The pigeons were trained to fly back to a place called home base. When a pigeon flew into its special cage at home base, it would ring a bell. The bell would alert the soldiers at home base that a message had arrived.

In 1918, during World War I, a group of American soldiers were surrounded in enemy territory. They had been there for more than two days. They did not have a lot to eat, and the mood was hopeless. The soldiers had already released three pigeons carrying messages back to the base. Still no help had come.

The soldiers brought out their last pigeon, named Cher Ami. In the French language, cher means "dear" and ami means "friend." The trapped soldiers attached a note to Cher Ami's leg, and they hoped the pigeon would be a dear friend to them. They hoped it would fly to home base. The note on Cher Ami's leg asked for help.

Enemy soldiers knew Cher Ami was carrying a note as soon as they saw him fly away. They tried to shoot the bird. Cher Ami was hit in the breast, eye, and leg, but he kept flying. Seeing Cher Ami fly away toward home base excited the trapped soldiers. But would the pigeon make it all the way there?

Cher Ami finally did arrive at home base, but he was badly wounded. The soldiers at the base felt mournful when they saw him, but they were happy to find the note he'd carried. Men were quickly sent from the base to help the trapped soldiers. Then, doctors helped mend Cher Ami's injuries.

Meanwhile, the trapped soldiers didn't know if Cher Ami had made it through. When help finally came, the soldiers felt many emotions. They felt joyful because they had been saved, and they felt thankful for their pigeon hero. Later, the United States government gave Cher Ami a medal as a reward.

You can see Cher Ami today at the Smithsonian Museum in Washington, D.C. After he died, he was preserved so people could see him forever. If you ever have the pleasure of seeing Cher Ami in person, you can look at him and remember his heroic flight to deliver a message that saved many lives.

COMPREHENSION Do you think soldiers use pigeons to communicate today? Why or why not? Which words help you understand the feelings that the soldiers had?

Days 3 and 4

"Cher Ami, the Brave Pigeon," Vol. 2, pp. 28–29

Assessment

Pretest/Posttest Administration p. 83
Pretest/Posttest Blackline Masters pp. 134–135

Day 1

Introduce Meanings

Assess To assess what word meanings children already know, copy and distribute the **Pretest/ Posttest** on pages 134–135. Use page 83 to administer the test.

Explain Write each oral vocabulary word below on the board. Read it aloud. Offer an explanation and a brief example for each word.

Words About Bad Behavior

disgust *n.* a feeling of dislike or of thinking something is wrong *I was filled with <u>disgust</u> when I saw the boy cheat on the test.*

embarrass *v.* to be made to feel shy or ashamed *My baby sister will <u>embarrass</u> me if she cries during the movie.*

insult *n.* mean words *His <u>insult</u> about my singing made me feel sad all day.*

scorn *n.* strong dislike and lack of respect *She gave a look of <u>scorn</u> when I said I was too scared to go.*

sneered *v.* spoke with scorn or gave a look of scorn *Her lip curled up as she <u>sneered</u> at the other team.*

treated *v.* acted toward *She <u>treated</u> everyone unkindly.*

Discuss Guide children to see the relationship between each word and the category. Ask questions such as this: What might make you feel **disgust**?

Read Aloud Explain that you will read aloud a story about a spoiled princess. Then read aloud "The Spoiled Princess." Discuss the Comprehension questions.

Day 2

Categorize and Classify

Reread and Explain Reread "The Spoiled Princess." At the end of each sentence that includes an oral vocabulary word, stop and repeat the explanation of the word. Then reread the sentence.

Use a Graphic Organizer Use the graphic organizer and the questions below to reinforce understanding of the relationship between each word and the category.

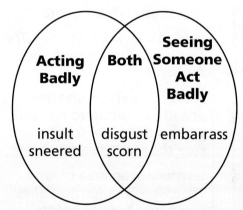

Acting Badly — Both — Seeing Someone Act Badly

insult
sneered

disgust
scorn

embarrass

1. Suppose you were looking at someone in a mean way. What word might describe that? **(sneered)**

2. How would you **treat** someone who was acting badly? (Sample answer: I would let them know that what they were doing was wrong.)

Day 3

Introduce Meanings

Explain Write each oral vocabulary word below on the board. Read it aloud. Offer an explanation and a brief example for each word.

Words About Feelings
emotions *n.* feelings *Happiness and sadness are both <u>emotions</u>.*
excite *v.* to be made to feel very happy *Going on vacation <u>excited</u> us.*
joyful *adj.* very happy *I felt <u>joyful</u> when my team won the game.*
mood *n.* the way you are feeling at a certain time *We were all in a good <u>mood</u> during the holidays.*
mournful *adj.* very sad *She felt <u>mournful</u> when she lost her favorite toy.*
pleasure *n.* something that is fun or makes you happy *It was a <u>pleasure</u> to see you.*

Discuss Guide children to see the relationship between each word and the category. Read each word and prompt children to describe a situation when they might feel each emotion.

Read Aloud Explain that you will read aloud a story about a very special pigeon. Then read aloud "Cher Ami, the Brave Pigeon." Discuss the Comprehension questions.

Day 4

Categorize and Classify

Reread and Explain Reread "Cher Ami, the Brave Pigeon." At the end of each sentence that includes an oral vocabulary word, stop and repeat the explanation of the word. Then reread the sentence.

Use a Graphic Organizer Use the graphic organizer and the questions below to reinforce understanding of the relationship between each word and the category.

Words About Happy Emotions	Words About Sad Emotions
excite joyful pleasure	mournful

1. Name some things that put you in a happy **mood**. (Sample answers: music; playing outside)

2. What are some other sad **emotions**? Add these to the graphic organizer as children suggest them. (Sample answers: hurt; lonely)

Day 5

Deepen Understanding

Review Review word meanings for all oral vocabulary words. Use the definitions and examples from Day 1 and Day 3.

Guide Partner Activities Have partners work together to complete each of the activities below. Circulate and listen to partners as they work. Provide corrective feedback.

Categorize Work with a partner. List three things you think are a **pleasure** to do. Then list three things that **embarrass** you.

Examples What is something that puts you in a good **mood**? Tell your partner. Now tell about something that puts you in a bad mood.

Describe Talk to your partner. Describe something that might **excite** you.

Word Parts The suffix *-ful* means "full of." The word **joyful** means "full of joy." The word **mournful** means "full of mourning or sadness." Use a dictionary or glossary. Work with your partner to find and list two other examples of words with *-ful* meaning "full of."

Draw Draw three faces that show different **emotions**.

Write Now write a description of the faces. Use these words: **disgust, insult, scorn, sneered, treated**.

Assess To assess what word meanings children have learned, copy and distribute the **Pretest/Posttest** on pages 134–135. Use page 83 to administer the test. Compare scores with Day 1 assessment.

THE FISH PRINCE

A long time ago, a young married couple lived by a river. They were very poor, but fishing together on the peaceful river made them happy.

One day, the woman caught a very large fish. As she picked it up, its head turned. The fish looked straight at her and spoke. "I am not a fish, but a prince," the fish said. "Please let me go."

The woman threw the fish back into the river at once. She looked at her husband, but he had not heard the fish speak.

Later, the husband and wife returned to their tiny hut on the bank of the river. They had few possessions in their home, but it was warm nonetheless. They were happy there. That night, the wife told her husband about the talking fish.

The husband became very excited. "That fish is magical! You had great fortune to catch that fish. He will give you anything you ask for. Go back to him and ask him to give us a palace and endless riches."

The woman did as her husband asked. She knew that this was their only chance to gain money and security.

She went down to the river and called out to the fish. "Oh, fish prince. I am the one who freed you today. Please come and reward me for my good deed. My husband and I want to be wealthy."

The fish appeared at once and said, "Go back to your home. It has now become a palace filled with valuable things."

Sure enough, the woman returned and found a great palace where the small hut once stood. The palace was filled with expensive furniture and trinkets.

After the couple had lived in the palace for a few weeks, they found that they were less happy than they had been in the small hut. They no longer spent time together as they had when they were fishing. They had lots of empty space and nothing to do all day. After some time, the man said to his wife, "Go back to the fish, and ask him to make us happy again."

When the woman asked the fish for happiness, it said, "Go back home. You now have what you need to be happy." When the woman returned home, her husband was sitting in their tiny hut again. For the first time in weeks, he was smiling.

COMPREHENSION How does the couple's life change after they catch the fish? What words tell you about money?

30

Days 1 and 2

"The Fish Prince," Vol. 2, pp. 30–31

BABY RATTLESNAKE

Baby Rattlesnake lived with his family in the hot, dry desert. He couldn't wait to grow up to be a big rattler like his dad. His brothers and sisters already had their rattles.

Every day, Baby Rattlesnake asked, "When can I have my rattle?"

Every day, Mama Rattlesnake answered, "Not yet, Baby Rattlesnake."

But Baby Rattlesnake did not give up. He asked in the morning and the evening. He even asked in the middle of the night, just to disturb his parents. His whining became a huge annoyance to his family. Finally, he made himself such a nuisance that his parents gave in.

"You may have your rattle if you promise to use it wisely. Stay away from people!" they warned.

Baby Rattlesnake agreed to his parents' rules. But he was a mischievous snake. He couldn't wait to scare someone with his new rattle! So he slithered close to an eagle and sat quietly until it was almost asleep. Just as the eagle closed its eyes, Baby Rattlesnake shook his rattle hard and fast.

"Yikes! A snake!" the eagle screeched as it flapped into the air. Baby Rattlesnake laughed.

He was still chuckling to himself when he saw the village. He remembered that his parents told him not to interfere with people. "But why not scare just one?" he thought. "It would be funny."

He slithered into the village. It was hard to stop himself from laughing. "I bet they will scream and run, just like the eagle," he thought.

He slithered into a house that belonged to the chief. The chief's daughter was inside sleeping. He crept close to her and shook his rattle. She screamed, grabbed a stick, and chased Baby Rattlesnake. Baby Rattlesnake was lucky to get away, but he lost his rattle during the chase.

When he got home, his parents were terribly worried. Baby Rattlesnake began to cry. "I disobeyed you and lost my rattle. I'm sorry. I'll never do it again," he said. And he did not.

COMPREHENSION Which words help you understand how Baby Rattlesnake gets into trouble? Do you think Baby Rattlesnake learned his lesson? Why or why not?

32

Days 3 and 4

"Baby Rattlesnake," Vol. 2, pp. 32–33

Assessment

Pretest/Posttest Administration p. 84

Pretest/Posttest Blackline Masters pp. 136–137

Day 1

Introduce Meanings

Assess To assess what word meanings children already know, copy and distribute the **Pretest/Posttest** on pages 136–137. Use page 84 to administer the test.

Explain Write each oral vocabulary word below on the board. Read it aloud. Offer an explanation and a brief example for each word.

Words About Money

fortune *n.* luck *It was just good fortune that we found the money on the sidewalk.*

gain *v.* to get *He will wash his dad's car to gain money for a new video game.*

possessions *n.* things that are owned *The princess felt lucky to have all her possessions.*

reward *v.* to give someone a prize or payment *The king will reward the man who found his lost horse.*

valuable *adj.* having a lot of importance or worth *The queen kept her valuable jewelry locked in a safe.*

wealthy *adj.* rich; having a lot of money or things *The wealthy duke hosted the fancy party.*

Discuss Guide children to see the relationship between each word and the category. Ask: Describe two **possessions** of yours. Then tell about a time you **gained** some money of your own.

Read Aloud Explain that you will read aloud a story about a couple who suddenly become wealthy. Then read aloud "The Fish Prince." Discuss the Comprehension questions.

Day 2

Categorize and Classify

Reread and Explain Reread "The Fish Prince." At the end of each sentence that includes an oral vocabulary word, stop and repeat the explanation of the word. Then reread the sentence.

Use a Graphic Organizer Use the graphic organizer and the questions below to reinforce understanding of the relationship between each word and the category.

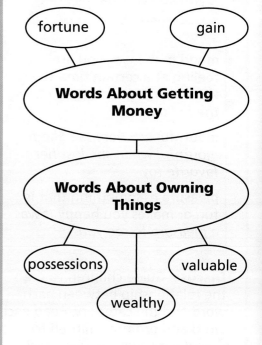

1. Someone who has a lot of money is _____. (**wealthy**)

2. Name some things that your parents might **reward** you for doing. (Sample answer: doing chores, behaving)

Day 3

Introduce Meanings

Explain Write each oral vocabulary word below on the board. Read it aloud. Offer an explanation and a brief example for each word.

Words About Trouble

annoyance *n.* something that bothers you *The flies were an annoyance to people trying to eat at the picnic.*

disobey *v.* to go against the rules *Sometimes she will disobey her parents by not telling them where she is going.*

disturb *v.* to bother *Please don't disturb me when I'm working.*

interfere *v.* get in the way of *My baby sister will interfere if we try to play a game.*

mischievous *adj.* naughty *The mischievous dog grabbed my sandwich off my plate.*

nuisances *n.* pests *Mosquitoes are terrible nuisances in the summer.*

Discuss Guide children to see the relationship between each word and the category. Prompt them to use the words to talk about characters they know.

Read Aloud Explain that you will read aloud a story about a baby snake that gets into lots of trouble. Then read aloud "Baby Rattlesnake." Discuss the Comprehension questions.

Day 4

Categorize and Classify

Reread and Explain Reread "Baby Rattlesnake." At the end of each sentence that includes an oral vocabulary word, stop and repeat the explanation of the word. Then reread the sentence.

Use a Graphic Organizer Use the graphic organizer and the questions below to reinforce understanding of the relationship between each word and the category.

Bothersome Things	Bothersome Actions
annoyance mischievous nuisances	disobey disturb interfere

1. You might get into trouble if you _____. (**disobey**)

2. Would you expect someone who is **mischievous** to be a **nuisance** or a helpful person? (**mischievous**)

3. What are some things that **interfere** with doing schoolwork? (Answers will vary.)

Day 5

Deepen Understanding

Review Repeat explanations for all oral vocabulary words. Use the definitions and examples from Day 1 and Day 3.

Guide Partner Activities Have partners work together to complete each of the activities below. Circulate and listen to partners as they work. Provide corrective feedback.

Describe Talk to a partner. Describe somebody you know who is **mischievous**. Use these words: **annoyance, disobey, disturb, nuisance**.

Draw Make a picture of your favorite **possession**. Then imagine it was lost. Tell a partner how you would **reward** the person who found it.

Compare Talk to your partner. Compare something that is **valuable** to something that is not valuable.

Role-Play With a partner, imagine that you have good **fortune**. Something happens that makes you very **wealthy**. Pretend that someone is trying to **gain** your money. Act out how that person tries to **interfere** with your happiness.

Assess To assess what word meanings children have learned, copy and distribute the **Pretest/Posttest** on pages 136–137. Use page 84 to administer the test. Compare scores with Day 1 assessment.

Days 1 and 2

"The Return of the Wolf," Vol. 2, pp. 34–35

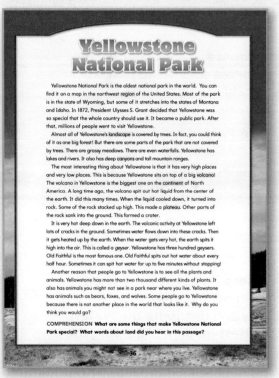

Days 3 and 4

"Yellowstone National Park," Vol. 2, pp. 36–37

Assessment

Pretest/Posttest Administration p. 85
Pretest/Posttest Blackline Masters pp. 138–139

Day 1

Introduce Meanings

Assess To assess what word meanings children already know, copy and distribute the **Pretest/Posttest** on pages 138–139. Use page 85 to administer the test.

Explain Write each word below on the board. Read it aloud. Then introduce the category. Explain that when animals are endangered, they are in danger of dying out completely. Offer an explanation and a brief example for each word.

Words About Endangered Animals

biological *adj.* having to do with living things *A biological book might have information about both plants and animals.*

rare *adj.* not seen often; unusual *It is rare to see raccoons awake during the daytime.*

scientific *adj.* related to science; tested *The scientific research shows that dolphins are mammals.*

species *n.* a kind of animal *Housecats are part of a different species than tigers.*

survival *n.* staying alive *Plants need water for their survival.*

vanished *v.* disappeared *The tiny mouse vanished as soon as the hungry cat looked away.*

Discuss Guide children to see the relationship between each word and the category. Discuss with them some things that animals do for **survival**.

Read Aloud Explain that you will read aloud a story about an endangered species. Then read aloud "The Return of the Wolf." Discuss the Comprehension questions.

Day 2

Categorize and Classify

Reread and Explain Reread "The Return of the Wolf." At the end of each sentence that includes an oral vocabulary word, stop and repeat the explanation of the word. Then reread the sentence.

Use a Graphic Organizer Use the graphic organizer and the questions below to reinforce understanding of the relationship between each word and the category.

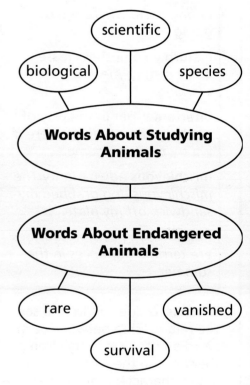

1. When scientists do careful research, what kind of study is it called? (**scientific**)

2. Name an animal that is **rare** in your neighborhood. (Answers will vary.)

3. What are some things animals need for **survival**? (Sample answer: food, sleep)

Day 3

Introduce Meanings

Explain Write each word below on the board. Read it aloud. Offer an explanation and a brief example for each word.

Words About Land

canyon *n.* a very deep, wide split in the ground *A river runs through the bottom of the canyon.*

continent *n.* one of seven large land areas in the world *The United States is on the continent of North America.*

landscape *n.* the way the land looks *The desert landscape is wide, long, and sandy colored.*

plateau *n.* a hill with a flat top; a tableland *We could see sheep grazing on the plateau.*

region *n.* an area of a country *Indiana is in the Midwest region of the United States.*

volcano *n.* a mountain that lets out heat from the center of the earth *The volcano spit lava when it erupted.*

Discuss Guide children to see the relationship between each word and the category. Discuss with them the size and shape of each landform on the list.

Read Aloud Explain that you will read aloud a story about the land in Yellowstone National Park. Then read aloud "Yellowstone National Park." Discuss the Comprehension questions.

Day 4

Categorize and Classify

Reread and Explain Reread "Yellowstone National Park." At the end of each sentence that includes an oral vocabulary word, stop and repeat the explanation of the word. Then reread the sentence.

Use a Graphic Organizer Use the graphic organizer and the questions below to reinforce understanding of the relationship between each word and the category.

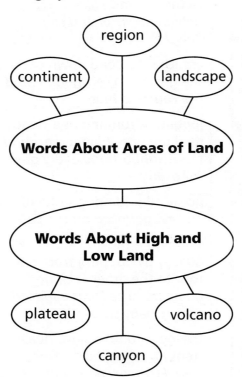

1. Which is bigger, a **region** or a **continent**? (a continent)

2. Describe a **landscape** that you think is beautiful. (Answers will vary.)

Day 5

Deepen Understanding

Review Repeat explanations for all oral vocabulary words. Use the definitions and examples from Day 1 and Day 3.

Guide Partner Activities Have partners work together to complete each of the activities below. Circulate and listen to partners as they work. Provide corrective feedback.

Role-Play Pretend you are doing **scientific** research on an endangered **species.** Explain your research to your partner. Use these words: **rare, survival, region, vanished.**

Compare Talk to your partner. Compare a **canyon** to a **plateau.** Then compare them each to a **volcano.**

Draw Imagine a **landscape,** such as a beach, a desert, or a forest. Then draw a picture of this landscape. Describe your picture to a partner.

Describe Pretend that you are doing **biological** studies of a **continent.** Describe the animals that live there. What do they look like? How do they act?

Assess To assess what word meanings children have learned, copy and distribute the **Pretest/ Posttest** on pages 138–139. Use page 85 to administer the test. Compare scores with Day 1 assessment.

The Turtle and the Rabbit

A turtle trudged along a trail one day when a rabbit raced up behind him and stopped. The turtle heard the rabbit snort, "How can anyone move so slowly?"

With a leap, the rabbit got in front of the turtle and stood in his way. "I feel sorry for you animals that creep so slowly. Don't you wish you were a fine, fast rabbit like me?"

"No," the turtle said, walking away, but the rabbit pounced in front of him again.

"I can outrun animals that want to eat me," said the rabbit.

The turtle said, "No animals want to eat me. Goodbye."

"Wait!" said the rabbit. "Let's have a race." The turtle thought for a minute.

"Are you slow at everything?" cried the rabbit. "How can you take so long to answer my question?"

"No," the turtle said. "I don't want to race."

"You're afraid!" said the rabbit. "You know I'd win!"

Now the turtle was angry. "If you want to race, we'll race," he said.

So the two animals decided upon a course and a finish line.

Then the rabbit crouched down to get a good start. "Ready? Go!" And with that, the rabbit jumped up and jogged away, moving at a steady pace. The turtle stumbled over a twig on the path.

"This is too easy," the rabbit said to himself. Up ahead, he saw a patch of lettuce and a lawn of soft green grass. "I'll stop there for lunch," he said. "Why hurry?"

After eating for a while, the rabbit looked for the turtle, who was still far behind him. He yawned. "I think I'll take a nap," he decided. So he lay down and fell asleep in the warm sun.

Meanwhile, the turtle kept trudging slowly along the path.

A long time later, the rabbit woke up and looked around. The turtle was nowhere to be seen. The rabbit smiled. "I bet that slowpoke turtle is only halfway around the course. Well, I'll run along now and catch up to him before he reaches the finish line."

The rabbit skipped quickly along the course—but he didn't see the turtle until he came to the finish line. The turtle was already there, waiting for him!

"Hello," the turtle said. "I won the race. Maybe next time you'll remember that even slow animals can win races, if they just keep moving."

COMPREHENSION Why does the rabbit decide that he can have lunch and then take a nap? What words tell you how the animals move?

38

Days 1 and 2

"The Turtle and the Rabbit," Vol. 2, pp. 38–39

The Wild Horses of Assateague Island

Usually when we see horses, they are grazing, or eating grass, in a small, fenced-in field called a pasture. But some horses are wild animals. Assateague Island is one place in America where you can still see wild horses.

Assateague Island is in the Atlantic Ocean, close to the states of Virginia and Maryland. It is currently the home of about three hundred wild horses. This kind of horse has been on the island for about two centuries, or about two hundred years.

No one knows for sure where the horses lived prior to arriving on the island. Some people think that the horses swam to the island from a ship that sank in a storm. Others think that they were owned by people who once lived on the island.

The wild horses are small compared to most horses. This is because they eat grass that isn't very healthy. If they were fed what tame horses eat, they would be taller. If you ever get to see one of these horses up close, you will notice in an instant that it looks a little chubby. This is because the grass that the horses eat is salty. The salty grass makes the horses thirsty. They drink a lot of water, and the extra water makes them look chubby.

People who live on the mainland help the horses. They are careful to control how many horses are on the island. This helps to protect the island. If there were too many horses on Assateague Island, they would eat all the grass. Controlling the number of horses on the island ensures that the horses always have enough to eat. One way of keeping the number of horses below three hundred is an annual event called Pony Penning Day.

Each year, on one day in July, some of the horses are rounded up by men and led to the water. The horses swim to Chincoteague Island, part of the state of Virginia. The swim takes only a few minutes. The youngest horses can easily swim across the channel. Once the horses cross, the town of Chincoteague immediately holds a huge celebration and the horses rest in a fenced pasture. To make the size of the herd even smaller, some of the young horses are sold. This is because they are easier to tame than older horses. But people who want to buy a young wild horse must show that they can give it a good home.

The wild horses of Assateague Island are interesting to see. Maybe someday you will get a chance to see them in person.

COMPREHENSION Which words helped you understand when things in the selection took place? How did the horses change as they adapted to life on Assateague Island?

40

Days 3 and 4

"The Wild Horses of Assateague Island," Vol. 2, pp. 40–41

Assessment

Pretest/Posttest Administration p. 86
Pretest/Posttest Blackline Masters
pp. 140–141

Day 1

Introduce Meanings

Assess To assess what word meanings children already know, copy and distribute the **Pretest/Posttest** on pages 140–141. Use page 86 to administer the test.

Explain Write each oral vocabulary word below on the board. Read it aloud. Offer an explanation and a brief example for each word.

Words About Ways to Move

creep v. to move quietly, close to the ground *I like to creep up behind my sister and say, "Boo!"*

crouch v. to bend down close to the ground *I crouched behind the couch to hide.*

jogging v. running at a steady, medium pace *I jogged around the neighborhood every day for exercise.*

pounced v. jumped suddenly *The cat pounced on the yarn.*

skipping v. moving along quickly by hopping from one foot to the other *I skipped home because I was eager to see my baby sister.*

trudge v. to take slow, heavy steps *I trudged home from school with my poor report card.*

Discuss Guide children to see the relationship between each word and the category. Prompt students to use the words to describe how people move while playing a sport.

Read Aloud Explain that you will read aloud a story about the way a turtle moves compared to a rabbit. Then read aloud "The Turtle and the Rabbit." Discuss the Comprehension questions.

Day 2

Categorize and Classify

Reread and Explain Reread "The Turtle and the Rabbit." At the end of each sentence that includes an oral vocabulary word, stop and repeat the explanation of the word. Then reread the sentence.

Use a Graphic Organizer Use the graphic organizer and the questions below to reinforce understanding of the relationship between each word and the category.

Words About Quick Movements	Words About Slow Movements
jogged pounced skipping	creep crouch trudge

1. How is **jogging** different from **skipping**? (Sample answer: When you **jog,** you do not hop from one foot to the other, as you do when you **skip.**)

2. What words might describe how you would move if you didn't want anyone to see you? (Sample answer: **creep, crouch**)

Day 3

Introduce Meanings

Explain Write each oral vocabulary word below on the board. Read it aloud. Offer an explanation and a brief example for each word.

Words About Time
annual *adj.* happening once a year *Our <u>annual</u> family reunion is in July.* **centuries** *n.* periods of one hundred years *People have lived in this country for many <u>centuries</u>.* **currently** *adv.* happening now *We are <u>currently</u> working on addition in math class.* **immediately** *adv.* now or at once *I need a drink of water <u>immediately</u>.* **instant** *n.* a very brief period of time *A computer can give you information in an <u>instant</u>.* **prior** *adj.* earlier *I have a dentist appointment <u>prior</u> to school.*

Discuss Guide children to see the relationship between each word and the category. Ask students: What do you do **prior** to getting into bed at night? What do you think people have done for **centuries**?

Read Aloud Explain that you will read aloud a story about wild horses and how long they have been on an island. Then read aloud "The Wild Horses of Assateague Island." Discuss the Comprehension questions.

Day 4

Categorize and Classify

Reread and Explain Reread "The Wild Horses of Assateague Island." At the end of each sentence that includes an oral vocabulary word, stop and repeat the explanation of the word. Then reread the sentence.

Use a Graphic Organizer Use the graphic organizer and the questions below to reinforce understanding of the relationship between each word and the category.

Words About Now	currently immediately instant
Words About a Long Time	centuries annual
Words About Before	prior

1. What are some other words for something that happened **prior** to something else? Add these to the graphic organizer as children suggest them. (Sample answers: past; earlier)

2. What word would you use instead of "hundreds of years"? (**centuries**)

3. Name something that is **annual**. (Sample answers: a birthday; a holiday)

Day 5

Deepen Understanding

Review Repeat explanations for all oral vocabulary words. Use the definitions and examples from Day 1 and Day 3.

Guide Partner Activities Have partners work together to complete each of the activities below. Circulate and listen to partners as they work. Provide corrective feedback.

Role-Play Show how you would **creep, crouch, jog, pounce,** and **skip.** Then pretend you are very tired. Show how you would **trudge.**

Compare Talk to your partner. Compare two events that happen on an **annual** basis. Do any of them happen in an **instant**?

Discuss Talk to your partner. Tell about something that happened **centuries** ago. Then tell about something that has to happen **immediately.**

Describe Talk to your partner. Describe what you do **prior** to going to school in the morning.

Word Parts The suffix *-ly* means "at a specific period of time." The word **currently** means "happening now." Work with a partner. List three words about time, such as *week*. Add *-ly* to each one. Talk about what you think each word means. Then try to find each new word in a dictionary.

Assess To assess what word meanings children have learned, copy and distribute the **Pretest/Posttest** on pages 140–141. Use page 86 to administer the test. Compare scores with Day 1 assessment.

Weird Records

Stop and think for a moment. Do you have an **extraordinary** talent? Something that no one else can do? You just might have a special skill that could get you into the book *Guinness World Records*. Many ordinary people are surprised to find they are talented enough to be a record holder. They are also surprised when others hear about their records and start to see them as important **popular figures**.

Some people don't set out to have a world record. For example, Charles Osborne got the hiccups in 1922, and he continued to hiccup for sixty-eight years! He now holds the record for the longest attack of hiccups. Jeanne Louise Calment was born in 1875. She would live for another 122 years and become the oldest person ever.

Other people set out to earn incredible records. Mark Sinclair of Bramley, England, ran marathons on all seven continents. A marathon is a twenty-six-mile race. At twenty-four years of age, he was the youngest person to ever do this. Temba Tsheri climbed to the top of Mount Everest, which is the world's tallest mountain, when he was only sixteen years old. And Michael Perham, at fourteen years of age, became the youngest person to sail a boat alone across the Atlantic Ocean.

Then there are record holders who have **superior** skills in sports. Pele, a Brazilian soccer player, scored 1,280 goals from 1956 to 1977, setting a world record. Free diver Tanya Streeter broke the world record when she dove underwater to a depth of 525 feet.

Some people do **sensational** things as a group. In 2004, a group of 15,851 people in Ontario, Canada, lay down at the same time and made a record number of snow angels. In 1998, 1,508 people gathered in Edinburgh, Scotland, and juggled for at least three minutes, setting the world record for the most people juggling at once. There was even a group of kids in South Africa who watched movies for almost sixty hours straight. That set a record, too.

Do you have any ideas about how you could be in the book *Guinness World Records*? Maybe your class can dream up something **tremendous** to do together.

COMPREHENSION Which words help you understand how amazing the world records are? What world record would you want to hold?

42

Days 1 and 2

"Weird Records," Vol. 2, pp. 42–43

Baby Bunyan

Paul Bunyan was a **gigantic**, heavy baby. It took fifty storks to deliver him to his parents. After the storks arrived at the Bunyan house in the deep woods of Minnesota, they were so tired they had to rest for a month.

"Oh my!" Mr. Bunyan said as he looked at baby Paul, who **towered** over their house. "What are we going to do?"

"We need to get to work," said Mrs. Bunyan, smiling.

Mr. Bunyan was a lumberjack. He cut down a whole forest of trees to make a crib for Paul to sleep in. When he finished, the crib was as big as twenty train cars. It took the strength of forty horses to pull the **immense** baby into his bed.

Mrs. Bunyan knit the wool from a hundred lambs into a blanket. And later, the fire department came with a tanker full of warm milk for Paul. After dinner, Paul yawned so enormously that he caused a tornado down in Kansas. Then he fell asleep.

"Well, that's that," said Mr. Bunyan to Mrs. Bunyan. "Let's go to bed."

Soon the whole Bunyan family was sleeping—but not for long. Late that night, there was a **mighty** cry. It was baby Paul wailing. People could hear Paul's crying from Maine to Texas.

His mother rushed outside to see if she could soothe him. Paul just kept on crying. His parents didn't know what to do. Finally, his mother had an idea.

"This baby needs to be rocked back and forth," she told Mr. Bunyan.

"You're right!" he shouted. "I know just what to do."

He ran into town to get some help and brought back a hundred people. They tied two hundred ropes to Paul's crib and started dragging it to Lake Superior. It was **extremely** hard to drag the crib. Paul was crying so loudly, they all had to stuff cotton in their ears.

The townsfolk pushed Paul's crib into the water. Mr. Bunyan had built that crib so well that it floated just like a boat. Ships looked like **miniature** toys next to the crib. Waves came in and out, rocking Paul back and forth until he fell asleep. Mr. and Mrs. Bunyan knew they would have their hands full with this baby!

COMPREHENSION In what ways does the new baby change the lives of Mr. and Mrs. Bunyan? Which words help you understand Paul Bunyan's size?

44

Days 3 and 4

"Baby Bunyan," Vol. 2, pp. 44–45

Assessment

Pretest/Posttest Administration p. 87

Pretest/Posttest Blackline Masters pp. 142–143

Day 1

Introduce Meanings

Assess To assess what word meanings children already know, copy and distribute the **Pretest/ Posttest** on pages 142–143. Use page 87 to administer the test.

Explain Write each oral vocabulary word below on the board. Read it aloud. Offer an explanation and a brief example for each word.

Words That Mean "Great"

extraordinary *adj.* beyond what is normal *Jane is an extraordinary piano player.*

incredible *adj.* so amazing it's hard to believe *That talking parrot is incredible!*

popular figure *n.* someone whom others consider to be great *Our mayor is a popular figure.*

sensational *adj.* exciting *Kim's song was sensational.*

superior *adj.* better than average *This bread is superior to all the others.*

tremendous *adj.* very impressive *The soccer goalie made some tremendous catches.*

Discuss Guide children to see the relationship between each word and the category. Ask questions such as these: What is the opposite of a **popular figure**? What are some examples of a **sensational** meal?

Read Aloud Explain that you will read aloud a story about unusual people and words that mean "great." Then read aloud "Weird Records." Discuss the Comprehension questions.

Day 2

Categorize and Classify

Reread and Explain Reread "Weird Records." At the end of each sentence that includes an oral vocabulary word, stop and repeat the explanation of the word. Then reread the sentence.

Use a Graphic Organizer Use the graphic organizer and the questions below to reinforce understanding of the relationship between each word and the category.

Words That Could Describe Your Favorite TV Show
- incredible
- superior
- extraordinary
- tremendous
- sensational

1. An actor on a hit television show is most likely a _____. **(popular figure)**

2. Can you describe an **extraordinary** event that happened on your favorite show? (Answers will vary.)

Day 3

Introduce Meanings

Explain Write each oral vocabulary word below on the board. Read it aloud. Offer an explanation and a brief example for each word.

Words About Size and Strength

extremely *adv.* very *We had to work extremely hard to finish the project on time.*

gigantic *adj.* huge *The building is so gigantic it can hold twelve large airplanes.*

immense *adj.* bigger than the usual size *The immense car was too big to fit into most garages.*

mighty *adj.* strong and powerful *The mighty African elephant can knock trees down by leaning on them.*

miniature *adj.* tiny *Some people buy miniature houses and collect small pieces of furniture to put inside them.*

towered *v.* so tall it stood high above others *The huge building towered over others in the area.*

Discuss Guide children to see the relationship between each word and the category. Ask questions such as these: What are some examples of things you **tower** over? What are some examples of things that are **gigantic**?

Read Aloud Explain that you will read aloud a story about Paul Bunyan and how words about size and strength are helpful in describing him. Then read aloud "Baby Bunyan." Discuss the Comprehension questions.

Day 4

Categorize and Classify

Reread and Explain Reread "Baby Bunyan." At the end of each sentence that includes an oral vocabulary word, stop and repeat the explanation of the word. Then reread the sentence.

Use a Graphic Organizer Use the graphic organizer and the questions below to reinforce understanding of the relationship between each word and the category.

Words About Size	Words About Strength
gigantic immense miniature towered	extremely mighty

1. What word might you use to describe something that is very small? **(miniature)**

2. Paul Bunyan was amazingly strong and _____. **(mighty)**

3. What word might you use to describe the size of an elephant? **(Sample answers: gigantic; immense)**

Day 5

Deepen Understanding

Review Repeat explanations for all oral vocabulary words. Use the definitions and examples from Day 1 and Day 3.

Guide Partner Activities Have partners work together to complete each of the activities below. Circulate and listen to partners as they work. Provide corrective feedback.

Categorize Work with a partner to list three **mighty** characters that you have read about. What does being **extremely** strong allow them to do? In what ways are they **superior** to other characters?

Draw Draw a picture of an **immense** thing that **towers** over other things. Make sure your drawing shows both **gigantic** and **miniature** things.

Write Write about an **extraordinary** experience you've had. Be sure to include the words **incredible** and **sensational**.

Describe With your partner, talk or write about what it would be like to be the strongest second grader in the world. Explain what you would do with your **tremendous** strength. Would others see you as a **popular figure**?

Assess To assess what word meanings children have learned, copy and distribute the **Pretest/Posttest** on pages 142–143. Use page 87 to administer the test. Compare scores with Day 1 assessment.

The La Brea Tar Pits

The La Brea Tar Pits in Los Angeles, California, are a window into ancient history. This site holds the remains of animals that died in these pits many thousands of years ago. The remains of many kinds of prehistoric animals have been found in the tar pits. Like dinosaurs, many of these animals do not live today. Scientists have found huge elephant-like mammoths. They have found fierce saber-toothed cats. They have even found dire wolves—animals that look like giant versions of the wolves you see today.

The tar pits are pools of black, sticky oil. They formed when tar from under the ground started to rise to the surface of the earth. It bubbled up to the surface and formed the tar pits. Tar has been bubbling to the surface at La Brea for forty thousand years!

So how did ancient animals die in these pits? Leaves, dust, and water often covered the tar pits. Sometimes an animal would go near the pits. The animal would not see the tar because it was covered. The animal would then walk into a tar pit and get stuck. For example, a mammoth would get its feet stuck in the tar and try to get free. The more it struggled, the deeper it would sink. Other animals might see the mammoth. They might think the mammoth looked like a tasty dinner. They would leap on it and get stuck, too. Eventually, the animals would sink all the way into the tar. Over the years, all but the animals' skeletons disappeared. Then the tar hardened around the bones, creating fossils. Much later, people found the fossils in the tar.

Scientists have also found fossils of plants in the tar pits. They have found hundreds of kinds of plants and animals. All together, they have found millions of fossils. Some of these fossils are big animals, such as mammoths. Others are too small to see with your eyes. All of them can help people learn about the past. So if you are ever in Los Angeles, stop by the La Brea Tar Pits for a look into ancient history!

COMPREHENSION Retell how ancient animals got stuck in the tar pits. Which words help you understand what people have found in the tar pits?

46

Days 1 and 2

"The La Brea Tar Pits," Vol. 2, pp. 46–47

A Real Pigsty

Mark's room was very messy. It was scary, even. Huge piles of dirty clothes and yucky old apples littered his room. He even left rubbish, like candy bar wrappers and smelly cheese sandwiches, right on the floor.

One day his mother opened the door and peered inside. "I can't stand it anymore!" she cried angrily. "This room is a pigsty. I want you to clean it right now!"

"Yeah sure, Mom. Later," answered Mark.

Mark lay on his bed thinking about cleaning his room. He yawned. He stretched. Soon, he was fast asleep. Then he had a very strange dream.

In his dream, Mark's mother opened the door again. "Here, piggy. Come get your dinner," she said. Then she walked into his room carrying a bucket. The bucket was full of nasty table scraps.

"Where's your trough?" she asked. "All pigs have a trough. Oh, there it is." Right beside his bed was a large wooden box. She poured the nasty table scraps into the box.

Mark tried to talk, but the only sound he could make was a loud "Oink!" He quickly looked down at his feet. What was this? His feet had been replaced by hard, sharp hooves! He trotted over to the mirror. There, staring back at him, was a big pig. "Oh no!" he tried to say out loud, but the only sound he made was a frightened "Oink!"

Mark's room had not always been messy. His room had looked so nice before he spoiled it with garbage. Mark thought about how his mom told him not to waste things. He thought about how she told him to clean up and recycle. Now it was too late. He began to cry. He longed for a clean, unspoiled room. He wanted another chance.

Then he woke up. He was a little boy once again. "Oh, I didn't like that," he said. "I did not like being a pig. Not at all." Then he began to clean his room. He put the trash in the garbage can. He even made his bed.

Soon his mother came back. "You cleaned your room!" she cried. "Thank you so much."

COMPREHENSION How does turning into a pig change Mark's life? Which words help you understand how messy Mark's room is?

48

Days 3 and 4

"A Real Pigsty," Vol. 2, pp. 48–49

Assessment

Pretest/Posttest Administration p. 88

Pretest/Posttest Blackline Masters pp. 144–145

Day 1

Introduce Meanings

Assess To assess what word meanings children already know, copy and distribute the **Pretest/Posttest** on pages 144–145. Use page 88 to administer the test.

Explain Write each word below on the board. Read it aloud. Offer an explanation and a brief example for each word.

Words About Digging into the Past
ancient adj. very old *The ancient city was built thousands of years ago.*
fossils n. parts of animals and plants from long ago that have hardened in mud or tar. *Scientists found fossils of huge dinosaurs.*
prehistoric adj. from a time before people wrote down their history *Some prehistoric people lived in caves.*
remains n. parts of what were once living things *That museum is filled with the remains of dinosaurs.*
site n. a place where something is or where something happened *There is a park on the site of the battle.*
skeletons n. groups of bones that support animals' bodies *At the museum, we saw skeletons of many animals.*

Discuss Guide children to see the relationship between each word and the category.

Read Aloud Explain that you will read aloud a story about fossils in California. Then read aloud "The La Brea Tar Pits." Discuss the Comprehension questions.

Day 2

Categorize and Classify

Reread and Explain Reread "The La Brea Tar Pits." At the end of each sentence that includes an oral vocabulary word, stop and repeat the explanation of the word. Then reread the sentence.

Use a Graphic Organizer Use the graphic organizer and the questions below to reinforce understanding of the relationship between each word and the category.

Words About Long Ago	Words About Animals from Long Ago
ancient prehistoric	fossils remains skeletons

1. Long ago, there was a village on this _____. **(site)**

2. What word might you use to describe an event that took place before anyone was around to write about it? **(prehistoric)**

3. There are no dinosaurs alive today; all that is left of them are their _____. **(remains)**

Day 3

Introduce Meanings

Explain Write each word below on the board. Read it aloud. Offer an explanation and a brief example for each word.

Words About Trash

litter *v.* to carelessly throw pieces of paper or other garbage around *It makes me angry when people litter in the park.*

recycle *v.* to collect old paper, glass, and plastic so they can be made into other things *We will gather the empty cans and recycle them.*

rubbish *n.* trash; garbage *Please place your rubbish in the trash can.*

spoil *v.* to ruin *Garbage will spoil the beauty of the beach.*

unspoiled *adj.* clean; not messed up *The forest was once unspoiled, but now it is full of trash.*

waste *v.* to use or spend something carelessly *Be careful not to waste water when you brush your teeth.*

Discuss Guide children to see the relationship between each word and the category. Prompt them to use the words to describe how they get rid of things they no longer need.

Read Aloud Explain that you will read aloud a story about a boy who learns a lesson about not letting his room get too messy. Then read aloud "A Real Pigsty." Discuss the Comprehension questions.

Day 4

Categorize and Classify

Reread and Explain Reread "A Real Pigsty." At the end of each sentence that includes an oral vocabulary word, stop and repeat the explanation of the word. Then reread the sentence.

Use a Graphic Organizer Use the graphic organizer and the questions below to reinforce understanding of the relationship between each word and the category.

	Being Careless	Being Careful
litter	yes	no
recycle	no	yes
rubbish	yes	no
spoil	yes	no
un-spoiled	no	yes
waste	yes	no

1. If we take care of natural areas, they can remain _____. **(unspoiled)**

2. What is it called when you donate old items to be made into new items? **(recycling)**

Day 5

Deepen Understanding

Review Repeat explanations for all oral vocabulary words. Use the definitions and examples from Day 1 and Day 3.

Guide Partner Activities Have partners work together to complete each of the activities below. Circulate and listen to partners as they work. Provide corrective feedback.

Categorize Work with a partner to list five things that you might call **rubbish** or that someone might **litter**. Could you **recycle** any of these items?

Examples Create a list of places that are **unspoiled**. What could happen to **spoil** them?

Compare Make a list of activities that **waste** time. Then make a list of activities that make good use of time.

Role Play Pretend you are a scientist. Show your partner how you would dig for **fossils**. Use these words: **ancient, prehistoric, remains, site, skeletons.**

Word Parts The prefix *un-* means "not." The word **spoiled** means "ruined." Together, they make the word **unspoiled,** which means "not spoiled; not ruined." Use a dictionary or a glossary. Work with a partner to find and list three other examples of words with *un-* meaning "not."

Assess To assess what word meanings children have learned, copy and distribute the **Pretest/Posttest** on pages 144–145. Use page 88 to administer the test. Compare scores with Day 1 assessment.

Space Girl

Isabel rode with her parents to the liftoff site in a special bus. The giant rocket up ahead seemed to get bigger and bigger as they drove closer.

"You are going to be famous," her father said, smiling at her.

This would be an exciting day. It was the day of the launch. Not only was Isabel about to become the first kid astronaut, she was also going to be the first kid to walk on the Moon. Her parents were scientists. The whole family was going to live at the new International Moon Base. Today they were flying from Earth to the Moon.

The mission would last for a whole year. Isabel was both excited and sad. She was excited because she would get to fly in a rocket and explore the Moon. She was sad because she knew she would miss her friends at school.

People in white suits helped them into the rocket and strapped them into their seats. Isabel's heart was beating fast as they started the countdown. The astronauts checked and double-checked their instruments. Everything had to be perfect.

When the countdown was over, Isabel felt the rocket begin to shake. The engines roared. Soon they were speeding through the sky and up through the atmosphere.

"Everything is going exactly as planned, Isabel," her dad reassured her. "Are you OK?"

"I'm fine, Dad," Isabel responded.

Soon they were up in space, circling the Earth. Isabel looked down at the blue oceans and white clouds. "I need to write about this in my diary," she thought. Then she looked out a window on the other side of the spaceship. The void of space seemed empty and endless.

Suddenly, her mom's face was upside down in front of her.

"Do you want to unstrap and float around?" her mom asked.

Isabel took off the straps and felt weightless. She drifted around the rocket.

"This is awesome!" she said, beaming at her mom.

"Come over here," her mom said. "I want to show you something."

Isabel floated to the window and looked outside at the Moon. She'd never seen the Moon look so big. It felt as if she could reach out and touch the craters.

"Those craters were made when asteroids hit the Moon long ago," said her mom.

"And in just a few days, you will be playing in the craters!"

Isabel couldn't wait.

COMPREHENSION Do you think Isabel will have fun on the Moon? Why or why not? Which words help you understand space?

50

Days 1 and 2

"Space Girl," Vol. 2, pp. 50–51

Maria Mitchell
A Great Example

Maria Mitchell was a woman who loved to learn. She especially loved science, and it was science that made Mitchell famous.

Mitchell was born in 1818 on an island called Nantucket, which is part of the state of Massachusetts. She was lucky to be born where she was. At that time, girls faced many obstacles. People often treated girls differently than boys. Girls did not always go to school or learn things that boys learned. But on the island where Mitchell was born, girls did go to school and they learned the same things that boys learned. Mitchell's father was the principal of her school. He was also an astronomer. He liked to study planets, stars, and other things in outer space. Mitchell's father taught her to love outer space, too.

When Mitchell was young, she memorized the names of the stars. Mitchell was very smart, and her father encouraged her to work hard. As she grew up, she worked as a schoolteacher and a librarian. But Mitchell's dream was to be an astronomer like her father.

When she was twenty-nine years old, Mitchell's dream came true. She was using a telescope to look far away into space, and she saw something she had never seen before. It looked like a star was moving. She had discovered a comet! Mitchell was only the second woman ever to discover a comet. This made her very famous! They named the comet "Miss Mitchell's Comet" after her. She was also given a gold medal. Mitchell had achieved her goal of becoming a famous astronomer.

But even though she was famous, Mitchell knew that many women still struggled to get the chance to learn. In 1865, she became a professor of astronomy at Vassar College. At Vassar, Mitchell challenged young women to study astronomy. She wished that women could learn just as much about science as men did.

Mitchell worked at Vassar for twenty-three years. During this time, she did a lot to help women. She helped start the American Association for the Advancement of Women. She also studied other parts of outer space. Mitchell died in 1889, but women still worked hard to study and learn just as she did. The Maria Mitchell Observatory was opened in 1908, in her honor.

Maria Mitchell's life is proof that people can work past challenges, as long as they have a dream.

COMPREHENSION Why did Mitchell want to help other women learn? What words about dreams did you hear in this passage?

52

Days 3 and 4

"Maria Mitchell: A Great Example," Vol. 2, pp. 52–53

Assessment

Pretest/Posttest Administration p. 89

Pretest/Posttest Blackline Masters pp. 146–147

Day 1

Introduce Meanings

Assess To assess what word meanings children already know, copy and distribute the **Pretest/Posttest** on pages 146–147. Use page 89 to administer the test.

Explain Write each oral vocabulary word below on the board. Read it aloud. Offer an explanation and a brief example for each word.

Words About Space

asteroid *n.* a rocky object in space that is smaller than a planet *The asteroid just missed hitting Mars.*

craters *n.* large holes in the ground caused by things hitting the ground very hard *The Moon is covered with craters.*

instruments *n.* tools for doing certain jobs *They studied Mars with special instruments.*

launch *n.* the sending of something into the air or into space *The rocket is ready for launch.*

mission *n.* a special task, often involving travel *The astronauts went on a mission to study the Moon.*

weightless *adj.* not pulled to the ground by gravity *She floated weightless in space.*

Discuss Guide children to see the relationship between each word and the category. Ask questions such as these: Have you ever seen the **launch** of a spaceship? How do you think it would feel to be **weightless**?

Read Aloud Explain that you will read aloud a story about a girl who goes to the Moon. Then read aloud "Space Girl." Discuss the Comprehension questions.

Day 2

Categorize and Classify

Reread and Explain Reread "Space Girl." At the end of each sentence that includes an oral vocabulary word, stop and repeat the explanation of the word. Then reread the sentence.

Use a Graphic Organizer Use the graphic organizer and the questions below to reinforce understanding of the relationship between each word and the category.

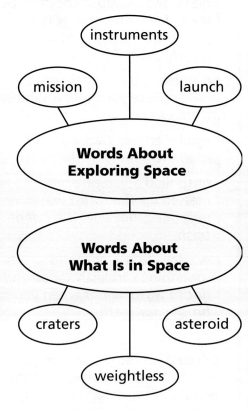

1. If you could go on a mission into space, where would you go? (Answers will vary.)

2. What other words can you use to talk about what is in space? Add these to the graphic organizer as children suggest them. (Sample answers: planets; comets; stars)

Day 3

Introduce Meanings

Explain Write each oral vocabulary word below on the board. Read it aloud. Offer an explanation and a brief example for each word.

Words About Dreams

challenge *v.* to try to get someone to do something new or difficult *I* *challenge* *you to run from here to there without stopping.*

dream *n.* something you want to have happen *Stan's* *dream* *is to become President of the United States.*

encourage *v.* to try to get someone to do something and to support them in doing it *Mary tried to* *encourage* *him to do his best.*

goal *n.* something you want to do *Fran's* *goal* *was to win the race.*

obstacles *n.* things in the way *She needed to get around the* *obstacles* *in the road.*

wish *v.* to want something to be true *I* *wish* *I could play the guitar.*

Discuss Guide children to see the relationship between each word and the category. Prompt them to talk about their hopes and dreams using the words.

Read Aloud Explain that you will read aloud a story about a woman who achieved her dream of becoming a scientist. Then read aloud "Maria Mitchell: A Great Example." Discuss the Comprehension questions.

Day 4

Categorize and Classify

Reread and Explain Reread "Maria Mitchell: A Great Example." At the end of each sentence that includes an oral vocabulary word, stop and repeat the explanation of the word. Then reread the sentence.

Use a Graphic Organizer Use the graphic organizer and the questions below to reinforce understanding of the relationship between each word and the category.

Words About What You Want	Words About What You Do to Get What You Want
dream goal wish	challenge encourage

1. What words refer to trying to get people to do things? **(encourage, challenge)**

2. Have you ever had to find a way around an **obstacle**? (Answers will vary.)

3. What is something you **wish** you had? (Answers will vary.)

Day 5

Deepen Understanding

Review Review word meanings for all oral vocabulary words. Use the definitions and examples from Day 1 and Day 3.

Guide Partner Activities Have partners work together to complete each of the activities below. Circulate and listen to partners as they work. Provide corrective feedback.

Examples Work with a partner. Make a list of three **goals** you have for the future.

Draw Draw a picture of a rocket ship **launch**. Then draw a picture of an astronaut floating **weightless** in outer space. Show an **asteroid** in the distance.

Describe Talk to your partner about a person who **challenges** you to make your **dreams** come true. Use these words: **encourage, obstacles, wish.**

Role-Play Imagine that you are an astronaut. Your **mission** is to study the Moon and its **craters.** Show how you would use your **instruments** to study it.

Word Parts The suffix *-less* means "without." The word **weightless** means "without weight." Work with a partner. Think of three other words that you could be "without," such as *sleep.* Add *-less* to each one. Then use a dictionary or a glossary to check the words you made.

Assess To assess what word meanings children have learned, copy and distribute the **Pretest/Posttest** on pages 146–147. Use page 89 to administer the test. Compare scores with Day 1 assessment.

Stone Soup

Once, in the middle of the coldest winter anyone could remember, an old man walked into a village. The snow was piled along the road like mounds of mashed potatoes. But there was hardly any food to eat. In fact, the old man was reaching the point of **starvation**. Hunger made him feel weak and sad.

He decided to go from house to house to ask for some food.

"Pardon me," he said to the villagers at the first home. "Could you spare a few crumbs of bread for a hungry old man?"

"We don't have any food here," the villagers told him. But from their doorstep, the old man could smell the **aroma** of fresh cabbage.

The old man was turned away from every home he went to. He could smell food from each doorstep. He was hungry, but he was also very wise. So the old man thought of a plan. He walked to the center of town, built a fire, and hung his old iron pot over it. Then he heaped snow into the pot until it melted into water and began to boil. Finally, he placed a stone into the pot.

Just then, a villager walked by. "What are you making?" he asked the old man.

"I am making stone soup," he replied. "Doesn't it smell wonderful?"

The villager thought he truly could smell wonderful soup. "It does smell delicious, but I have something that will make it better," he said.

"Then please bring it here," said the old man.

The villager ran to his house and brought back some sweet red beets. Soon, another villager came along. "That soup smells tasty, but I have something that will make it better," she said.

"Then please bring it here," said the old man, smiling.

The second villager ran to her house and brought back fresh green cabbage. Another villager brought onions. Another brought potatoes. Soon the entire village had added food to the pot of stone soup. Now it truly did smell wonderful.

They all sat together and ate the **nourishing** soup. It was a **feast** for the whole village. Everyone had **plenty**, and there was even soup left over. As they allowed the meal to **digest** and warm their bodies, the villagers thanked the old man for showing them the great thing that can happen when everyone shares what little they have.

COMPREHENSION Which words help you understand what the soup is like? Why do the villagers change their minds about giving away their food?

54

Days 1 and 2

"Stone Soup," Vol. 2, pp. 54–55

LAZY BONES

Many hundreds of years ago, a boy named Taro lived in the country of Japan. Laziness was the **theme** of Taro's life. Taro was so lazy that he thought lifting his head off a pillow was hard work. He would daydream all through the school day, and he never helped his mother with the tea **ceremony**, even when she had guests.

"I think you would sleep for three years if I let you," his mother teased.

Aside from his laziness, Taro was very smart. He did well in all his classes, except math. Taro disliked math because it was a lot of hard work, and he would rather spend time sleeping. One day Taro came home from school with a plan.

A girl named Akiko lived next door to Taro. She had a friendly **spirit** and was kind to everyone. She was also good at math. Taro thought that if he made up a good story, Akiko would agree to do his homework.

Taro waited until it was nighttime and then dressed in a dark robe. He went to Akiko's house and knocked on her window.

"Who's there? Taro, is that you?" asked Akiko, opening the window.

"I am a creature from the forest," Taro answered in his best scary voice. "I have brought you something important."

He handed her a delicate piece of wood that looked very old. The wood had strange **inscriptions** carved into it. They looked like made-up words.

"I can't read the inscriptions," said Akiko, smiling slyly. "I can't understand this writing."

Taro pointed to the shapes. "These shapes are **symbols**. They mean something very important." Then he pointed to the inscription. "It says you must **dedicate** your spare time to doing Taro's math homework."

"Oh, then I suppose I should do it," said Akiko, smiling strangely.

So Akiko did Taro's homework, and Taro went home and slept all night. Akiko handed Taro his homework just before school. He was so happy his idea worked! Finally, it was time for math class. Taro had his homework ready.

"Instead of turning in your homework, I want you all to get ready for a surprise quiz," his teacher announced.

Taro felt a lump in his throat. Akiko smiled.

COMPREHENSION Do you think the surprise quiz will make Taro work harder? Why? Which words help you understand Taro's trick?

56

Days 3 and 4

"Lazy Bones," Vol. 2, pp. 56–57

Assessment

Pretest/Posttest Administration p. 90

Pretest/Posttest Blackline Masters pp. 148–149

Day 1

Introduce Meanings

Assess To assess what word meanings children already know, copy and distribute the **Pretest/ Posttest** on pages 148–149. Use page 90 to administer the test.

Explain Write each oral vocabulary word below on the board. Read it aloud. Offer an explanation and a brief example for each word.

Words About Eating

aroma *n.* a smell, usually good *I love the <u>aroma</u> of ham.*

digested *v.* what our bodies do to the food we eat so that we can have energy *When food is <u>digested</u> by your body, it is broken down into smaller parts that your body can use to keep you healthy.*

feast *n.* a large, fancy meal *Tom made a huge <u>feast</u> for his dad's birthday.*

nourishing *adj.* helping to support life, growth, or strength *Bob began every day with a <u>nourishing</u> breakfast.*

plenty *n.* a large amount *The squirrels hid <u>plenty</u> of nuts to eat during the winter.*

starvation *n.* suffering because of a lack of food *After a week without eating, the lost camper was close to <u>starvation</u>.*

Discuss Guide children to see the relationship between each word and the category of eating.

Read Aloud Explain that you will read aloud a story about an old man who makes other people change their minds. Then read aloud "Stone Soup." Discuss the Comprehension questions.

Day 2

Categorize and Classify

Reread and Explain Reread "Stone Soup." At the end of each sentence that includes an oral vocabulary word, stop and repeat the explanation of the word. Then reread the sentence.

Use a Graphic Organizer Use the graphic organizer and the questions below to reinforce understanding of the relationship between each word and the category.

Words for Describing Food	Words About Amounts of Food
aroma nourishing	feast plenty starvation

1. What word might you use to describe what happens to food after it is eaten? **(digested)**

2. Before we entered the kitchen, we could tell that good food was cooking from the _____. **(aroma)**

3. Healthful food is _____. **(nourishing)**

Day 3

Introduce Meanings

Explain Write each oral vocabulary word below on the board. Read it aloud. Offer an explanation and a brief example for each word.

Words About Something Very Special

ceremony *n.* a serious event for a special purpose, often acted out in front of many people. *A wedding is one kind of ceremony.*

dedicate *v.* to set apart for a special purpose *Henry chose to dedicate one hour of every day to practicing the piano.*

inscriptions *n.* special written or carved messages *The builders put inscriptions on the library walls with sayings from famous books.*

spirit *n.* what someone is like; their personality *Amanda had a playful spirit and was always joking around at recess.*

symbols *n.* shapes or marks that stand for something *The stars on our flag are symbols; each star stands for one state.*

theme *n.* the idea behind something *The theme of the principal's speech was that all students should do their homework.*

Discuss Guide children to see the relationship between each word and the category.

Read Aloud Explain that you will read aloud a story about a boy who tries to trick someone into doing his homework. Then read aloud "Lazy Bones." Discuss the Comprehension questions.

Day 4

Categorize and Classify

Reread and Explain Reread "Lazy Bones." At the end of each sentence that includes an oral vocabulary word, stop and repeat the explanation of the word. Then reread the sentence.

Use a Graphic Organizer Use the graphic organizer and the questions below to reinforce understanding of the relationship between each word and the category.

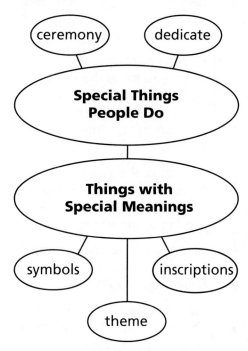

1. Name an example of a **ceremony.** (Sample answers: a wedding; a funeral; a graduation)

2. A person who is always laughing has a fun _____. (**spirit**)

Day 5

Deepen Understanding

Review Repeat explanations for all oral vocabulary words. Use the definitions and examples from Day 1 and Day 3.

Guide Partner Activities Have partners work together to complete each of the activities below. Circulate and listen to partners as they work. Provide corrective feedback.

Examples Work with a partner. List three **ceremonies** that you have been to or have read about. What special purpose did they each have?

Categorize Work with a partner. List three things you would like to **dedicate** some time to. Would they include a hobby? A sport? Would you like to help other people?

Draw Make a message or a sign for your partner by drawing some shapes or pictures that stand for words. Then describe the **symbols.** What is the **theme** of your message?

Write Write an **inscription** that you would like the builders to put on some public building, such as a school or a library. What kind of **spirit** will you have when you write your inscription?

Describe Work with a partner. Write a description of a **feast** you would like to prepare. Use these words: **aroma, digest, nourishing, plenty, starvation.**

Assess To assess what word meanings children have learned, copy and distribute the **Pretest/Posttest** on pages 148–149. Use page 90 to administer the test. Compare scores with Day 1 assessment.

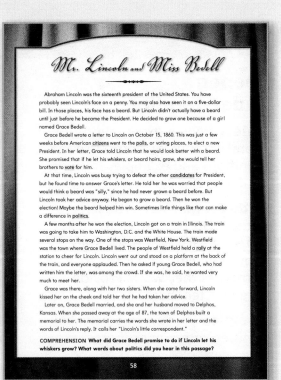

Days 1 and 2

"Mr. Lincoln and Miss Bedell," Vol. 2, pp. 58–59

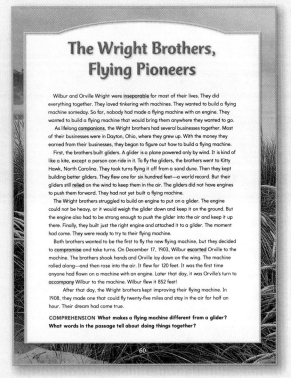

Days 3 and 4

"The Wright Brothers, Flying Pioneers," Vol. 2, pp. 60–61

Assessment

Pretest/Posttest Administration p. 91
Pretest/Posttest Blackline Masters
pp. 150–151

Day 1

Introduce Meanings

Assess To assess what word meanings children already know, copy and distribute the **Pretest/Posttest** on pages 150–151. Use page 91 to administer the test.

Explain Write each oral vocabulary word below on the board. Read it aloud. Offer an explanation and a brief example for each word.

Words About Politics

candidates *n.* people others vote for *Two candidates wish to become the mayor.*

citizens *n.* people who live in a place and have the right to vote when they grow up *Citizens of the United States can vote when they are 18 years old.*

politics *n.* the work of running a government *Joan liked politics and wanted to get a job in the government.*

poll *n.* a place where people go to vote *We went to the polls to choose a new President.*

rally *n.* a gathering of people to show support *We went to a rally to support a new law.*

vote *v.* to make a choice in an election *Every four years, we vote to choose a President.*

Discuss Guide children to see the relationship between each word and the category.

Read Aloud Explain that you will read aloud a story about how a girl may have helped Abraham Lincoln become President. Then read aloud "Mr. Lincoln and Miss Bedell." Discuss the Comprehension questions.

Day 2

Categorize and Classify

Reread and Explain Reread "Mr. Lincoln and Miss Bedell." At the end of each sentence that includes an oral vocabulary word, stop and repeat the explanation of the word. Then reread the sentence.

Use a Graphic Organizer Use the graphic organizer and the questions below to reinforce understanding of the relationship between each word and the category.

Words About What Happens in Politics	Words About People in Politics
poll rally vote	candidates citizens

1. The right to **vote** is enjoyed by all _____. **(citizens)**

2. When people go to vote, they usually do it at a _____. **(poll)**

3. Hundreds of people showed their support for the **candidate** by holding a huge _____. **(rally)**

Day 3

Introduce Meanings

Explain Write each oral vocabulary word below on the board. Read it aloud. Offer an explanation and a brief example for each word.

Words About Friendship

accompany *v.* to go along with *George will accompany me to the doctor's office.*

companion *n.* a person who often goes with someone else *When Ken took hikes in the park, Will was his usual companion.*

compromise *v.* to make an agreement in which each side gives up something *Ted and Ann agreed to compromise on the movie they would see.*

escorted *v.* went along with someone to guide or protect *A nurse escorted Norma to the waiting room.*

inseparable *adj.* unable to be apart *Mandy and Lucy are best friends and have been inseparable since they were five years old.*

relied *v.* needed the help or support of *The people who lived near the river relied on it for their drinking water.*

Discuss Guide children to see the relationship between each word and the category. Prompt children to tell how each word tells about friendship.

Read Aloud Explain that you will read aloud a story about the Wright brothers. Then read aloud "The Wright Brothers, Flying Pioneers." Discuss the Comprehension questions.

Day 4

Categorize and Classify

Reread and Explain Reread "The Wright Brothers, Flying Pioneers." At the end of each sentence that includes an oral vocabulary word, stop and repeat the explanation of the word. Then reread the sentence.

Use a Graphic Organizer Use the graphic organizer and the questions below to reinforce understanding of the relationship between each word and the category.

Words to Describe Friends	Words About What Friends Do
companion inseparable	accompany compromise escorted relied

1. Suppose you want to play tag and your friend wants to play catch. What are some ways you each can **compromise**? (Answers will vary.)

2. What word might you use to talk about going along with someone? **(accompany; escorted)**

Day 5

Deepen Understanding

Review Repeat explanations for all oral vocabulary words. Use the definitions and examples from Day 1 and Day 3.

Guide Partner Activities Have partners work together to complete each of the activities below. Circulate and listen to partners as they work. Provide corrective feedback.

Examples Work with a partner. Make a list of people you have **relied** on. Explain why you relied on them.

Describe Work with a partner. Write a description of an election. Use these words: **candidates, citizens, politics, poll, rally, vote.**

Draw Draw a picture of a family member or a friend. Is this person your **companion?** Are the two of you **inseparable?**

Write Have you ever agreed to **compromise** to end an argument? Write a description about what you gave up and what you got.

Role-Play Show how you might **accompany** a visitor around your school. Have you or your partner ever **escorted** someone?

Assess To assess what word meanings children have learned, copy and distribute the **Pretest/ Posttest** on pages 150–151. Use page 91 to administer the test. Compare scores with Day 1 assessment.

Unit 1, Lesson 1

Copy and distribute **Pretest/Posttest** pages 92–93. Also see directions, page 1.

Day 1–Day 2: Words About Solving Mysteries

1. **clues** *We used **clues** to find the bike.* What are **clues**?
   - ○ parts
   - ○ places
   - ● hints

2. **detective** *The **detective** learned who had taken the dog.* What is the job of a **detective**?
   - ○ to help dogs
   - ● to figure things out
   - ○ to drive a truck

3. **mysterious** *A **mysterious** picture was drawn on the wall.* When something is **mysterious,** it is
   - ○ easy to find
   - ● hard to explain
   - ○ simple to erase

4. **prove** *Joseph wants to **prove** that he can study hard.* When a person wants to **prove** something, he or she will
   - ● show it is true
   - ○ follow instructions
   - ○ make something up

5. **puzzling** *The noise in the basement is **puzzling** to the family.* If something is **puzzling** to people, they are feeling
   - ○ tired
   - ○ excited
   - ● confused

6. **suspicious** *The police officer was **suspicious** of the boy.* If the police are **suspicious** of someone, they think that person
   - ● did something wrong
   - ○ is hurt
   - ○ looks lost

Day 3–Day 4: Words About Traveling

7. **arrival** *We saw the mayor after his **arrival** at the meeting.* What does the word **arrival** mean?
   - ○ leaving a place
   - ● getting to a place
   - ○ finding a seat in a place

8. **route** *I know the **route** we will take for our trip.* What is a **route**?
   - ● a way from one place to another
   - ○ a bunch of stuff you bring to a place
   - ○ a person who knows a place

9. **send** *We will **send** flowers to my mother on her birthday.* When people **send** something, they
   - ○ keep it in one place
   - ○ hide it in a place
   - ● make it go to another place

10. **tour** *Our class went on a **tour** of the museum.* When you go on a **tour** of a museum, you will probably see
    - ● most of it
    - ○ one part of it
    - ○ only pictures of it

11. **transport** *The company used a truck to **transport** the fruit.* What does the word **transport** mean?
    - ● to carry
    - ○ to sell
    - ○ to pile up

12. **travel** *We have to **travel** to visit my grandparents.* When people **travel,** they
    - ○ stay where they are
    - ○ live at home
    - ● go to another place

62

Unit 1, Lesson 2

Copy and distribute **Pretest/Posttest** pages 94–95. Also see directions, page 1.

Day 1–Day 2: Words About Families

1. **ancestors** *His ancestors came from Africa.* Your **ancestors** are family members who
   - ○ live with you now
   - ● lived before you
   - ○ live far away

2. **bond** *The cousins have a strong bond.* When you have a strong **bond** with someone, you
   - ● like them a lot
   - ○ hardly know them
   - ○ hate them

3. **inheritance** *Blond hair is an inheritance from my mother.* An **inheritance** is something that
   - ○ you wish you had
   - ○ only one person in your family has
   - ● your parents passed on to you

4. **memories** *My grandmother's memories are important to her.* When people have **memories,** they have
   - ○ special gifts from relatives
   - ● thoughts about past times
   - ○ clothing they used to wear

5. **reunion** *We will have a family reunion at our house.* How often might a family **reunion** happen?
   - ○ every night
   - ○ every month
   - ● every few years

6. **unusual** *It was unusual for my cousins to visit.* Something **unusual** happens
   - ● not very often
   - ○ every year
   - ○ all the time

Day 3–Day 4: Words About Being Fair

7. **boycott** *People decided to boycott the company.* When people **boycott** a company, they
   - ○ buy everything from it
   - ● refuse to buy from it
   - ○ write letters about it

8. **cause** *Some people support the cause of recycling.* Which of these is an example of a **cause**?
   - ● feeding people who are hungry
   - ○ doing all your schoolwork
   - ○ buying presents for your family

9. **injustice** *Homework sometimes seems like an injustice.* An **injustice** makes a person feel that he or she is being treated
   - ○ in a special way
   - ○ in just the right way
   - ● in an unfair way

10. **picket** *The workers started to picket their company.* What does the word **picket** mean?
    - ● to speak out about something unfair
    - ○ to work hard to make money
    - ○ to quit a bad job

11. **rights** *Free speech is one of the rights of all Americans.* When people have **rights,** they are
    - ○ kept from doing things
    - ● allowed to do things
    - ○ told how to do things

12. **strike** *The workers want to strike because they think that their workday is too long.* When workers **strike,** they
    - ○ work more
    - ○ work less
    - ● stop working

Unit 1, Lesson 3

Copy and distribute **Pretest/Posttest** pages 96–97. Also see directions, page 1.

Day 1–Day 2: Words About Places to Live

1. **basement** *Dad has a workshop in the **basement** of the house.* To get to a **basement**, people most likely
   - ○ go outside
   - ● go downstairs
   - ○ go upstairs

2. **city center** *Our library is in the **city center**.* A **city center** is the
   - ○ whole of a city
   - ● middle of a city
   - ○ edge of a city

3. **cottage** *They stayed in a **cottage** on the edge of the lake.* What is a **cottage**?
   - ○ a large hotel
   - ○ a kind of boat
   - ● a small, simple house

4. **country** *Kiko had never been to the **country** before.* The **country** is land that is
   - ○ far from your home
   - ○ near the ocean
   - ● outside of the city

5. **farmland** *Farmland needs to have good soil.* **Farmland** most likely has
   - ○ trees or bushes
   - ● fruits or vegetables
   - ○ sand or rocks

6. **mansion** *The family moved into their new **mansion**.* A **mansion** is a
   - ● big house with many rooms
   - ○ farm with many buildings
   - ○ home in a building of many homes

Day 3–Day 4: Words About the Government

7. **capitol** *We got to meet the governor in his office in the **capitol**.* What does the word **capitol** mean?
   - ○ the tallest building in a city
   - ○ the house of a governor
   - ● the main government building

8. **federal** *Making coins is a job of the **federal** government.* The **federal** government does things for
   - ● everyone in the country
   - ○ people in only one part of the country
   - ○ people only in your city

9. **landmark** *You can see more than one **landmark** in Washington, D.C.* Which of these might be a **landmark**?
   - ● a building
   - ○ a car or truck
   - ○ a picture

10. **legislate** *The lawmakers will **legislate** to build schools.* When lawmakers **legislate**, they
    - ○ work very hard
    - ○ ask for help
    - ● make laws

11. **memorial** *The mayor built a **memorial** in the center of town.* A **memorial** can help people
    - ● remember someone
    - ○ play and have fun
    - ○ work to make money

12. **official** *We received an **official** letter in the mail.* Who sends an **official** letter?
    - ○ parents or grandparents
    - ● the people in charge of something
    - ○ your friends from school

Unit 1, Lesson 4

Copy and distribute **Pretest/Posttest** pages 98–99. Also see directions, page 1.

Day 1–Day 2: Words About Being Smart

1. **clever** *Filling an ice cube tray with fruit juice is a **clever** way to make frozen treats.* Something that is **clever** is
   - ○ slow
   - ● smart
   - ○ old-fashioned

2. **deceive** *The wolf tried to **deceive** Little Red Riding Hood.* What does the word **deceive** mean?
   - ● trick
   - ○ meet
   - ○ change

3. **devise** *Kristen will **devise** a way to win the contest.* When people **devise** something, they
   - ● think of a plan
   - ○ copy another idea
   - ○ read something in a book

4. **intelligence** *The boy's **intelligence** helped him win the prize.* If someone has **intelligence,** he or she is a
   - ○ friendly person
   - ● good thinker
   - ○ fast runner

5. **scheme** *The girl had a **scheme** for getting enough money to buy a new toy.* A **scheme** is a
   - ○ special tool
   - ○ team of people
   - ● plan

6. **trickster** *We never knew what that **trickster** would do next.* A **trickster** is someone who
   - ○ loves to help out
   - ○ moves around a lot
   - ● tries to fool people

Day 3–Day 4: Words About Digging

7. **buried** *My friend **buried** a box.* If someone **buried** something, what was the first thing he or she did?
   - ○ tied a rope
   - ○ drew a picture
   - ● dug a hole

8. **chamber** *The ants dug out a large **chamber** for the queen.* What does the word **chamber** mean?
   - ● a room
   - ○ a building
   - ○ a bed

9. **trench** *He found his missing glove in a **trench** by the side of the road.* A **trench** is a
   - ○ deep hole
   - ● long, narrow ditch
   - ○ pile of dirt

10. **tunnel** *The workers will **tunnel** to the other side of the mountain.* When workers **tunnel,** they
    - ○ build a bridge
    - ○ climb a ladder
    - ● dig under the ground

11. **uncovering** *After **uncovering** the rock, Dad pulled it out of the hole.* If a person is **uncovering** something, he or she is
    - ○ finding out how heavy it is
    - ○ moving it back and forth
    - ● taking something off the top of it

12. **underground** *We eat the **underground** part of a carrot plant.* If you pick the **underground** part of a carrot plant, your hands will probably get
    - ○ dry
    - ● dirty
    - ○ hurt

Unit 1, Lesson 5

Copy and distribute **Pretest/Posttest** pages 100–101. Also see directions, page 1.

Day 1–Day 2: Words About Good Manners

1. **apologize** *She decided to* **apologize** *to her friend.* When people **apologize,** they
   - ● say they are sorry
   - ○ act in a mean way
   - ○ tell a big secret

2. **civil** *The boys were* **civil** *when they were at the restaurant.* What does the word **civil** mean?
   - ○ hungry
   - ○ rude
   - ● polite

3. **introduce** *The teacher will* **introduce** *the new student to the class.* When you **introduce** someone, you
   - ○ show them where to go
   - ● say who they are
   - ○ teach them something

4. **invite** *We will* **invite** *our friends to the party.* What does the word **invite** mean?
   - ● ask someone to come
   - ○ give someone a ride
   - ○ give orders to someone

5. **note** *The girl sent a* **note** *to her grandmother.* Someone who sent a **note**
   - ○ drew a picture
   - ○ made a phone call
   - ● wrote words

6. **self-control** *Jenny needs to behave with more* **self-control.** When someone has **self-control,** they
   - ● think before they act
   - ○ act proud of themselves
   - ○ do whatever they want

Day 3–Day 4: Words About Scary Things

7. **fierce** *The animals watched out for the* **fierce** *lion.* If an animal is **fierce,** it probably
   - ○ helps other animals
   - ● hurts other animals
   - ○ runs very fast

8. **frightening** *The boy closed his eyes during the* **frightening** *movie.* When someone sees something **frightening,** he or she feels
   - ● scared
   - ○ bored
   - ○ tired

9. **horrifying** *A* **horrifying** *monster chased everyone in the book.* What does the word **horrifying** mean?
   - ○ very strong
   - ● very scary
   - ○ very big

10. **panicking** *The* **panicking** *bird squawked and quickly flew away.* What does the word **panicking** mean?
    - ○ very noisy
    - ○ very brave
    - ● very scared

11. **savage** *He thought the jungle was full of* **savage** *animals.* A **savage** animal might
    - ● try to hurt people
    - ○ be friendly to people
    - ○ hide from people

12. **terror** *The little girl always felt* **terror** *during a thunderstorm.* What does the word **terror** mean?
    - ○ strong excitement
    - ○ strong dislike
    - ● strong fear

Unit 2, Lesson 6

Copy and distribute **Pretest/Posttest** pages 102–103. Also see directions, page 1.

Day 1–Day 2: Words About Birds

1. **gliding** *We saw hawks **gliding** over the field.* What does the word **gliding** mean?
   ○ hunting small animals
   ● flying without moving wings
   ○ sitting on a branch

2. **greeting** *The teacher gave us a friendly **greeting.*** You give someone a **greeting** when you want to
   ● say *hello*
   ○ make them go away
   ○ tell them you are sorry

3. **hatch** *The baby birds will **hatch** any day now.* When animals **hatch,** they
   ○ learn to fly
   ○ eat
   ● come out of eggs

4. **migrate** *Some whales **migrate** each winter.* What does the word **migrate** mean?
   ○ grow larger
   ○ sleep for a long time
   ● travel a long way

5. **molt** *Birds **molt** at different times of the year.* What does the word **molt** mean?
   ● lose feathers
   ○ make nests
   ○ eat leaves

6. **nocturnal** *Most owls are **nocturnal.*** **Nocturnal** animals are
   ○ awake all the time
   ● awake at night
   ○ asleep all night

Day 3–Day 4: Words About Building

7. **brace** *Mom built a **brace** for the shelf.* A **brace** is a
   ○ wall
   ○ handle
   ● support

8. **construct** *I want to **construct** a tree house.* What does the word **construct** mean?
   ● build
   ○ sleep in
   ○ plan

9. **reinforce** *The workers must **reinforce** the roof.* When people **reinforce** something, they
   ○ cover it up
   ● make it stronger
   ○ tear it down

10. **slab** *He used a **slab** of stone to make the porch step.* A **slab** is a
    ○ small, round piece
    ● large, flat piece
    ○ tall, thin piece

11. **splintering** *Lightning struck the tree, **splintering** it.* **Splintering** something means
    ○ burning it up
    ○ cutting it down
    ● breaking it apart

12. **timber** *That barn is made of old **timber.*** What does the word **timber** mean?
    ○ bricks
    ● wood
    ○ metal

Unit 2, Lesson 7

Copy and distribute **Pretest/Posttest** pages 104–105. Also see directions, page 1.

Day 1–Day 2: Words About the Environment

1. **atmosphere** *The atmosphere wraps around Earth.* What is the **atmosphere** made of?
   - ○ land and water
   - ● air and sky
   - ○ rain and snow

2. **electricity** *The electricity went off during the storm.* Which of these is powered by **electricity**?
   - ○ a kite
   - ○ a skateboard
   - ● a television

3. **excess** *An excess of smoke can pollute the air.* What does the word **excess** mean?
   - ● too much of something
   - ○ the right amount of something
   - ○ not enough of something

4. **global** *Hunger is a global problem.* What does the word **global** mean?
   - ○ in your town
   - ○ in our country
   - ● around the world

5. **planet** *There is more water than land on our planet.* Which of these things is a **planet**?
   - ○ the Sun
   - ● Earth
   - ○ the Moon

6. **pollution** *People should try to make less pollution.* Which of these things is more likely to cause **pollution**?
   - ● chemicals
   - ○ mud
   - ○ wood

Day 3–Day 4: Words About Speaking

7. **insisted** *Mrs. Kim insisted that we stay for dinner.* What does the word **insisted** mean?
   - ○ refused angrily
   - ○ apologized sadly
   - ● said firmly

8. **mention** *I did not mention that I lost my sweater.* What does the word **mention** mean?
   - ● say
   - ○ remember
   - ○ care

9. **muttered** *Brett muttered that he wanted to go home.* What does the word **muttered** mean?
   - ○ wrote quickly
   - ○ thought suddenly
   - ● spoke quietly

10. **praise** *Lucy was surprised to hear her aunt's praise.* **Praise** is something you might get if you
    - ○ forgot to do your homework
    - ● did well on a test
    - ○ watched a lot of TV

11. **snapped** *She snapped at me when I asked about the math test.* If someone **snapped** at you, he or she was probably
    - ○ happy
    - ○ curious
    - ● angry

12. **utter** *I heard the twins utter their thanks.* What does the word **utter** mean?
    - ○ listen
    - ● speak
    - ○ laugh

Unit 2, Lesson 8

Copy and distribute **Pretest/Posttest** pages 106–107. Also see directions, page 1.

Day 1–Day 2: Words About Volcanoes

1. **erupt** *No one thought that the volcano would* **erupt.**
What does the word **erupt** mean?
   - ○ sit quietly
   - ● burst violently
   - ○ shake gently

2. **exploding** *We saw the volcano* **exploding** *in the distance.* What does the word **exploding** mean?
   - ● blowing up
   - ○ standing tall
   - ○ leaking slowly

3. **fiery** *The wind blew* **fiery** *ashes from the volcano.* Where else could you see **fiery** ashes?
   - ○ in a cold fireplace
   - ● in a burning campfire
   - ○ in a damp sandbox

4. **lava** *A river of* **lava** *ran down the mountain.* What happens to **lava** when it cools down?
   - ○ It turns into ice.
   - ○ It turns into a volcano.
   - ● It turns into solid rock.

5. **molten** *Volcanoes are filled with* **molten** *rock.* What does the word **molten** mean?
   - ○ hard
   - ● melted
   - ○ old

6. **volcanic** **Volcanic** *ash covered the hillside.* Which is probably true of something **volcanic**?
   - ○ People dug it up from underground.
   - ○ It came out very cold from underground.
   - ● It exploded upward from underground.

Day 3–Day 4: Words About Earthquakes

7. **collapse** *The earthquake made the tall building* **collapse.** What does the word **collapse** mean?
   - ○ catch on fire
   - ○ explode loudly
   - ● fall down suddenly

8. **disaster** *Many kinds of* **disasters** *can happen to a forest.* What best describes what a **disaster** could do to a forest?
   - ○ help it grow
   - ● destroy it
   - ○ bring visitors to it

9. **earthquake** *The books fell off the shelf during the* **earthquake.** An **earthquake** happens when
   - ○ there is a bad storm
   - ○ someone runs indoors
   - ● the ground shakes

10. **impact** *The earthquake made an* **impact** *on the city's buildings.* How many people would notice something that had an **impact** on a city's buildings?
    - ● almost everyone
    - ○ some people
    - ○ only a few people

11. **trembles** *I almost fell because of the* **trembles** *going through the ground.* What do **trembles** feel like?
    - ● shaking
    - ○ heat
    - ○ bumps

12. **wreckage** *The storm left a great deal of* **wreckage.** Which of these things is a kind of **wreckage**?
    - ● broken fences
    - ○ big puddles
    - ○ strong wind

Unit 2, Lesson 9

Copy and distribute **Pretest/Posttest** pages 108–109. Also see directions, page 1.

Day 1–Day 2: Words About Snakes

1. **attack** *I saw a bird attack a snake.* What does the word **attack** mean?
   - ○ get away from
   - ○ hide from
   - ● try to hurt

2. **creatures** *The jungle is filled with all kinds of creatures.* What does the word **creatures** mean?
   - ○ green plants
   - ● living things
   - ○ rivers and streams

3. **poison** *Some animals hunt by using poison.* **Poison** is often
   - ● wet
   - ○ sharp
   - ○ hard

4. **rodent** *We saw a rodent behind the house.* A **rodent** is an animal with
   - ○ wings
   - ○ four hooves
   - ● large front teeth

5. **slimy** *Snakes are not actually slimy.* Which of these animals might feel **slimy**?
   - ● a fish
   - ○ a bird
   - ○ a dog

6. **slither** *The snake turned and slithered away.* When snakes **slither**, they
   - ○ dive and swim
   - ○ run and jump
   - ● wiggle and slide

Day 3–Day 4: Words About Water

7. **dripping** *Water was dripping from the hose.* What does the word **dripping** mean?
   - ● coming down in drops
   - ○ pouring out
   - ○ spraying around

8. **liquid** *I want something liquid with dinner.* Which of these things is a **liquid**?
   - ○ bread
   - ● milk
   - ○ meat

9. **moist** *This towel feels moist.* What does the word **moist** mean?
   - ○ soft
   - ○ warm
   - ● damp

10. **monsoon** *Some countries have a monsoon season.* A **monsoon** is a time of heavy
    - ● rain
    - ○ fog
    - ○ snow

11. **rainfall** *He saw that there had been a rainfall last night.* **Rainfall** is water from
    - ○ a hose
    - ● a cloud
    - ○ a stream

12. **soggy** *She came home with soggy socks.* What does the word **soggy** mean?
    - ○ worn out
    - ● soaked
    - ○ dirty

Unit 2, Lesson 10

Copy and distribute **Pretest/Posttest** pages 110–111. Also see directions, page 1.

Day 1–Day 2: Words About Weather Conditions

1. **cooling** *The fan started* **cooling** *the kitchen.* Which of these would you use for **cooling** a drink?
   - ● ice
   - ○ an oven
   - ○ sugar

2. **deserts** *Many* **deserts** *are far from the ocean.* What does the word **deserts** mean?
   - ○ long, muddy rivers
   - ● large, dry, sandy areas
   - ○ tall mountain ranges

3. **drought** *Farmers worry about their crops whenever there is a* **drought.** A **drought** happens when there is
   - ● little or no rain
   - ○ a lot of flooding
   - ○ a group of insects

4. **evaporation** *Evaporation made the puddle disappear.* Which of these things causes **evaporation**?
   - ○ a rainy day
   - ● heat from the sun
   - ○ smoke from a fire

5. **overheated** *Our car's engine got* **overheated** *on our trip.* What does the word **overheated** mean?
   - ○ worn out
   - ○ out of gas
   - ● too hot

6. **shade** *We had our picnic in the* **shade.** You would most likely find **shade**
   - ● under a big, leafy tree
   - ○ on a warm, sunny street
   - ○ at the top of a long, icy hill

Day 3–Day 4: Words About Mountains

7. **avalanches** *Sometimes this mountain has* **avalanches.** What does the word **avalanches** mean?
   - ○ rushing streams or rivers
   - ○ people skiing or hiking
   - ● snow falling down a mountain

8. **cliffs** *The eagles made their nests in the high* **cliffs.** **Cliffs** are found
   - ○ in the tops of large trees
   - ● on the steep sides of mountains
   - ○ inside deep caves

9. **descend** *Hold my hand as you* **descend** *the mountain.* What does the word **descend** mean?
   - ○ move across
   - ○ move up
   - ● move down

10. **elevation** *I learned the* **elevation** *of that hill.* If you learn the **elevation** of a place you know how
    - ● high it is
    - ○ wet it is
    - ○ old it is

11. **slopes** *We saw the* **slopes** *in the distance.* If you can see **slopes,** you are close to
    - ○ beaches
    - ● hills
    - ○ fields

12. **summit** *We reached the* **summit** *before sunset.* What does the word **summit** mean?
    - ○ valley
    - ○ hotel
    - ● top

Unit 3, Lesson 11

Copy and distribute **Pretest/Posttest** pages 112–113. Also see directions, page 1.

Day 1–Day 2: Words About Teamwork

1. **assist** *She tried to assist me when I had a lot of homework.* When someone tries to **assist** you, they try to
   - ● help you
   - ○ punish you
   - ○ slow you down

2. **association** *My dad worked in association with my teacher to build a bird feeder.* If you work in **association** with someone, you work
   - ○ for a long time
   - ● together
   - ○ quickly

3. **collaborate** *We can work faster if we collaborate.* If two people **collaborate,** they
   - ○ stay away from each other
   - ○ fight with each other
   - ● agree with each other

4. **cooperate** *When my sister and I cooperate, we get our jobs done quickly.* What does the word **cooperate** mean?
   - ○ have fun
   - ● to work together
   - ○ to work hard

5. **plan** *You can plan how you will do your homework.* When you **plan** something, you
   - ● decide how you will do it
   - ○ do not worry about how you will do it
   - ○ ask someone how you will do it

6. **task** *There are some tasks that I do not enjoy.* What is a **task**?
   - ○ a meal
   - ○ a game
   - ● a job

Day 3–Day 4: Words About Being Well Known

7. **admiration** *She had a look of admiration when she watched the dancers.* If you look at people with **admiration,** you probably
   - ○ find them boring
   - ● think they are great
   - ○ hate them

8. **expert** *He is an expert at fixing bicycles.* If someone is an **expert,** he or she
   - ○ gets a lot of exercise by doing something
   - ○ is still learning how to do something
   - ● knows a lot about doing something

9. **fame** *He had a lot of fame for being a singer and an actor.* What does the word **fame** mean?
   - ● being well known
   - ○ being wealthy
   - ○ being talented

10. **honor** *I received an honor for my grades.* What does the word **honor** mean?
    - ○ a treat
    - ● an award
    - ○ a punishment

11. **prominent** *She is a prominent writer in our town.* If someone is **prominent,** it means he or she is
    - ● important
    - ○ mean
    - ○ forgotten

12. **respected** *Mark's dad is a respected teacher at the high school.* What does the word **respected** mean?
    - ○ creative
    - ○ not very good
    - ● well-liked

Unit 3, Lesson 12

Copy and distribute **Pretest/Posttest** pages 114–115. Also see directions, page 1.

Day 1–Day 2: Words About Music

1. **auditioning** *My sister is **auditioning** for the school play.* If you are **auditioning** for a play, you
   - ○ are going to watch it
   - ○ are already part of it
   - ● want to be part of it

2. **band** *I enjoy watching the **band** perform at football games.* A **band** is a group of people playing different
   - ○ sports
   - ● instruments
   - ○ parts in a play

3. **concert** *We went to the **concert** at school.* What happens at a **concert**?
   - ○ You see a play.
   - ● You hear music.
   - ○ You watch dancing.

4. **debut** *She made her **debut** in front of a huge crowd.* A **debut** is
   - ○ the last time you do something
   - ○ the second time you do something
   - ● the first time you do something

5. **orchestra** *I hope to play the cello in the **orchestra**.* A person who plays in an **orchestra** is playing
   - ● with a group
   - ○ outside
   - ○ alone

6. **vocal** *She has a great deal of **vocal** talent.* If someone has **vocal** talent, they have a nice
   - ● voice
   - ○ personality
   - ○ smile

Day 3–Day 4: Words About Noises

7. **blare** *You will hear city noises **blare** outside your window.* Which of these things would **blare**?
   - ○ a hammer
   - ○ an engine
   - ● a horn

8. **peaceful** *My bedroom is a **peaceful** place to read.* If a place is **peaceful**, it is usually
   - ○ messy
   - ● quiet
   - ○ noisy

9. **racket** *My little brother makes quite a **racket** when he plays.* What does the word **racket** mean?
   - ● a loud noise
   - ○ a quiet sound
   - ○ a big mess

10. **rumble** *We heard the **rumble** of a marching band.* What would make a **rumble**?
   - ○ a whistle
   - ○ a guitar
   - ● a drum

11. **thunderous** *Our class made a **thunderous** noise when we went to recess.* What is a **thunderous** sound?
   - ● a loud, deep sound
   - ○ a high, musical sound
   - ○ a quiet, humming sound

12. **volume** *"Please turn up the **volume**," she said.* What does the word **volume** mean?
   - ○ the picture on a television
   - ● the loudness of sound
   - ○ the button on a radio

Unit 3, Lesson 13

Copy and distribute **Pretest/Posttest** pages 116–117. Also see directions, page 1.

Day 1–Day 2: Words About Artists

1. **artist** *The artist was well known.* What does an **artist** do?
   - ○ reads about art
   - ● makes art
   - ○ buys art

2. **exhibition** *Tanya is having an exhibition.* If a person is having an **exhibition,** he or she is
   - ○ taking pictures
   - ● showing something
   - ○ offering classes

3. **inspired** *She inspired me to write a book.* If someone **inspired** you, he or she
   - ● gave you an idea
   - ○ said you were doing a good job
   - ○ told you to do something

4. **studio** *Her studio had large windows and bright paint.* A **studio** is a place where
   - ○ children play
   - ○ people sell things
   - ● artists work

5. **talent** *She has a lot of talent as a dancer.* If someone has a lot of **talent,** they are very
   - ○ unhappy about doing something
   - ● good at doing something
   - ○ tired after doing something

6. **techniques** *Many people admire his painting techniques.* The word **techniques** tells
   - ○ why you do something
   - ○ where you do something
   - ● how you do something

Day 3–Day 4: Words About Acting

7. **autograph** *The movie star gave his autograph to a fan.* If someone gives you an **autograph,** they
   - ● write their name
   - ○ draw a picture
   - ○ shake your hand

8. **bravo** *We shouted "Bravo!" at the end of the play.* What does the word **bravo** mean?
   - ○ thank you
   - ○ it's over
   - ● well done

9. **dialogue** *The dialogue in the movie was realistic.* **Dialogue** is
   - ○ what actors do
   - ○ what actors look like
   - ● what actors say

10. **dramatic** *The end of the movie was very dramatic.* What does the word **dramatic** mean?
    - ● exciting
    - ○ boring
    - ○ musical

11. **performs** *He performs every afternoon.* If someone **performs,** they are probably
    - ○ reading silently
    - ● acting on stage
    - ○ playing board games

12. **scene** *The characters became friends in the last scene.* What does the word **scene** mean?
    - ○ a television show
    - ○ a movie
    - ● a part of a play

Unit 3, Lesson 14

Copy and distribute **Pretest/Posttest** pages 118–119. Also see directions, page 1.

Day 1–Day 2: Words About Competing

1. **contest** *We are having a **contest** at school. A **contest** is most like a*
   - ○ test
   - ● game
   - ○ sale

2. **defeated** *We **defeated** the other team in the last few minutes.* If a team is **defeated,** they have
   - ● lost the game
   - ○ won the game
   - ○ tied the game

3. **opposing** *My best friend is on the **opposing** team.* If someone is on an **opposing** team, they are on
   - ○ the best team
   - ● another team
   - ○ your team

4. **overcome** *I will **overcome** my fear of speaking in front of a large group.* If you **overcome** a fear, you
   - ○ let it keep you from doing something
   - ● control it and do something anyway
   - ○ feel embarrassed by it

5. **succeed** *If you want to **succeed**, you must work hard.* What does the word **succeed** mean?
   - ○ practice a lot
   - ○ take a test
   - ● reach a goal

6. **triumph** *It was a **triumph** when she crossed the finish line.* If you have a **triumph,** you have probably
   - ○ lost something easy
   - ○ forgot to do something important
   - ● won something hard

Day 3–Day 4: Words About Love

7. **affection** *My cat shows **affection** by licking me.* If a cat shows you **affection,** it probably
   - ● likes you
   - ○ misses you
   - ○ likes someone else

8. **appreciate** *He will **appreciate** all of their work.* If you **appreciate** someone, you want to say
   - ○ sorry to them
   - ● thank you to them
   - ○ goodbye to them

9. **beloved** *My **beloved** pet is a puppy.* If a pet is **beloved,** it means that it is
   - ○ fun to play with
   - ○ brand new
   - ● cared for very much

10. **devote** *I need to **devote** more time to my homework.* What does the word **devote** mean?
    - ○ to refuse
    - ● to give
    - ○ to ask for help

11. **emotional** *The movie made her **emotional**.* If someone feels **emotional,** they
    - ● have strong feelings
    - ○ get a new idea
    - ○ are tired

12. **endeared** *My mom **endeared** herself to all my friends.* If you **endeared** yourself, you made
    - ○ food for someone
    - ○ someone mad at you
    - ● someone love you

Unit 3, Lesson 15

Copy and distribute **Pretest/Posttest** pages 120–121. Also see directions, page 1.

Day 1–Day 2: Words About Crimes and Criminals

1. **burglaries** *The police are investigating several* **burglaries.** **Burglaries** happen when people
   - ○ throw a ball through a window
   - ● break into a house and steal things
   - ○ drive through a red light

2. **illegal** *Driving too fast is* **illegal.** Something **illegal** is
   - ○ easy to do
   - ○ helpful to others
   - ● against the law

3. **inspector** *The* **inspector** *asked if anyone saw what happened.* An **inspector** is
   - ○ a thief
   - ○ a neighbor
   - ● a police officer

4. **interrogate** *The police will* **interrogate** *people who saw the accident.* When people **interrogate** you, they
   - ○ arrest you
   - ● ask you questions
   - ○ take your photograph

5. **intruder** *The* **intruder** *in the kitchen was a mouse.* If an animal is an **intruder,** it is
   - ○ running away from another animal
   - ○ trapped and held in a cage
   - ● somewhere it doesn't belong

6. **suspect** *The* **suspect** *had muddy boots.* If someone is a **suspect,** it means people believe he or she
   - ● did something wrong
   - ○ solves crimes and arrests people
   - ○ likes to go for long walks

Day 3–Day 4: Words About Guilty and Not Guilty

7. **alibi** *What was your* **alibi** *when the lamp broke?* If you tell people your **alibi,** you tell them that you
   - ○ had a good reason for what you did
   - ○ need help learning right from wrong
   - ● were somewhere else at the time

8. **courthouse** *The judge works at the* **courthouse.** A **courthouse** is a place where people
   - ● decide who broke the law
   - ○ write stories about breaking the law
   - ○ try to break the law

9. **evidence** *There is no* **evidence** *to show that I broke the lamp.* If someone has **evidence,** he or she has
   - ○ an excuse
   - ○ a helper
   - ● proof

10. **innocent** *The unopened bottle proved that he was* **innocent.** If someone is **innocent,** it means that he or she
    - ○ did something wrong
    - ● is not guilty
    - ○ is in danger

11. **justice** *Everyone should be treated with* **justice.** If you are treated with **justice,** it means you are treated with
    - ○ hatred
    - ○ kindness
    - ● fairness

12. **witnesses** *Several* **witnesses** *saw her steal a cookie.* **Witnesses** are people who
    - ○ get into trouble
    - ● see something happen
    - ○ wait a long time

Unit 4, Lesson 16

Copy and distribute **Pretest/Posttest** pages 122–123. Also see directions, page 1.

Day 1–Day 2: Words About Buying and Selling

1. **advertise** *We decided to **advertise** the bake sale in the newspaper.* When you **advertise** something, you are
   ○ asking where to buy it
   ● telling people about it
   ○ keeping it a secret

2. **hired** *The doctor **hired** my sister.* When you are **hired**, you start a new
   ○ home
   ○ medicine
   ● job

3. **market** *Many new customers came to the store when it started to **market** its special products.* What does the word **market** mean?
   ○ to buy
   ○ to find
   ● to sell

4. **merchant** *The **merchants** held a special event for kids.* If someone is a **merchant**, he or she might own
   ○ an airplane
   ● a bookstore
   ○ a zoo

5. **product** *The new **product** at the store was very popular.* A **product** is
   ○ something that decorates a store
   ○ someone who works in a store
   ● something that is sold in a store

6. **promote** *The store printed a special poster to **promote** the banana sale.* What does the word **promote** mean?
   ● to tell people about something
   ○ to sell more of something
   ○ to get rid of something

Day 3–Day 4: Words About Winter

7. **blizzard** *The **blizzard** during the night closed roads for miles around.* What does the word **blizzard** mean?
   ○ a mighty wind storm
   ● a powerful snowstorm
   ○ a strong rainstorm

8. **chilly** *After swimming in the ocean, I got **chilly**.* If you are **chilly**, one thing that might make you feel better is
   ○ a fan
   ○ a swimsuit
   ● a coat

9. **freeze** *The cold made the water in the pond **freeze**.* When water **freezes**, it turns to
   ○ wood
   ● ice
   ○ rock

10. **haze** *A morning **haze** covered the fields.* When something is covered by **haze**, it becomes
    ○ easy to smell
    ○ cold and stiff
    ● hard to see

11. **melt** *The ice cream is beginning to **melt**.* What does the word **melt** mean?
    ○ turn to snow
    ● turn to water
    ○ turn to grass

12. **wintry** *I put on my coat because of the **wintry** wind.* If something is **wintry**, it feels
    ● cold
    ○ comfortable
    ○ hard

Unit 4, Lesson 17

Copy and distribute **Pretest/Posttest** pages 124–125. Also see directions, page 1.

Day 1–Day 2: Words About Baseball

1. **baseball** *My family went to a baseball game.* Which of these do you need to play **baseball**?
   - ● a bat and a small ball
   - ○ a basket and a large ball
   - ○ a racket and a small ball

2. **bleachers** *I got a sunburn while sitting on the bleachers.* What does the word **bleachers** mean?
   - ● seats for watching a sport
   - ○ large rocks at a beach
   - ○ benches in a park

3. **compete** *Mai decided to compete in the big game.* When a person **competes,** he or she is trying to
   - ○ watch
   - ○ quit
   - ● win

4. **manager** *My science teacher is also the baseball team's manager.* Another word for **manager** is
   - ○ referee
   - ● coach
   - ○ pitcher

5. **umpire** *The umpire said the player was out.* A good **umpire**
   - ○ helps one team play better
   - ● is always fair
   - ○ throws the ball back to the pitcher

6. **warm-up** *Chuck was late joining the team's warm-up.* What do players do during a **warm-up**?
   - ○ put on extra clothing
   - ○ talk about a game
   - ● exercise carefully

Day 3–Day 4: Words About Soldiers

7. **advanced** *The soldiers advanced quietly.* If soldiers **advanced,** they
   - ● moved forward
   - ○ spoke softly
   - ○ turned around

8. **armed forces** *The armed forces protected the small children.* What are **armed forces**?
   - ○ a large group of helpful people
   - ● a large group of soldiers
   - ○ a large group of politicians

9. **battle** *The battle lasted for days.* What is a **battle**?
   - ○ a trip
   - ○ a meeting
   - ● a fight

10. **conquer** *The army will conquer the city.* If an army does **conquer** a city, then it will
    - ● control the city
    - ○ free the city
    - ○ leave the city

11. **shield** *The soldiers used their shields.* What does a **shield** do?
    - ○ scares someone
    - ○ moves someone
    - ● protects someone

12. **warrior** *A warrior walked down the street.* What has a **warrior** been taught how to do?
    - ○ help sick people
    - ● fight other people
    - ○ arrest bad people

Unit 4, Lesson 18

Copy and distribute **Pretest/Posttest** pages 126–127. Also see directions, page 1.

Day 1–Day 2: Words About Getting Hurt

1. **ambulance** *An **ambulance** arrived at the hospital.* An **ambulance** is a type of
   ○ medicine
   ○ sick person
   ● truck

2. **condition** *The doctor says Rena is in good **condition** and can come home soon.* What does the word **condition** mean?
   ○ the way someone looks
   ● the way someone is
   ○ the way someone speaks

3. **injured** *I visited my **injured** friend.* What does the word **injured** mean?
   ○ healthy
   ● hurt
   ○ lonely

4. **precaution** *Sam's mom always wears an oven mitt as a **precaution** when taking food out of the oven.* A **precaution** will keep you from getting
   ○ cold
   ● hurt
   ○ wet

5. **treatment** *She got **treatment** after she scraped her foot.* Which of the following could be **treatment** for a scrape?
   ● a bandage
   ○ a punishment
   ○ a shoe

6. **wound** *The cat had a **wound** on its nose.* What does the word **wound** mean?
   ○ a whisker
   ● a cut
   ○ a cold

Day 3–Day 4: Words About Feeling Hurt or Sick

7. **ache** *My thumb started to **ache**.* If something starts to **ache**, it
   ○ doesn't hurt very much
   ● hurts for a while
   ○ hurts a lot for a very short time

8. **comfort** *The card gave my aunt **comfort**.* When you give someone **comfort**, that person feels
   ● a little better
   ○ really confused
   ○ even worse

9. **faint** *David felt like he might **faint** from the heat in the room.* What does the word **faint** mean?
   ○ to sweat
   ○ to breathe fast
   ● to pass out

10. **recover** *Darnell was very sick, and then he began to **recover**.* When someone begins to **recover**, he or she
    ○ gets worse
    ● gets better
    ○ stays the same

11. **suffered** *Toby **suffered** all afternoon.* Someone who **suffered** probably felt
    ● weak and unhappy
    ○ hopeful and strong
    ○ funny and friendly

12. **swell** *Maddy's finger began to **swell** after the car door slammed on it.* What does the word **swell** mean?
    ○ to get smaller
    ● to puff up
    ○ to bleed a lot

Unit 4, Lesson 19

Copy and distribute **Pretest/Posttest** pages 128–129. Also see directions, page 1.

Day 1–Day 2: Words That Tell What People Are Like

1. **feisty** *The gymnast is small but* **feisty**. If someone is **feisty**, he or she probably
   - ● does not give up easily
   - ○ is not very fast
   - ○ cannot win any games

2. **jealous** *My cousin was* **jealous** *of me.* If people are **jealous** of you, they
   - ○ help you with something
   - ● want something you have
   - ○ try to be your friend

3. **restless** *My sister was* **restless** *while we watched the game.* If a person is **restless**, he or she cannot
   - ○ feel better
   - ○ get warm
   - ● sit still

4. **sensitive** *The teacher is very* **sensitive** *to her students' feelings.* What does the word **sensitive** mean?
   - ● aware of
   - ○ afraid of
   - ○ tired of

5. **sincere** *When I said I liked your picture, I was being* **sincere**. If someone is **sincere**, he or she is
   - ○ fake
   - ● honest
   - ○ funny

6. **stubborn** *Angie was a* **stubborn** *runner.* If Angie is a **stubborn** runner, she probably
   - ○ wins every single race
   - ● keeps running when she is tired
   - ○ helps other runners

Day 3–Day 4: More Words That Tell What People Are Like

7. **clumsy** *Although he thought he was* **clumsy**, *Tim was a good dancer.* If someone is **clumsy**, he or she is
   - ● awkward
   - ○ lazy
   - ○ confused

8. **genuine** *Her happiness at seeing us seemed* **genuine**. When you say people seem **genuine**, you mean they are
   - ○ making a joke
   - ● telling the truth
   - ○ faking it

9. **modest** *Misha was* **modest** *about winning the prize.* If Misha was **modest** about winning a prize, he probably told
   - ● only a few people what he won
   - ○ lies about how many prizes he won
   - ○ everyone what he won

10. **negative** *Dari's* **negative** *comments made us angry.* When someone is **negative**, he or she talks about
    - ○ strange things
    - ● unhappy things
    - ○ silly things

11. **quality** *Shari complained about the* **quality** *of this jacket.* If people complain about the **quality** of a jacket, they think it is
    - ● badly made
    - ○ not big enough
    - ○ too ugly to wear

12. **reluctant** *The child was* **reluctant** *to go into the doctor's office.* What might a **reluctant** child do?
    - ○ run ahead into the office
    - ○ refuse to leave the office
    - ● walk slowly into the office

Unit 4, Lesson 20

Copy and distribute **Pretest/Posttest** pages 130–131. Also see directions, page 1.

Day 1–Day 2: Words About Superheroes

1. **captured** *The hero was captured.* When people are **captured**, they
   - ● cannot get away
   - ○ come back again
   - ○ leave on a trip

2. **distress** *The small children were in distress.* Someone who is in **distress** is
   - ○ happy
   - ○ impatient
   - ● upset

3. **feat** *The man performed a feat for the crowd.* What does the word **feat** mean?
   - ○ an interesting talk
   - ● a brave act
   - ○ a beautiful song

4. **muscular strength** *My friend has a lot of muscular strength.* If someone has a lot of **muscular strength**, what can he or she do better than other people?
   - ○ solve problems
   - ● lift heavy things
   - ○ put together tiny pieces

5. **rescue** *The girl rescued her little brother.* When you **rescue** someone, you
   - ○ tease them
   - ○ help them rest
   - ● save them

6. **villain** *In the movie, it was the dog who found the villain.* What is a **villain**?
   - ● a bad guy
   - ○ a hero
   - ○ a funny actor

Day 3–Day 4: Words About Moving Quickly

7. **charged** *The runners charged forward at the beginning of the race.* What does the word **charged** mean?
   - ○ fell
   - ● rushed
   - ○ jumped

8. **hastened** *Abby hastened to pick up the books I had dropped.* If someone has **hastened**, he or she has
   - ○ refused
   - ● hurried
   - ○ waited

9. **momentum** *The roller coaster has more momentum as it speeds downhill.* If something has more **momentum**, it can
   - ○ be hotter
   - ○ be louder
   - ● be faster

10. **pursuing** *That dog was pursuing Mrs. Whatley's cat!* If you are **pursuing** something, you are
    - ● following it
    - ○ biting it
    - ○ holding it

11. **retreat** *We decided to retreat to our room.* When you **retreat**, you
    - ○ line up
    - ● go back
    - ○ move over

12. **streak** *The frightened squirrel streaked away from us.* What does **streak** mean?
    - ○ climbed high
    - ○ jumped down
    - ● ran fast

Unit 5, Lesson 21

Copy and distribute **Pretest/Posttest** pages 132–133. Also see directions, page 1.

Day 1–Day 2: Words About Sailing

1. **aboard** *We walked **aboard** when the captain said it was okay.* If you walk **aboard** a ship, you walk
   - ● on the ship
   - ○ off the ship
   - ○ around the ship

2. **anchor** *The **anchor** of a ship is very heavy.* What is an **anchor** used for?
   - ○ to help steer a ship
   - ○ to make a ship move faster
   - ● to keep a ship from moving

3. **Antarctic Circle** *Our captain told us when our ship had crossed the **Antarctic Circle.*** If you were on a ship near the **Antarctic Circle,** you would probably see
   - ○ jungles
   - ● ice
   - ○ sand

4. **bay** *Our boat sailed into the **bay.*** A **bay** is
   - ○ a deep river
   - ● a part of the sea
   - ○ a wooden dock

5. **current** *We could see the **current** in the ocean.* Water in a **current** always
   - ○ looks cloudy
   - ○ gets warmer
   - ● keeps moving

6. **voyage** *We are going on a long **voyage.*** If you are going on a **voyage**, you will probably take a
   - ● boat
   - ○ train
   - ○ car

Day 3–Day 4: Words About Explorers

7. **expedition** *She will make an **expedition** to the rain forest.* When people make an **expedition,** they
   - ○ build a road
   - ● go on a journey
   - ○ draw a map

8. **frontier** *They began a new life on the **frontier.*** What kind of place is a **frontier**?
   - ○ a crowded place
   - ○ an old-fashioned place
   - ● an empty place

9. **guided** *Ben **guided** the visitors around our school.* What does the word **guided** mean?
   - ○ listened carefully to
   - ● showed the way
   - ○ followed closely

10. **scout** *We listened as the **scout** explained what we had to do.* What does a **scout** do?
    - ● goes ahead of a group
    - ○ follows a group
    - ○ cooks for a group

11. **territory** *They explored the new **territory.*** A **territory** is
    - ○ a small playground
    - ○ a big house
    - ● an area of land

12. **wilderness** *She likes to explore the **wilderness.*** If a place is a **wilderness,** it probably has almost no
    - ○ trees
    - ● people
    - ○ rivers

Unit 5, Lesson 22

Copy and distribute **Pretest/Posttest** pages 134–135. Also see directions, page 1.

Day 1–Day 2: Words About Bad Behavior

1. **disgust** *She was filled with **disgust** when she saw trash on the side of the road.* If people are filled with **disgust,** they
   - ○ don't care about things
   - ○ are filled with joy
   - ● think something is wrong

2. **embarrass** *I try not to **embarrass** my parents.* To **embarrass** someone is to make that person feel
   - ○ proud
   - ● ashamed
   - ○ angry

3. **insult** *His **insult** took me by surprise.* An **insult** uses words that are
   - ○ kind
   - ○ hard
   - ● mean

4. **scorn** *After the cat ripped up the rug, its owner gave it a look of **scorn.*** If you give a pet a look of **scorn,** you look as if you
   - ● don't like it
   - ○ know it well
   - ○ are afraid of it

5. **sneered** *The boy **sneered** at his brother.* When the boy **sneered,** he
   - ○ yelled loudly
   - ● gave a mean look
   - ○ ran toward something

6. **treated** *I didn't like the way our neighbor **treated** us when we moved in.* What does the word **treated** mean?
   - ○ brought food
   - ○ asked questions
   - ● acted toward

Day 3–Day 4: Words About Feelings

7. **emotions** *Her **emotions** changed when her friend came to visit.* **Emotions** are
   - ● feelings
   - ○ thoughts
   - ○ dreams

8. **excite** *I can always **excite** my dog by showing him his leash.* Something that **excites** an animal makes it
   - ○ sleepy
   - ● happy
   - ○ sad

9. **joyful** *I felt **joyful** when my dog had puppies.* If you feel **joyful,** it means you feel very
   - ○ afraid
   - ○ worried
   - ● happy

10. **mood** *Her **mood** changed when she came home from school.* Your **mood** is how you
    - ○ dress
    - ● feel
    - ○ speak

11. **mournful** *I felt **mournful** when summer vacation ended.* If you feel **mournful,** you probably look
    - ● sad
    - ○ worried
    - ○ happy

12. **pleasure** *It was a **pleasure** to swim in the river.* If something was a **pleasure,** you
    - ○ forgot it
    - ○ feared it
    - ● enjoyed it

Unit 5, Lesson 23

Copy and distribute **Pretest/Posttest** pages 136–137. Also see directions, page 1.

Day 1–Day 2: Words About Money

1. **fortune** *Good* **fortune** *brought him some extra money.* The word **fortune** tells about
   - ○ what job you get
   - ● what luck you have
   - ○ what gifts you open

2. **gain** *We talked about different ways to* **gain** *money.* If you **gain** money, you
   - ● get it
   - ○ wish for it
   - ○ give it

3. **possessions** *My friends are more important than my* **possessions.** Which of these might be one of your **possessions**?
   - ○ your mother
   - ○ your street
   - ● your bicycle

4. **reward** *Our teacher will* **reward** *us for the way we behaved.* To give a **reward** is to give a
   - ○ punishment
   - ● prize
   - ○ quiz

5. **valuable** *It is not a good idea to bring anything* **valuable** *to school.* Something that is **valuable**
   - ○ is easily lost
   - ● cost a lot of money
   - ○ looks shiny and colorful

6. **wealthy** *His grandfather was a* **wealthy** *man.* If a man is **wealthy,** what kind of house might he live in?
   - ○ an old, run-down house
   - ○ a house in the woods
   - ● a large, beautiful house

Day 3–Day 4: Words About Trouble

7. **annoyance** *My little sister can be such an* **annoyance**! If you are an **annoyance,** it means you
   - ○ hurt people
   - ● bother people
   - ○ help people

8. **disobey** *He would never* **disobey** *his teacher.* If you **disobey** someone, it means you
   - ○ follow his or her rules
   - ○ make his or her rules
   - ● break his or her rules

9. **disturb** *I did not want to* **disturb** *the baby.* What does the word **disturb** mean?
   - ○ to feed
   - ○ to dress
   - ● to bother

10. **interfere** *The dog's barking will* **interfere** *with the party.* If a dog were to **interfere** with a party, the people there would probably
    - ○ feel very tired later
    - ● have less fun
    - ○ talk a lot more

11. **mischievous** *The* **mischievous** *cat pounced on my head.* What does the word **mischievous** mean?
    - ● naughty
    - ○ hungry
    - ○ furry

12. **nuisances** *We had to deal with many* **nuisances** *on our camping trip.* **Nuisances** are things that
    - ○ everyone loves to do
    - ○ might hurt you badly
    - ● bother you but don't hurt you badly

Unit 5, Lesson 24

Copy and distribute **Pretest/Posttest** pages 138–139. Also see directions, page 1.

Day 1–Day 2: Words About Endangered Animals

1. **biological** *There is a biological reason why animals need to eat.* Something **biological** has to do with
   - ○ outer space
   - ● living things
   - ○ making food

2. **rare** *The rare butterfly is found only in South America.* If something is **rare,** it is
   - ● unusual
   - ○ normal
   - ○ beautiful

3. **scientific** *The scientific study proved that hawks can live in the city.* The word **scientific** can be used to describe something that is
   - ● tested
   - ○ new
   - ○ healthy

4. **species** *That species of butterfly lives in the countryside.* A **species** is
   - ● one kind of animal
   - ○ a scientist who studies an animal
   - ○ an animal that eats other animals

5. **survival** *Many animals need trees for their survival.* What does the word **survival** mean?
   - ○ being happy
   - ○ looking pretty
   - ● staying alive

6. **vanished** *The squirrel vanished into the forest.* If something **vanished,** it
   - ○ climbed higher
   - ● disappeared
   - ○ moved closer

Day 3–Day 4: Words About Land

7. **canyon** *We hiked through a canyon on our vacation.* If you hiked through a **canyon,** it means you hiked through
   - ● a split in the ground
   - ○ a large open field
   - ○ a steep, rocky trail

8. **continent** *We live on the continent of North America.* A **continent** is
   - ○ an area covered with ice
   - ○ a large area with trees and mountains
   - ● one of seven large land areas in the world

9. **landscape** *We saw a landscape of fields and mountains.* The word **landscape** tells
   - ○ how big the land is
   - ● what the land looks like
   - ○ how far away the land is

10. **plateau** *Sheep were grazing on the plateau.* A **plateau** is a hill with a
    - ● flat top
    - ○ pointy top
    - ○ split in the middle

11. **region** *Our region of the country gets a lot of snow.* If you live in a **region,** you live in
    - ○ the capital of a country
    - ○ the coldest part of a country
    - ● an area of a country

12. **volcano** *The volcano has not been active in years.* A **volcano** is
    - ○ a cold, icy river
    - ● a mountain that lets out heat
    - ○ a hill covered with grass

Unit 5, Lesson 25

Copy and distribute **Pretest/Posttest** pages 140–141. Also see directions, page 1.

Day 1–Day 2: Words About Ways to Move

1. **creep** *I watched the cat* **creep** *up on a mouse.* When something **creeps,** it
   - ● moves close to the ground
   - ○ runs very quickly
   - ○ makes a lot of noise

2. **crouch** *I had to* **crouch** *to get through the gate.* What does the word **crouch** mean?
   - ○ to jump over
   - ○ to roll under
   - ● to bend down

3. **jogging** *I saw her* **jogging** *around the block.* When someone is **jogging,** he or she is
   - ○ walking fast
   - ● running steadily
   - ○ riding a bicycle

4. **pounced** *The lion* **pounced** *on the zebra.* If an animal **pounced,** what did it do?
   - ○ crawled quietly
   - ● jumped suddenly
   - ○ climbed quickly

5. **skipping** *After her team won the game, she started* **skipping** *home.* Which of these is most like **skipping**?
   - ● hopping
   - ○ running
   - ○ crawling

6. **trudge** *I could hear my sister* **trudge** *up the stairs to bed.* When you **trudge,** what kind of steps do you take?
   - ○ short, fast steps
   - ○ quick, quiet steps
   - ● slow, heavy steps

Day 3–Day 4: Words About Time

7. **annual** *Our* **annual** *trip is tomorrow.* If something is an **annual** event, it happens once a
   - ○ month
   - ○ week
   - ● year

8. **centuries** *Those people came to America several* **centuries** *ago.* **Centuries** are periods of
   - ● one hundred years
   - ○ fifty years
   - ○ one thousand years

9. **currently** *He is* **currently** *at his grandmother's house.* If you are doing something **currently,** you are doing it
   - ○ often
   - ● now
   - ○ soon

10. **immediately** *I will go to soccer practice* **immediately.** If you do something **immediately,** you do it
    - ● right away
    - ○ over and over
    - ○ sometimes

11. **instant** *It took her an* **instant** *to think of the answer.* What does the word **instant** mean?
    - ○ a very long time
    - ● a very short time
    - ○ many times

12. **prior** *My mom goes for a run* **prior** *to going to work.* If something happens **prior** to something else, then it happens
    - ○ in the middle of
    - ○ soon after
    - ● just before

Unit 6, Lesson 26

Copy and distribute **Pretest/Posttest** pages 142–143. Also see directions, page 1.

Days 1–2: Words That Mean "Great"

1. **extraordinary** *Leo is an extraordinary hockey player.*
   An **extraordinary** hockey player is very
   ○ excited by hockey
   ● good at hockey
   ○ unhappy about hockey

2. **incredible** *Rosa's talent for juggling is incredible.*
   Something that is **incredible** is
   ○ small
   ● amazing
   ○ normal

3. **popular figure** *Mrs. Hooper is a popular figure at the school.* A **popular figure** is someone who everyone
   ● likes
   ○ forgets
   ○ dislikes

4. **sensational** *The action movie they watched was sensational.* The word **sensational** means very
   ○ bad
   ● exciting
   ○ strange

5. **superior** *This restaurant is superior to every other one in town.* Something that is **superior** is
   ○ more expensive than others
   ○ smaller than others
   ● better than others

6. **tremendous** *The chef made a tremendous meal.* The word **tremendous** means
   ○ frightening
   ● impressive
   ○ surprising

Days 3–4: Words About Size and Strength

7. **extremely** *My sister is extremely strong.* The word **extremely** means
   ○ a little bit
   ● very
   ○ sometimes

8. **gigantic** *The wedding cake was gigantic.* A **gigantic** cake is
   ● huge
   ○ delicious
   ○ pretty

9. **immense** *We sat under an immense tree.* The word **immense** means very
   ○ skinny
   ○ beautiful
   ● large

10. **mighty** *A mighty wind blew against the trees.* The word **mighty** means
    ● powerful
    ○ cold
    ○ surprising

11. **miniature** *My aunt loves miniature trains.* Something that is **miniature** is
    ○ old
    ○ fancy
    ● tiny

12. **towered** *Patty towered over most of the people she met.* If Patty **towered** over other people, she was
    ○ smarter than them
    ○ louder than them
    ● taller than them

Unit 6, Lesson 27

Copy and distribute **Pretest/Posttest** pages 144–145. Also see directions, page 1.

Day 1–Day 2: Words About Digging Into the Past

1. **ancient** *Meg is studying an **ancient** volcano.* The word **ancient** means very
   - ● old
   - ○ dangerous
   - ○ big

2. **fossils** *The scientist studied **fossils** of tiny animals.* **Fossils** are
   - ○ foods that animals ate
   - ○ places that animals once lived
   - ● animal parts from long ago

3. **prehistoric** *I am interested in **prehistoric** animals such as dinosaurs.* **Prehistoric** animals
   - ● lived a long time ago
   - ○ hunted in very cold areas
   - ○ swam very deep in the ocean

4. **remains** *There were **remains** of animals in the cave.* The word **remains** means
   - ○ homes
   - ● parts
   - ○ pictures

5. **site** *There are many dinosaur footprints at this **site**.* A **site** is a
   - ○ beach
   - ● place
   - ○ classroom

6. **skeletons** *These dinosaurs had huge **skeletons**.* The **skeletons** of animals are made up of their
   - ● bones
   - ○ skin
   - ○ brains

Day 3–Day 4: Words About Trash

7. **litter** *It is against the law to **litter**.* The word **litter** means to
   - ○ steal people's things
   - ● throw trash around
   - ○ lie to the police

8. **recycle** *We **recycle** all of our bottles.* What does the word **recycle** mean?
   - ○ throw in the trash after using
   - ○ clean with soap and water
   - ● collect to make into something else

9. **rubbish** *We found a pile of **rubbish** on the grass.* Where should **rubbish** be?
   - ○ buried in the ground
   - ○ growing in a garden
   - ● thrown in a garbage can

10. **spoil** *A stain might **spoil** a shirt.* What does the word **spoil** mean?
    - ● ruin
    - ○ make beautiful
    - ○ wash

11. **unspoiled** *This beach is completely **unspoiled**.* What are you most likely to see on an **unspoiled** beach?
    - ● clean water and beautiful sand
    - ○ trucks dumping garbage
    - ○ houses and people

12. **waste** *Turn off the light so you don't **waste** electricity.* When you **waste** something, you use it
    - ○ carefully
    - ● carelessly
    - ○ dangerously

Unit 6, Lesson 28

Copy and distribute **Pretest/Posttest** pages 146–147. Also see directions, page 1.

Day 1–Day 2: Words About Space

1. **asteroid** *An asteroid floated through space.* The word **asteroid** means
   - ● a rocky object
   - ○ a spaceship
   - ○ an astronaut

2. **craters** *There are many craters on Earth.* **Craters** are caused by
   - ○ water running through rivers
   - ● objects hitting the ground
   - ○ ice moving across land

3. **instruments** *Scientists use special instruments when studying space.* **Instruments** are special
   - ● tools
   - ○ books
   - ○ skills

4. **launch** *The launch of a rocket is an amazing sight.* When there is a **launch,** something
   - ○ burns up
   - ○ falls down
   - ● takes off

5. **mission** *We have a mission to study Mars.* The word **mission** means a
   - ○ toy
   - ○ team
   - ● job

6. **weightless** *It is a strange feeling to be weightless.* The word **weightless** means not being
   - ○ busy or tired
   - ● pulled down by gravity
   - ○ able to move around

Day 3–Day 4: Words About Dreams

7. **challenge** *Our coaches challenge us to do our best.* When adults **challenge** children, they are asking them to do something
   - ● difficult
   - ○ boring
   - ○ wrong

8. **dream** *I have a dream of working at a zoo.* The word **dream** means a
   - ○ fear
   - ○ secret
   - ● hope

9. **encourage** *Steve's teacher tried to encourage him.* If someone is trying to **encourage** you, they are probably
   - ● helping you do something
   - ○ punishing you for something
   - ○ tricking you into something

10. **goal** *Inez has the goal of going to college.* A **goal** is something you
    - ○ are afraid of
    - ○ get mad about
    - ● want to do

11. **obstacles** *We all face obstacles in life.* When people face **obstacles,** they are most likely to feel
    - ○ satisfied
    - ● frustrated
    - ○ grateful

12. **wish** *I wish that I could speak more than one language.* When you **wish** for something, you
    - ○ don't care about it
    - ● want it to happen
    - ○ think it can't happen

Unit 6, Lesson 29

Copy and distribute **Pretest/Posttest** pages 148–149. Also see directions, page 1.

Day 1–Day 2: Words About Eating

1. **aroma** *There was a great* **aroma** *in the kitchen.*
   An **aroma** is a
   ○ chef
   ● smell
   ○ meal

2. **digested** *It took a while before I fully* **digested** *my lunch.*
   What happens when you have **digested** food?
   ○ You have paid for food at a restaurant.
   ○ You have cooked a delicious meal.
   ● Your body has started using food for strength.

3. **feast** *On Thanksgiving, my cousin made an enormous* **feast.** The word **feast** means a
   ● large meal
   ○ huge cake
   ○ big mistake

4. **nourishing** *The cook made us a* **nourishing** *meal.* The word **nourishing** means
   ○ delicious
   ○ big
   ● healthy

5. **plenty** *We have* **plenty** *of soup for lunch.* If you have **plenty** of something, there is
   ○ a small amount
   ● a large amount
   ○ the right kind

6. **starvation** *The farmers were in danger of* **starvation.**
   Starvation happens when people don't have
   ● anything to eat
   ○ a home
   ○ enough rain

Day 3–Day 4: Words About Something Very Special

7. **ceremony** *The school held a* **ceremony** *for its best students.* A **ceremony** is usually a
   ● special event
   ○ large prize
   ○ difficult test

8. **dedicate** *Our class decided to* **dedicate** *an hour each day for quiet reading.* The word **dedicate** means to
   ○ ask for
   ● set aside
   ○ get rid of

9. **inscriptions** *There are many* **inscriptions** *on the wall of the old building.* **Inscriptions** are
   ○ pictures
   ● words
   ○ windows

10. **spirit** *José has a friendly* **spirit.** When you describe someone's **spirit,** you are telling about what kind of
    ○ pet they have
    ○ people they know
    ● person they are

11. **symbols** *Signs often use* **symbols** *to tell drivers where to go.* **Symbols** are things that
    ○ have bright colors
    ● stand for something
    ○ light up at night

12. **theme** *The* **theme** *of the article is that people should create less pollution.* The **theme** of something is its
    ● main idea
    ○ title
    ○ writer

Unit 6, Lesson 30

Copy and distribute **Pretest/Posttest** pages 150–151. Also see directions, page 1.

Day 1–Day 2: Words About Politics

1. **candidates** *I am not sure which of the* **candidates** *will win.* **Candidates** want to
   - ○ win at sports
   - ● become leaders
   - ○ get prizes

2. **citizens** *People who are born in the U.S. are* **citizens** *of this country.* **Citizens** are people who
   - ● help choose their leaders
   - ○ do not have the right to vote
   - ○ are born in other countries

3. **politics** *Her work in* **politics** *brought her to Washington, D.C.* People who work in **politics** work for
   - ● the government
   - ○ the mall
   - ○ a restaurant

4. **poll** *The* **poll** *is in the town hall this year.* A **poll** is a place where people
   - ○ play
   - ○ gather
   - ● vote

5. **rally** *Jane went to a* **rally** *for the mayor.* The word **rally** means
   - ○ a large building where people work
   - ● a gathering to show support for someone
   - ○ a show with lots of music and dancing

6. **vote** *I will* **vote** *for the person I trust the most.* If you **vote** for someone, you
   - ○ tell them your secrets
   - ● choose them in an election
   - ○ tell people about them

Day 3–Day 4: Words About Friendship

7. **accompany** *Vera asked her cousin to* **accompany** *her to the show.* The word **accompany** means
   - ○ lead ahead
   - ○ follow behind
   - ● go along with

8. **companion** *George was my* **companion** *that year.* A **companion** is someone
   - ● you spend time with
   - ○ you work for
   - ○ you don't like

9. **compromise** *After arguing for hours, we decided to* **compromise**. To **compromise** is to
   - ○ lose
   - ○ win
   - ● agree on certain things

10. **escorted** *Lydia* **escorted** *us to the bus stop.* The word **escorted** means
    - ○ sent
    - ● guided
    - ○ followed

11. **inseparable** *The two brothers were* **inseparable**. If two people are **inseparable**, they are
    - ○ usually fighting
    - ○ exactly alike
    - ● always together

12. **relied** *I have always* **relied** *on my grandfather.* If you **relied** on someone, you
    - ● needed their help
    - ○ told them everything
    - ○ did things for them

Words About Solving Mysteries

Listen as I read each question to you. Then listen as I read each answer choice. Fill in the bubble for the correct answer.

1 Ⓐ parts

  Ⓑ places

  Ⓒ hints

2 Ⓐ to help dogs

  Ⓑ to figure things out

  Ⓒ to drive a truck

3 Ⓐ easy to find

  Ⓑ hard to explain

  Ⓒ simple to erase

4 Ⓐ show it is true

  Ⓑ follow instructions

  Ⓒ make something up

5 Ⓐ tired

  Ⓑ excited

  Ⓒ confused

6 Ⓐ did something wrong

  Ⓑ is hurt

  Ⓒ looks lost

Words About Traveling

Pretest/Posttest
Curious About Words

Listen as I read each question to you. Then listen as I read each answer choice. Fill in the bubble for the correct answer.

7 (A) leaving a place

(B) getting to a place

(C) finding a seat in a place

8 (A) a way from one place to another

(B) a bunch of stuff you bring to a place

(C) a person who knows a place

9 (A) keep it in one place

(B) hide it in a place

(C) make it go to another place

10 (A) most of it

(B) one part of it

(C) only pictures of it

11 (A) to carry

(B) to sell

(C) to pile up

12 (A) stay where they are

(B) live at home

(C) go to another place

Words About Families

Listen as I read each question to you. Then listen as
I read each answer choice. Fill in the bubble for the
correct answer.

1 Ⓐ live with you now

Ⓑ lived before you

Ⓒ live far away

2 Ⓐ like them a lot

Ⓑ hardly know them

Ⓒ hate them

3 Ⓐ you wish you had

Ⓑ only one person in your
family has

Ⓒ your parents passed
on to you

4 Ⓐ special gifts from relatives

Ⓑ thoughts about past times

Ⓒ clothing they used to wear

5 Ⓐ every night

Ⓑ every month

Ⓒ every few years

6 Ⓐ not very often

Ⓑ every year

Ⓒ all the time

Words About Being Fair

Listen as I read each question to you. Then listen as I read each answer choice. Fill in the bubble for the correct answer.

7
- (A) buy everything from it
- (B) refuse to buy from it
- (C) write letters about it

8
- (A) feeding people who are hungry
- (B) doing all your schoolwork
- (C) buying presents for your family

9
- (A) in a special way
- (B) in just the right way
- (C) in an unfair way

10
- (A) to speak out about something unfair
- (B) to work hard to make money
- (C) to quit a bad job

11
- (A) kept from doing things
- (B) allowed to do things
- (C) told how to do things

12
- (A) work more
- (B) work less
- (C) stop working

Words About Places to Live

Listen as I read each question to you. Then listen as I read each answer choice. Fill in the bubble for the correct answer.

1 (A) go outside

(B) go downstairs

(C) go upstairs

2 (A) whole of a city

(B) middle of a city

(C) edge of a city

3 (A) a large hotel

(B) a kind of boat

(C) a small, simple house

4 (A) far from your home

(B) near the ocean

(C) outside of the city

5 (A) trees or bushes

(B) fruits or vegetables

(C) sand or rocks

6 (A) big house with many rooms

(B) farm with many buildings

(C) home in a building of many homes

96

Words About the Government

Listen as I read each question to you. Then listen as I read each answer choice. Fill in the bubble for the correct answer.

7 Ⓐ the tallest building in a city

Ⓑ the house of a governor

Ⓒ the main government building

8 Ⓐ everyone in the country

Ⓑ people in only one part of the country

Ⓒ people only in your city

9 Ⓐ a building

Ⓑ a car or truck

Ⓒ a picture

10 Ⓐ work very hard

Ⓑ ask for help

Ⓒ make laws

11 Ⓐ remember someone

Ⓑ play and have fun

Ⓒ work to make money

12 Ⓐ parents or grandparents

Ⓑ the people in charge of something

Ⓒ your friends from school

Words About Being Smart

Listen as I read each question to you. Then listen as
I read each answer choice. Fill in the bubble for the
correct answer.

1 Ⓐ slow

Ⓑ smart

Ⓒ old-fashioned

2 Ⓐ trick

Ⓑ meet

Ⓒ change

3 Ⓐ think of a plan

Ⓑ copy another idea

Ⓒ read something in a book

4 Ⓐ friendly person

Ⓑ good thinker

Ⓒ fast runner

5 Ⓐ special tool

Ⓑ team of people

Ⓒ plan

6 Ⓐ loves to help out

Ⓑ moves around a lot

Ⓒ tries to fool people

Words About Digging

Listen as I read each question to you. Then listen as I read each answer choice. Fill in the bubble for the correct answer.

7 (A) tied a rope

(B) drew a picture

(C) dug a hole

8 (A) a room

(B) a building

(C) a bed

9 (A) deep hole

(B) long, narrow ditch

(C) pile of dirt

10 (A) build a bridge

(B) climb a ladder

(C) dig under the ground

11 (A) finding out how heavy it is

(B) moving it back and forth

(C) taking something off the top of it

12 (A) dry

(B) dirty

(C) hurt

Words About Good Manners

Listen as I read each question to you. Then listen as
I read each answer choice. Fill in the bubble for the
correct answer.

1 Ⓐ say they are sorry

Ⓑ act in a mean way

Ⓒ tell a big secret

2 Ⓐ hungry

Ⓑ rude

Ⓒ polite

3 Ⓐ show them where to go

Ⓑ say who they are

Ⓒ teach them something

4 Ⓐ ask someone to come

Ⓑ give someone a ride

Ⓒ give orders to someone

5 Ⓐ drew a picture

Ⓑ made a phone call

Ⓒ written words

6 Ⓐ think before they act

Ⓑ act proud of themselves

Ⓒ do whatever they want

Words About Scary Things

Listen as I read each question to you. Then listen as I read each answer choice. Fill in the bubble for the correct answer.

7
Ⓐ helps other animals
Ⓑ hurts other animals
Ⓒ runs very fast

8
Ⓐ scared
Ⓑ bored
Ⓒ tired

9
Ⓐ very strong
Ⓑ very scary
Ⓒ very big

10
Ⓐ very noisy
Ⓑ very brave
Ⓒ very scared

11
Ⓐ try to hurt people
Ⓑ be friendly to people
Ⓒ hide from people

12
Ⓐ strong excitement
Ⓑ strong dislike
Ⓒ strong fear

Words About Birds

Listen as I read each question to you. Then listen as
I read each answer choice. Fill in the bubble for the
correct answer.

1 (A) hunting small animals

(B) flying without moving wings

(C) sitting on a branch

2 (A) say *hello*

(B) make them go away

(C) tell them you are sorry

3 (A) learn to fly

(B) eat

(C) come out of eggs

4 (A) grow larger

(B) sleep for a long time

(C) travel a long way

5 (A) lose feathers

(B) make nests

(C) eat leaves

6 (A) awake all the time

(B) awake at night

(C) asleep all night

Words About Building

Listen as I read each question to you. Then listen as I read each answer choice. Fill in the bubble for the correct answer.

7 Ⓐ wall

Ⓑ handle

Ⓒ support

8 Ⓐ build

Ⓑ sleep in

Ⓒ plan

9 Ⓐ cover it up

Ⓑ make it stronger

Ⓒ tear it down

10 Ⓐ small, round piece

Ⓑ large, flat piece

Ⓒ tall, thin piece

11 Ⓐ burning it up

Ⓑ cutting it down

Ⓒ breaking it apart

12 Ⓐ bricks

Ⓑ wood

Ⓒ metal

Words About the Environment

Listen as I read each question to you. Then listen as I read each answer choice. Fill in the bubble for the correct answer.

1
Ⓐ land and water
Ⓑ air and sky
Ⓒ rain and snow

2
Ⓐ a kite
Ⓑ a skateboard
Ⓒ a television

3
Ⓐ too much of something
Ⓑ the right amount of something
Ⓒ not enough of something

4
Ⓐ in your town
Ⓑ in our country
Ⓒ around the world

5
Ⓐ the Sun
Ⓑ Earth
Ⓒ the Moon

6
Ⓐ chemicals
Ⓑ mud
Ⓒ wood

Words About Speaking

Listen as I read each question to you. Then listen as
I read each answer choice. Fill in the bubble for the
correct answer.

7 Ⓐ refused angrily

Ⓑ apologized sadly

Ⓒ said firmly

8 Ⓐ say

Ⓑ remember

Ⓒ care

9 Ⓐ wrote quickly

Ⓑ thought suddenly

Ⓒ spoke quietly

10 Ⓐ forgot to do your homework

Ⓑ did well on a test

Ⓒ watched a lot of TV

11 Ⓐ happy

Ⓑ curious

Ⓒ angry

12 Ⓐ listen

Ⓑ speak

Ⓒ laugh

Unit 2, Lesson 8
BLACKLINE MASTER 2-15

Pretest/Posttest
Curious About Words

Words About Volcanoes

Listen as I read each question to you. Then listen as I read each answer choice. Fill in the bubble for the correct answer.

1 (A) sit quietly
(B) burst violently
(C) shake gently

2 (A) blowing up
(B) standing tall
(C) leaking slowly

3 (A) in a cold fireplace
(B) in a burning campfire
(C) in a damp sandbox

4 (A) It turns into ice.
(B) It turns into a volcano.
(C) It turns into solid rock.

5 (A) hard
(B) melted
(C) old

6 (A) People dug it up from underground.
(B) It came out very cold from underground.
(C) It exploded upward from underground.

Words About Earthquakes

Listen as I read each question to you. Then listen as I read each answer choice. Fill in the bubble for the correct answer.

7 Ⓐ catch on fire

Ⓑ explode loudly

Ⓒ fall down suddenly

8 Ⓐ help it grow

Ⓑ destroy it

Ⓒ bring visitors to it

9 Ⓐ there is a bad storm

Ⓑ someone runs indoors

Ⓒ the ground shakes

10 Ⓐ almost everyone

Ⓑ some people

Ⓒ only a few people

11 Ⓐ shaking

Ⓑ heat

Ⓒ bumps

12 Ⓐ broken fences

Ⓑ big puddles

Ⓒ strong wind

Words About Snakes

Listen as I read each question to you. Then listen as I read each answer choice. Fill in the bubble for the correct answer.

1 Ⓐ get away from
   Ⓑ hide from
   Ⓒ try to hurt

2 Ⓐ green plants
   Ⓑ living things
   Ⓒ rivers and streams

3 Ⓐ wet
   Ⓑ sharp
   Ⓒ hard

4 Ⓐ wings
   Ⓑ four hooves
   Ⓒ large front teeth

5 Ⓐ a fish
   Ⓑ a bird
   Ⓒ a dog

6 Ⓐ dive and swim
   Ⓑ run and jump
   Ⓒ wiggle and slide

Pretest/Posttest
Curious About Words

Words About Water

Listen as I read each question to you. Then listen as I read each answer choice. Fill in the bubble for the correct answer.

7 Ⓐ coming down in drops

Ⓑ pouring out

Ⓒ spraying around

8 Ⓐ bread

Ⓑ milk

Ⓒ meat

9 Ⓐ soft

Ⓑ warm

Ⓒ damp

10 Ⓐ rains

Ⓑ fog

Ⓒ snow

11 Ⓐ a hose

Ⓑ a cloud

Ⓒ a stream

12 Ⓐ worn out

Ⓑ soaked

Ⓒ dirty

Words About Weather Conditions

Listen as I read each question to you. Then listen as I read each answer choice. Fill in the bubble for the correct answer.

1 Ⓐ ice

Ⓑ an oven

Ⓒ sugar

2 Ⓐ long, muddy rivers

Ⓑ large, dry, sandy areas

Ⓒ tall mountain ranges

3 Ⓐ little or no rain

Ⓑ a lot of flooding

Ⓒ a group of insects

4 Ⓐ a rainy day

Ⓑ heat from the sun

Ⓒ smoke from a fire

5 Ⓐ worn out

Ⓑ out of gas

Ⓒ too hot

6 Ⓐ under a big, leafy tree

Ⓑ on a warm, sunny street

Ⓒ at the top of a long, icy hill

Words About Mountains

Listen as I read each question to you. Then listen as I read each answer choice. Fill in the bubble for the correct answer.

7 Ⓐ rushing streams or rivers

Ⓑ people skiing or hiking

Ⓒ snow falling down a mountain

8 Ⓐ in the tops of large trees

Ⓑ on the steep sides of mountains

Ⓒ inside deep caves

9 Ⓐ move across

Ⓑ move up

Ⓒ move down

10 Ⓐ high it is

Ⓑ wet it is

Ⓒ old it is

11 Ⓐ beaches

Ⓑ hills

Ⓒ fields

12 Ⓐ valley

Ⓑ hotel

Ⓒ top

Pretest/Posttest
Curious About Words

Words About Teamwork

Listen as I read each question to you. Then listen as I read each answer choice. Fill in the bubble for the correct answer.

1 Ⓐ help you

Ⓑ punish you

Ⓒ slow you down

2 Ⓐ for a long time

Ⓑ together

Ⓒ quickly

3 Ⓐ stay away from each other

Ⓑ fight with each other

Ⓒ agree with each other

4 Ⓐ to have fun

Ⓑ to work together

Ⓒ to work hard

5 Ⓐ decide how you will do it

Ⓑ do not worry about how you will do it

Ⓒ ask someone how you will do it

6 Ⓐ a meal

Ⓑ a game

Ⓒ a job

Words About Being Well Known

Listen as I read each question to you. Then listen as I read each answer choice. Fill in the bubble for the correct answer.

7 Ⓐ find them boring

Ⓑ think they are great

Ⓒ hate them

8 Ⓐ gets a lot of exercise by doing something

Ⓑ is still learning how to do something

Ⓒ knows a lot about doing something

9 Ⓐ being well known

Ⓑ being wealthy

Ⓒ being talented

10 Ⓐ a treat

Ⓑ an award

Ⓒ a punishment

11 Ⓐ important

Ⓑ mean

Ⓒ forgotten

12 Ⓐ creative

Ⓑ not very good

Ⓒ well-liked

Words About Music

Listen as I read each question to you. Then listen as I read each answer choice. Fill in the bubble for the correct answer.

1 Ⓐ are going to watch it

Ⓑ are already part of it

Ⓒ want to be part of it

2 Ⓐ sports

Ⓑ instruments

Ⓒ parts in a play

3 Ⓐ You see a play.

Ⓑ You hear music.

Ⓒ You watch dancing.

4 Ⓐ the last time you do something

Ⓑ the second time you do something

Ⓒ the first time you do something

5 Ⓐ with a group

Ⓑ outside

Ⓒ alone

6 Ⓐ voice

Ⓑ personality

Ⓒ smile

Words About Noises

Listen as I read each question to you. Then listen as I read each answer choice. Fill in the bubble for the correct answer.

7 Ⓐ a hammer

Ⓑ an engine

Ⓒ a horn

8 Ⓐ messy

Ⓑ quiet

Ⓒ noisy

9 Ⓐ a loud noise

Ⓑ a quiet sound

Ⓒ a big mess

10 Ⓐ a whistle

Ⓑ a guitar

Ⓒ a drum

11 Ⓐ a loud, deep sound

Ⓑ a high, musical sound

Ⓒ a quiet, humming sound

12 Ⓐ the picture on a television

Ⓑ the loudness of sound

Ⓒ the button on a radio

Words About Artists

Pretest/Posttest
Curious About Words

Listen as I read each question to you. Then listen as
I read each answer choice. Fill in the bubble for the
correct answer.

1 Ⓐ reads about art

Ⓑ makes art

Ⓒ buys art

2 Ⓐ taking pictures

Ⓑ showing something

Ⓒ offering classes

3 Ⓐ gave you an idea

Ⓑ said you were doing a good job

Ⓒ told you to do something

4 Ⓐ children play

Ⓑ people sell things

Ⓒ artists work

5 Ⓐ unhappy about doing something

Ⓑ good at doing something

Ⓒ tired after doing something

6 Ⓐ why you do something

Ⓑ where you do something

Ⓒ how you do something

Words About Acting

Pretest/Posttest
Curious About Words

Listen as I read each question to you. Then listen as I read each answer choice. Fill in the bubble for the correct answer.

7   Ⓐ write their name

    Ⓑ draw a picture

    Ⓒ shake your hand

8   Ⓐ thank you

    Ⓑ it's over

    Ⓒ well done

9   Ⓐ what actors do

    Ⓑ what actors look like

    Ⓒ what actors say

10   Ⓐ exciting

    Ⓑ boring

    Ⓒ musical

11   Ⓐ reading silently

    Ⓑ acting on stage

    Ⓒ playing board games

12   Ⓐ a television show

    Ⓑ a movie

    Ⓒ a part of a play

Words About Competing

Listen as I read each question to you. Then listen as
I read each answer choice. Fill in the bubble for the
correct answer.

1 Ⓐ test

Ⓑ game

Ⓒ sale

2 Ⓐ lost the game

Ⓑ won the game

Ⓒ tied the game

3 Ⓐ the best team

Ⓑ another team

Ⓒ your team

4 Ⓐ let it keep you from doing
something

Ⓑ control it and do something
anyway

Ⓒ feel embarrassed by it

5 Ⓐ practice a lot

Ⓑ take a test

Ⓒ reach a goal

6 Ⓐ lost something easy

Ⓑ forgot to do something
important

Ⓒ won something hard

Words About Love

Listen as I read each question to you. Then listen as I read each answer choice. Fill in the bubble for the correct answer.

7 Ⓐ likes you

Ⓑ misses you

Ⓒ likes someone else

8 Ⓐ sorry to them

Ⓑ thank you to them

Ⓒ goodbye to them

9 Ⓐ fun to play with

Ⓑ brand new

Ⓒ cared for very much

10 Ⓐ to refuse

Ⓑ to give

Ⓒ to ask for help

11 Ⓐ have strong feelings

Ⓑ get a new idea

Ⓒ are tired

12 Ⓐ food for someone

Ⓑ someone mad at you

Ⓒ someone love you

Words About Crimes and Criminals

Listen as I read each question to you. Then listen as I read each answer choice. Fill in the bubble for the correct answer.

1 Ⓐ throw a ball through a window

Ⓑ break into a house and steal things

Ⓒ drive through a red light

2 Ⓐ easy to do

Ⓑ helpful to others

Ⓒ against the law

3 Ⓐ a thief

Ⓑ a neighbor

Ⓒ a police officer

4 Ⓐ arrest you

Ⓑ ask you questions

Ⓒ take your photograph

5 Ⓐ running away from another animal

Ⓑ trapped and held in a cage

Ⓒ somewhere it doesn't belong

6 Ⓐ did something wrong

Ⓑ solves crimes and arrests people

Ⓒ likes to go for long walks

Pretest/Posttest
Curious About Words

Words About Guilty and Not Guilty

Listen as I read each question to you. Then listen as I read each answer choice. Fill in the bubble for the correct answer.

7 Ⓐ had a good reason for what you did

　 Ⓑ need help learning right from wrong

　 Ⓒ were somewhere else at the time

8 Ⓐ decide who broke the law

　 Ⓑ write stories about breaking the law

　 Ⓒ try to break the law

9 Ⓐ an excuse

　 Ⓑ a helper

　 Ⓒ proof

10 Ⓐ did something wrong

　 Ⓑ is not guilty

　 Ⓒ is in danger

11 Ⓐ hatred

　 Ⓑ kindness

　 Ⓒ fairness

12 Ⓐ get into trouble

　 Ⓑ see something happen

　 Ⓒ wait a long time

Words About Buying and Selling

Listen as I read each question to you. Then listen as I read each answer choice. Fill in the bubble for the correct answer.

1 Ⓐ asking where to buy it

Ⓑ telling people about it

Ⓒ keeping it a secret

2 Ⓐ home

Ⓑ medicine

Ⓒ job

3 Ⓐ to buy

Ⓑ to find

Ⓒ to sell

4 Ⓐ an airplane

Ⓑ a bookstore

Ⓒ a zoo

5 Ⓐ something that decorates a store

Ⓑ someone who works in a store

Ⓒ something that is sold in a store

6 Ⓐ to tell people about something

Ⓑ to sell more of something

Ⓒ to get rid of something

Words About Winter

Listen as I read each question to you. Then listen as I read each answer choice. Fill in the bubble for the correct answer.

7 Ⓐ a mighty wind storm

Ⓑ a powerful snowstorm

Ⓒ a strong rainstorm

8 Ⓐ a fan

Ⓑ a swimsuit

Ⓒ a coat

9 Ⓐ wood

Ⓑ ice

Ⓒ rock

10 Ⓐ easy to smell

Ⓑ cold and stiff

Ⓒ hard to see

11 Ⓐ turn to snow

Ⓑ turn to water

Ⓒ turn to grass

12 Ⓐ cold

Ⓑ comfortable

Ⓒ hard

Words About Baseball

Listen as I read each question to you. Then listen as I read each answer choice. Fill in the bubble for the correct answer.

1
- Ⓐ a bat and a small ball
- Ⓑ a basket and a large ball
- Ⓒ a racket and a small ball

2
- Ⓐ seats for watching a sport
- Ⓑ large rocks at a beach
- Ⓒ benches in a park

3
- Ⓐ watch
- Ⓑ quit
- Ⓒ win

4
- Ⓐ referee
- Ⓑ coach
- Ⓒ pitcher

5
- Ⓐ helps one team play better
- Ⓑ is always fair
- Ⓒ throws the ball back to the pitcher

6
- Ⓐ put on extra clothing
- Ⓑ talk about a game
- Ⓒ exercise carefully

Name _____ Date _____

Words About Soldiers

Listen as I read each question to you. Then listen as I read each answer choice. Fill in the bubble for the correct answer.

7 Ⓐ moved forward

Ⓑ spoke softly

Ⓒ turned around

8 Ⓐ a large group of helpful people

Ⓑ a large group of soldiers

Ⓒ a large group of politicians

9 Ⓐ a trip

Ⓑ a meeting

Ⓒ a fight

10 Ⓐ control the city

Ⓑ free the city

Ⓒ leave the city

11 Ⓐ scares someone

Ⓑ moves someone

Ⓒ protects someone

12 Ⓐ help sick people

Ⓑ fight other people

Ⓒ arrest bad people

Words About Getting Hurt

Listen as I read each question to you. Then listen as
I read each answer choice. Fill in the bubble for the
correct answer.

1 Ⓐ medicine

　Ⓑ sick person

　Ⓒ truck

2 Ⓐ the way someone looks

　Ⓑ the way someone is

　Ⓒ the way someone speaks

3 Ⓐ healthy

　Ⓑ hurt

　Ⓒ lonely

4 Ⓐ cold

　Ⓑ hurt

　Ⓒ wet

5 Ⓐ a bandage

　Ⓑ a punishment

　Ⓒ a shoe

6 Ⓐ a whisker

　Ⓑ a cut

　Ⓒ a cold

Words About Feeling Hurt or Sick

Listen as I read each question to you. Then listen as I read each answer choice. Fill in the bubble for the correct answer.

7   Ⓐ doesn't hurt very much

    Ⓑ hurts for a while

    Ⓒ hurts a lot for a very short time

8   Ⓐ a little better

    Ⓑ really confused

    Ⓒ even worse

9   Ⓐ to sweat

    Ⓑ to breathe fast

    Ⓒ to pass out

10   Ⓐ gets worse

    Ⓑ gets better

    Ⓒ stays the same

11   Ⓐ weak and unhappy

    Ⓑ hopeful and strong

    Ⓒ funny and friendly

12   Ⓐ to get smaller

    Ⓑ to puff up

    Ⓒ to bleed a lot

Words That Tell What People Are Like

Listen as I read each question to you. Then listen as I read each answer choice. Fill in the bubble for the correct answer.

1
- Ⓐ does not give up easily
- Ⓑ is not very fast
- Ⓒ cannot win any games

2
- Ⓐ help you with something
- Ⓑ want something you have
- Ⓒ try to be your friend

3
- Ⓐ feel better
- Ⓑ get warm
- Ⓒ sit still

4
- Ⓐ aware of
- Ⓑ afraid of
- Ⓒ tired of

5
- Ⓐ fake
- Ⓑ honest
- Ⓒ funny

6
- Ⓐ wins every single race
- Ⓑ keeps running when she is tired
- Ⓒ helps other runners

More Words That Tell What People Are Like

Listen as I read each question to you. Then listen as I read each answer choice. Fill in the bubble for the correct answer.

7 (A) awkward

(B) lazy

(C) confused

8 (A) making a joke

(B) telling the truth

(C) faking it

9 (A) only a few people what he won

(B) lies about how many prizes he won

(C) everyone what he won

10 (A) strange things

(B) unhappy things

(C) silly things

11 (A) badly made

(B) not big enough

(C) too ugly to wear

12 (A) run ahead into the office

(B) refuse to leave the office

(C) walk slowly into the office

Name _____ Date _____

Words About Superheroes

Listen as I read each question to you. Then listen as I read each answer choice. Fill in the bubble for the correct answer.

1
Ⓐ cannot get away

Ⓑ come back again

Ⓒ leave on a trip

2
Ⓐ happy

Ⓑ impatient

Ⓒ upset

3
Ⓐ an interesting talk

Ⓑ a brave act

Ⓒ a beautiful song

4
Ⓐ solve problems

Ⓑ lift heavy things

Ⓒ put together tiny pieces

5
Ⓐ tease them

Ⓑ help them rest

Ⓒ save them

6
Ⓐ a bad guy

Ⓑ a hero

Ⓒ a funny actor

Words About Moving Quickly

Listen as I read each question to you. Then listen as I read each answer choice. Fill in the bubble for the correct answer.

7 Ⓐ fell
   Ⓑ rushed
   Ⓒ jumped

8 Ⓐ refused
   Ⓑ hurried
   Ⓒ waited

9 Ⓐ be hotter
   Ⓑ be louder
   Ⓒ be faster

10 Ⓐ following it
   Ⓑ biting it
   Ⓒ holding it

11 Ⓐ line up
   Ⓑ go back
   Ⓒ move over

12 Ⓐ climbed high
   Ⓑ jumped down
   Ⓒ ran fast

Words About Sailing

Listen as I read each question to you. Then listen as
I read each answer choice. Fill in the bubble for the
correct answer.

1 Ⓐ on the ship

  Ⓑ off the ship

  Ⓒ around the ship

2 Ⓐ to help steer a ship

  Ⓑ to make a ship move faster

  Ⓒ to keep a ship from moving

3 Ⓐ jungles

  Ⓑ ice

  Ⓒ sand

4 Ⓐ a deep river

  Ⓑ a part of the sea

  Ⓒ a wooden dock

5 Ⓐ looks cloudy

  Ⓑ gets warmer

  Ⓒ keeps moving

6 Ⓐ boat

  Ⓑ train

  Ⓒ car

Words About Explorers

Listen as I read each question to you. Then listen as I read each answer choice. Fill in the bubble for the correct answer.

7 Ⓐ build a road

Ⓑ go on a journey

Ⓒ draw a map

8 Ⓐ a crowded place

Ⓑ an old-fashioned place

Ⓒ an empty place

9 Ⓐ listened carefully to

Ⓑ showed the way

Ⓒ followed closely

10 Ⓐ goes ahead of a group

Ⓑ follows a group

Ⓒ cooks for a group

11 Ⓐ a small playground

Ⓑ a big house

Ⓒ an area of land

12 Ⓐ trees

Ⓑ people

Ⓒ rivers

Words About Bad Behavior

Listen as I read each question to you. Then listen as I read each answer choice. Fill in the bubble for the correct answer.

1 (A) don't care about things

(B) are filled with joy

(C) think something is wrong

2 (A) proud

(B) ashamed

(C) angry

3 (A) kind

(B) hard

(C) mean

4 (A) don't like it

(B) know it well

(C) are afraid of it

5 (A) yelled loudly

(B) gave a mean look

(C) ran toward something

6 (A) brought food

(B) asked questions

(C) acted toward

Words About Feelings

Listen as I read each question to you. Then listen as I read each answer choice. Fill in the bubble for the correct answer.

7 Ⓐ feelings

Ⓑ thoughts

Ⓒ dreams

8 Ⓐ sleepy

Ⓑ happy

Ⓒ sad

9 Ⓐ afraid

Ⓑ worried

Ⓒ happy

10 Ⓐ dress

Ⓑ feel

Ⓒ speak

11 Ⓐ sad

Ⓑ worried

Ⓒ happy

12 Ⓐ forgot it

Ⓑ feared it

Ⓒ enjoyed it

Words About Money

Listen as I read each question to you. Then listen as I read each answer choice. Fill in the bubble for the correct answer.

1 Ⓐ what job you get

Ⓑ what luck you have

Ⓒ what gifts you open

2 Ⓐ get it

Ⓑ wish for it

Ⓒ give it

3 Ⓐ your mother

Ⓑ your street

Ⓒ your bicycle

4 Ⓐ punishment

Ⓑ prize

Ⓒ quiz

5 Ⓐ is easily lost

Ⓑ cost a lot of money

Ⓒ looks shiny and colorful

6 Ⓐ an old, run-down house

Ⓑ a house in the woods

Ⓒ a large, beautiful house

Words About Trouble

Listen as I read each question to you. Then listen as I read each answer choice. Fill in the bubble for the correct answer.

7 Ⓐ hurt people

Ⓑ bother people

Ⓒ help people

8 Ⓐ follow his or her rules

Ⓑ make his or her rules

Ⓒ break his or her rules

9 Ⓐ to feed

Ⓑ to dress

Ⓒ to bother

10 Ⓐ feel very tired later

Ⓑ have less fun

Ⓒ talk a lot more

11 Ⓐ naughty

Ⓑ hungry

Ⓒ furry

12 Ⓐ everyone loves to do

Ⓑ might hurt you badly

Ⓒ bother you but don't hurt you badly

Words About Endangered Animals

Listen as I read each question to you. Then listen as I read each answer choice. Fill in the bubble for the correct answer.

1 Ⓐ outer space

Ⓑ living things

Ⓒ making food

2 Ⓐ unusual

Ⓑ normal

Ⓒ beautiful

3 Ⓐ tested

Ⓑ new

Ⓒ healthy

4 Ⓐ one kind of animal

Ⓑ a scientist who studies an animal

Ⓒ an animal that eats other animals

5 Ⓐ being happy

Ⓑ looking pretty

Ⓒ staying alive

6 Ⓐ climbed higher

Ⓑ disappeared

Ⓒ moved closer

Words About Land

Listen as I read each question to you. Then listen as
I read each answer choice. Fill in the bubble for the
correct answer.

7 Ⓐ a split in the ground

  Ⓑ a large open field

  Ⓒ a steep, rocky trail

8 Ⓐ an area covered with ice

  Ⓑ a large area with trees and
  mountains

  Ⓒ one of seven large land
  areas in the world

9 Ⓐ how big the land is

  Ⓑ what the land looks like

  Ⓒ how far away the land is

10 Ⓐ flat top

  Ⓑ pointy top

  Ⓒ split in the middle

11 Ⓐ the capital of a country

  Ⓑ the coldest part of a country

  Ⓒ an area of a country

12 Ⓐ a cold, icy river

  Ⓑ a mountain that lets out heat

  Ⓒ a hill covered with grass

Name _____ Date _____

Unit 5, Lesson 25
BLACKLINE MASTER 5–49

Pretest/Posttest
Curious About Words

Words About Ways to Move

Listen as I read each question to you. Then listen as
I read each answer choice. Fill in the bubble for the
correct answer.

1 (A) moves close to the ground

(B) runs very quickly

(C) makes a lot of noise

2 (A) to jump over

(B) to roll under

(C) to bend down

3 (A) walking fast

(B) running steadily

(C) riding a bicycle

4 (A) crawled quietly

(B) jumped suddenly

(C) climbed quickly

5 (A) hopping

(B) running

(C) crawling

6 (A) short, fast steps

(B) quick, quiet steps

(C) slow, heavy steps

Name _____ Date _____

Words About Time

Pretest/Posttest
Curious About Words

Listen as I read each question to you. Then listen as I read each answer choice. Fill in the bubble for the correct answer.

7 Ⓐ month
   Ⓑ week
   Ⓒ year

8 Ⓐ one hundred years
   Ⓑ fifty years
   Ⓒ one thousand years

9 Ⓐ often
   Ⓑ now
   Ⓒ soon

10 Ⓐ right away
   Ⓑ over and over
   Ⓒ sometimes

11 Ⓐ a very long time
   Ⓑ a very short time
   Ⓒ many times

12 Ⓐ in the middle of
   Ⓑ soon after
   Ⓒ just before

Words That Mean "Great"

Listen as I read each question to you. Then listen as I read each answer choice. Fill in the bubble for the correct answer.

1
- Ⓐ excited by hockey
- Ⓑ good at hockey
- Ⓒ unhappy about hockey

2
- Ⓐ small
- Ⓑ amazing
- Ⓒ normal

3
- Ⓐ likes
- Ⓑ forgets
- Ⓒ dislikes

4
- Ⓐ bad
- Ⓑ exciting
- Ⓒ strange

5
- Ⓐ more expensive than others
- Ⓑ smaller than others
- Ⓒ better than others

6
- Ⓐ frightening
- Ⓑ impressive
- Ⓒ surprising

Pretest/Posttest
Curious About Words

Words About Size and Strength

Listen as I read each question to you. Then listen as I read each answer choice. Fill in the bubble for the correct answer.

7 Ⓐ a little bit

Ⓑ very

Ⓒ sometimes

8 Ⓐ huge

Ⓑ delicious

Ⓒ pretty

9 Ⓐ skinny

Ⓑ beautiful

Ⓒ large

10 Ⓐ powerful

Ⓑ cold

Ⓒ surprising

11 Ⓐ old

Ⓑ fancy

Ⓒ tiny

12 Ⓐ smarter than them

Ⓑ louder than them

Ⓒ taller than them

Words About Digging Into the Past

Listen as I read each question to you. Then listen as I read each answer choice. Fill in the bubble for the correct answer.

1 Ⓐ old

Ⓑ dangerous

Ⓒ big

2 Ⓐ foods that animals ate

Ⓑ places that animals once lived

Ⓒ animal parts from long ago

3 Ⓐ lived a long time ago

Ⓑ hunted in very cold areas

Ⓒ swam very deep in the ocean

4 Ⓐ homes

Ⓑ parts

Ⓒ pictures

5 Ⓐ beach

Ⓑ place

Ⓒ classroom

6 Ⓐ bones

Ⓑ skin

Ⓒ brains

Words About Trash

Listen as I read each question to you. Then listen as
I read each answer choice. Fill in the bubble for the
correct answer.

7 Ⓐ steal people's things

Ⓑ throw trash around

Ⓒ lie to the police

8 Ⓐ throw in the trash after using

Ⓑ clean with soap and water

Ⓒ collect to make into something else

9 Ⓐ buried in the ground

Ⓑ growing in a garden

Ⓒ thrown in a garbage can

10 Ⓐ ruin

Ⓑ make beautiful

Ⓒ wash

11 Ⓐ clean water and beautiful sand

Ⓑ trucks dumping garbage

Ⓒ houses and people

12 Ⓐ carefully

Ⓑ carelessly

Ⓒ dangerously

Words About Space

Listen as I read each question to you. Then listen as I read each answer choice. Fill in the bubble for the correct answer.

1
- (A) a rocky object
- (B) a spaceship
- (C) an astronaut

2
- (A) water running through rivers
- (B) objects hitting the ground
- (C) ice moving across land

3
- (A) tools
- (B) books
- (C) skills

4
- (A) burns up
- (B) falls down
- (C) takes off

5
- (A) toy
- (B) team
- (C) job

6
- (A) busy or tired
- (B) pulled down by gravity
- (C) able to move around

Words About Dreams

Listen as I read each question to you. Then listen as I read each
answer choice. Fill in the bubble for the correct answer.

7 Ⓐ difficult

Ⓑ boring

Ⓒ wrong

8 Ⓐ fear

Ⓑ secret

Ⓒ hope

9 Ⓐ helping you do something

Ⓑ punishing you for something

Ⓒ tricking you into something

10 Ⓐ are afraid of

Ⓑ get mad about

Ⓒ want to do

11 Ⓐ satisfied

Ⓑ frustrated

Ⓒ grateful

12 Ⓐ don't care about it

Ⓑ want it to happen

Ⓒ think it can't happen

Name _____ Date _____

Words About Eating

Pretest/Posttest
Curious About Words

Listen as I read each question to you. Then listen as
I read each answer choice. Fill in the bubble for the
correct answer.

1 Ⓐ chef

Ⓑ smell

Ⓒ meal

2 Ⓐ You have paid for food
at a restaurant.

Ⓑ You have cooked a delicious
meal.

Ⓒ Your body has started
using food for strength.

3 Ⓐ large meal

Ⓑ huge cake

Ⓒ big mistake

4 Ⓐ delicious

Ⓑ big

Ⓒ healthy

5 Ⓐ a small amount

Ⓑ a large amount

Ⓒ the right kind

6 Ⓐ anything to eat

Ⓑ a home

Ⓒ enough rain

Pretest/Posttest
Curious About Words

Words About Something Very Special

Listen as I read each question to you. Then listen as I read each answer choice. Fill in the bubble for the correct answer.

7 Ⓐ special event

Ⓑ large prize

Ⓒ difficult test

8 Ⓐ ask for

Ⓑ set aside

Ⓒ get rid of

9 Ⓐ pictures

Ⓑ words

Ⓒ windows

10 Ⓐ pet they have

Ⓑ people they know

Ⓒ person they are

11 Ⓐ have bright colors

Ⓑ stand for something

Ⓒ light up at night

12 Ⓐ main idea

Ⓑ title

Ⓒ writer

Words About Politics

Listen as I read each question to you. Then listen as I read each answer choice. Fill in the bubble for the correct answer.

1 Ⓐ win at sports

Ⓑ become leaders

Ⓒ get prizes

2 Ⓐ help choose their leaders

Ⓑ do not have the right to vote

Ⓒ are born in other countries

3 Ⓐ the government

Ⓑ the mall

Ⓒ a restaurant

4 Ⓐ play

Ⓑ gather

Ⓒ vote

5 Ⓐ a large building where people work

Ⓑ a gathering to show support for someone

Ⓒ a show with lots of music and dancing

6 Ⓐ tell them your secrets

Ⓑ choose them in an election

Ⓒ tell people about them

Words About Friendship

Listen as I read each question to you. Then listen as I read each answer choice. Fill in the bubble for the correct answer.

7 Ⓐ lead ahead

Ⓑ follow behind

Ⓒ go along with

8 Ⓐ you spend time with

Ⓑ you work for

Ⓒ you don't like

9 Ⓐ lose

Ⓑ win

Ⓒ agree on certain things

10 Ⓐ sent

Ⓑ guided

Ⓒ followed

11 Ⓐ usually fighting

Ⓑ exactly alike

Ⓒ always together

12 Ⓐ needed their help

Ⓑ told them everything

Ⓒ did things for them

Word List

Unit 1

Lesson 1 (pp. T2–T3)

Words About Solving Mysteries	Words About Traveling
clues	arrival
detective	route
mysterious	send
prove	tour
puzzling	transport
suspicious	travel

Lesson 2 (pp. T4–T5)

Words About Families	Words About Being Fair
ancestors	boycott
bond	cause
inheritance	injustice
memories	picket
reunion	rights
unusual	strike

Lesson 3 (pp. T6–T7)

Words About Places to Live	Words About the Government
basement	capitol
city center	federal
cottage	landmark
country	legislate
farmland	memorial
mansion	official

Lesson 4 (pp. T8–T9)

Words About Being Smart	Words About Digging
clever	buried
deceive	chamber
devise	trench
intelligence	tunnel
scheme	uncovering
trickster	underground

Lesson 5 (pp. T10–T11)

Words About Good Manners	Words About Scary Things
apologize	fierce
civil	frightening
introduce	horrifying
invite	panicking
note	savage
self-control	terror

Unit 2

Lesson 6 (pp. T12–T13)

Words About Birds	Words About Building
gliding	brace
greeting	construct
hatch	reinforce
migrate	slab
molt	splintering
nocturnal	timber

Lesson 7 (pp. T14–T15)

Words About the Environment	Words About Speaking
atmosphere	insisted
electricity	mention
excess	muttered
global	praise
planet	snapped
pollution	utter

Lesson 8 (pp. T16–T17)

Words About Volcanoes	Words About Earthquakes
erupt	collapse
exploding	disaster
fiery	earthquake
lava	impact
molten	trembles
volcanic	wreckage

Lesson 9 (pp. T18–T19)

Words About Snakes	Words About Water
attack	dripping
creatures	liquid
poison	moist
rodent	monsoon
slimy	rainfall
slither	soggy

Lesson 10 (pp. T20–T21)

Words About Weather Conditions	Words About Mountains
cooling	avalanches
deserts	cliffs
drought	descend
evaporation	elevation
overheated	slopes
shade	summit

Unit 3

Lesson 11 (pp. T22–T23)

Words About Teamwork	Words About Being Well-Known
assist	admiration
association	expert
collaborate	fame
cooperate	honor
plan	prominent
task	respected

Lesson 12 (pp. T24–T25)

Words About Music	Words About Noises
auditioning	blare
band	peaceful
concert	racket
debut	rumble
orchestra	thunderous
vocal	volume

Lesson 13 (pp. T26–T27)

Words About Artists	Words About Acting
artist	autograph
exhibition	bravo
inspired	dialogue
studio	dramatic
talent	performs
techniques	scene

Lesson 14 (pp. T28–T29)

Words About Competing	Words About Love
contest	affection
defeated	appreciate
opposing	beloved
overcome	devote
succeed	emotional
triumph	endeared

Lesson 15 (pp. T30–T31)

Words About Crimes and Criminals	Words About Guilty and Not Guilty
burglaries	alibi
illegal	courthouse
inspector	evidence
interrogate	innocent
intruder	justice
suspect	witnesses

Unit 4

Lesson 16 (pp. T32–T33)

Words About Buying and Selling	Words About Winter
advertise	blizzard
hired	chilly
market	freeze
merchant	haze
product	melt
promote	wintry

Lesson 17 (pp. T34–T35)

Words About Baseball	Words About Soldiers
baseball	advanced
bleachers	armed forces
compete	battle
manager	conquer
umpire	shield
warm-up	warrior

Lesson 18 (pp. T36–T37)

Words About Getting Hurt	Words About Feeling Hurt or Sick
ambulance	ache
condition	comfort
injured	faint
precaution	recover
treatment	suffered
wound	swell

Lesson 19 (pp. T38–T39)

Words That Tell What People Are Like	More Words That Tell What People Are Like
feisty	clumsy
jealous	genuine
restless	modest
sensitive	negative
sincere	quality
stubborn	reluctant

Lesson 20 (pp. T40–T41)

Words About Superheroes	Words About Moving Quickly
captured	charged
distress	hastened
feat	momentum
muscular strength	pursuing
rescue	retreat
villain	streak

Unit 5

Lesson 21 (pp. T42–T43)

Words About Sailing	Words About Explorers
aboard	expedition
anchor	frontier
Antarctic Circle	guided
bay	scout
current	territory
voyage	wilderness

Lesson 22 (pp. T44–T45)

Words About Bad Behavior	Words About Feelings
disgust	emotions
embarrass	excite
insult	joyful
scorn	mood
sneered	mournful
treated	pleasure

Lesson 23 (pp. T46–T47)

Words About Money	Words About Trouble
fortune	annoyance
gain	disobey
possessions	disturb
reward	interfere
valuable	mischievous
wealthy	nuisances

Lesson 24 (pp. T48–T49)

Words About Endangered Animals	Words About Land
biological	canyon
rare	continent
scientific	landscape
species	plateau
survival	region
vanished	volcano

Lesson 25 (pp. T50–T51)

Words About Ways to Move	Words About Time
creep	annual
crouch	centuries
jogging	currently
pounced	immediately
skipping	instant
trudge	prior

Unit 6

Lesson 26 (pp. T52–T53)

Words That Mean "Great"	Words About Size and Strength
extraordinary	extremely
incredible	gigantic
popular figure	immense
sensational	mighty
superior	miniature
tremendous	towered

Lesson 27 (pp. T54–T55)

Words About Digging Into the Past	Words About Trash
ancient	litter
fossils	recycle
prehistoric	rubbish
remains	spoil
site	unspoiled
skeletons	waste

Lesson 28 (pp. T56–T57)

Words About Space	Words About Dreams
asteroid	challenge
craters	dream
instruments	encourage
launch	goal
mission	obstacles
weightless	wish

Lesson 29 (pp. T58–T59)

Words About Eating	Words About Something Very Special
aroma	ceremony
digested	dedicate
feast	inscriptions
nourishing	spirit
plenty	symbols
starvation	theme

Lesson 30 (pp. T60–T61)

Words About Politics	Words About Friendship
candidates	accompany
citizens	companion
politics	compromise
poll	escorted
rally	inseparable
vote	relied

Research Sources for Words Taught

Dale, E., & O'Rourke, J. (1981). *The living word vocabulary.* Chicago: World Book/Childcraft International.

Hiebert, E.H. (2005). WordZones™ based on "In pursuit of an effective, efficient vocabulary curriculum for elementary students," in E. H. Hiebert & M. Kamil (Eds.) *Teaching and learning vocabulary: bringing research to practice.* Mahwah, NJ: Lawrence Erlbaum Associates.

Marzano, Robert (2004). *Building background knowledge for academic achievement.* Alexandria, VA: Association for Supervision and Curriculum Development.

Templeton, S. (2006). "Derivationally related word families among the most frequently occurring words in English." (Unpublished)

Zeno, S.M, Ivens, S.H., Millard, R.T., & Duvvuri, R. (1995.) *The educator's word frequency guide.* New York: Touchstone Applied Science Associates, Inc.